OTHER TITLES IN THE LONG

Sports Talk

Sports Talk

LISA BECKELHIMER
University of Cincinnati

PEARSON
Longman

New York San Francisco Boston
London Toronto Sydney Tokyo Singapore Madrid
Mexico City Munich Paris Cape Town Hong Kong Montreal

Senior Sponsoring Editor: Virginia L. Blanford
Senior Marketing Manager: Sandra McGuire
Production Manager: Stacey Kulig
Project Coordination, Text Design, and Electronic Page Makeup:
    S4Carlisle Publishing Services
Senior Cover Design Manager: Nancy Danahy
Cover Image: Chris Whitehead, photographer © Digital Vision/Getty
    Images, Inc.
Senior Manufacturing Buyer: Dennis J. Para
Printer and Binder: Courier Corporation
Cover Printer: Coral Graphics

For permission to use copyrighted material, grateful
acknowledgment is made to the copyright holders on pp. 233–236,
which are hereby made part of this copyright page.

Library of Congress Cataloging-in-Publication Data

Beckelhimer, Lisa.
    Sports talk / Lisa Beckelhimer.
        p. cm.—(Longman topics reader)
    Includes bibliographical references.
    ISBN-13: 978-0-205-58337-9
    ISBN-10:   0-205-58337-7
    1. Sports—Social aspects. 2.   Sports in popular culture. I. Title.
    GV706.5.B43 2009
    306.4'83—dc22   2008030603

Please visit us at www.ablongman.com

ISBN 13: 978-0-205-58337-9
ISBN 10:   0-205-58337-7

1 2 3 4 5 6 7 8 9 10—CRW—11 10 09 08

For my home team,
Tim, Josh, and Jake

CONTENTS

**CHAPTER 5   Barriers or Breakthroughs:
What Role Does Gender
Play in Sports?**   *159*

egendary sports author and commentator Frank DeFord once said that people hear the first half of the word *sportswriter*, not the second half. He takes the opposite view—the writing is more important to him. Most of us fall into the group of people DeFord was referring to—we are fans, critics, athletes, or spectators, but rarely do we stop to consider the rhetorical, cultural, and sociological implications of sportswriting. According to Eric Dunning, author of *Sport Matters: Sociological Studies of Sport, Violence and Civilization*, sports infiltrate nearly every aspect of our society: mass media, the economy, our bonds with friends and strangers, our language, politics, industry, and international relations. Analyzing sports, then, goes far beyond keeping up with players' and teams' statistics, and even beyond reading books or magazines about sports or athletes. This reader is intended to give students the apparatus to analyze sports and sportswriting in a more critical context.

Sports Talk is an anthology meant to help students read carefully, think critically, and discuss and write analytically about sports. The readings provide the foundation for critical discussions on contemporary issues, cultural considerations, historical foundations, and rhetorical concerns in sports. The readings and discussion questions prompt a variety of thinking and writing skills including research, comparison, analysis, reflection, argument, and synthesis—skills that will be helpful to students in college and in the work force.

Each of the six chapters focuses on important rhetorical, sociological, and cultural issues examined through sports-related texts, including nonfiction essays, newspaper and magazine articles, sociological examinations, professional sportswriting, historical critiques, and analyses. Each chapter presents ideas for discussion, plus various writing assignments to help students hone a range of composition skills. Each chapter also includes lists of books, films, and Web sites worthy of further research and study. Chapter 1, Playing or Competing: What Do Sports Mean to America? offers various views of the role of sports in the United States, ranging from a justification of the mesmerizing power of sports' place in American culture to criticism of sports as "addictive" for Americans. Reading selections include scholarly analysis, mainstream journalism, and sportswriting. Chapter 2, Popular or Political: What Do Sports Mean to the World? broadens the perspective offered in Chapter 1 by examining sports in cultures outside of the United States, such as the importance of buzkashi in Afghanistan's culture. Writing ranges from a thought-provoking essay to articles from several reputable publications. Chapter 3, Offensive or on the Defense: What Role Does Violence Play in Sports? begins to examine controversial issues and prompts thinking from multiple perspectives about the impact of violence—real or perceived—in sports, with readings on sports ranging from boxing to hockey. Writers of some of the selections in this chapter analyze from objective perspectives, while other writers criticize or defend sports violence from firsthand experience. Chapter 4, Discrimination or Opportunity: What Role Does Race Play in Sports? includes readings revolving around racial issues in sports. The reading selections discuss both positive and negative issues of race and one pair of readings poses an argument and a rebuttal on the same controversial topic. Chapter 5, Barriers or Breakthroughs: What Role Does Gender Play in Sports? asks readers to think about issues of gender in sports. The reading selections provide students with models of scholarly, narrative, and argumentative writing. Finally, Chapter 6, Trash-Talk or Free Speech: What Do Words Mean in Sports? includes readings on a variety of rhetorical issues in sports, from free speech on college campuses to sports metaphors in our culture. Reading selections run the gamut from articles in academic sports journals to those from mainstream sports publications that students will recognize immediately.

With its variety of reading selections, this reader strives to fulfill instructors' need for a variety of writing models. Readings are from renowned sports publications like *Sports Illustrated* and *Sporting News,* from mainstream publications like *The New York Times* and *USA Today*, and from scholarly journals and books. Authors range from sports "outsiders" like scientist Carl Sagan and cultural commentator Roger Rosenblatt, to former athletes and sportswriters like S. L. Price and Mariah Burton Nelson, to literary greats like Ernest Hemingway and Joyce Carol Oates. Some of the readings examine historical context, while many focus on contemporary issues that are relevant to students' lives right now.

Sports Talk also includes these features:

- Thirty-two reading selections organized into six chapters focusing on particular rhetorical and cultural issues in sports that demand critical thinking.
- Reading selections that address the diversity of sports and readers' interests by covering a variety of sports, ranging from mainstream sports like football, baseball, and basketball to less common sports like bullfighting, mountain climbing, and martial arts.
- Reading selections that represent a range of opinions, from avid endorsement to outright criticism of sports, providing teachers with the apparatus for teaching multiple perspectives, debate, and counterargument.
- Reading selections that reflect a variety of styles—essays, articles, sports reporting, and more—and a variety of disciplines—writing, sociology, business, and more, that provide a rich variety for teachers and experiences for student readers.
- Introductions before each reading that inform students about the author, publication, or issue at hand and place the selection into context for readers.
- Lists of recommended readings, films, and Web sites that offer a springboard for encouraging students to continue their research and study.
- Questions for discussion and writing after each reading selection with prompts for use in class or as homework.

Sports Talk provides an excellent foundation for courses in writing, English composition, special topics, cultural studies, sociology, and elective courses in sports programs such as administration, marketing, and athletic training. The book encourages readers to expand notions of sport as simply a "game" and examine the impact of sport on rhetoric, on society, on culture, and on our own identities.

ACKNOWLEDGMENTS

Teaching English composition sometimes seems as grueling as working out at the gym or training for a marathon. Just when we think we're caught up with grading, another essay or portfolio is due and hundreds of pages of student work appear on our desks or in our e-mail inboxes. Of course, we must find time for our own writing—even when we have papers to grade and faculty meetings to attend. Just as athletes have many other people to thank for their successes—trainers, agents, and teammates, not to mention families and friends—I have many people to thank for their help with this book. My dad tops the list.

As a child growing up in St. Louis, I had many opportunities to learn and appreciate sports. For those opportunities, I would like to thank my father, Larry, who never considered having daughters rather than sons as a disadvantage. He and my mother, Judy, had two daughters, and faithfully attended our track meets and volleyball games, and even the traditionally-female events such as dance team and cheerleading competitions. But it was my dad who, even before my sister was born, exposed me to sports that many dads don't share with their daughters. I remember willingly tagging along with him to hockey games and enthusiastically cheering alongside him for our favorite boxers fighting on TV. Years later, my parents were blessed with two boys, and they taught all four of us many skills valuable in both sports and life, such as self-motivation, pride in our work, and the endurance to finish even the longest and most difficult tasks.

Now that I'm grown, I and my husband are the leaders of our own team, responsible for teaching those same values to our sons. I want to thank my husband, Tim, for his patience and support as I worked to grade papers and write a book at the same time. He has been my constant coach and trainer, encouraging me and motivating me to go the extra mile. Thanks also to my sons, Josh and Jake, for all they bring to my life. Whether I'm watching one of them learn karate, play soccer, or swim, I continue to learn about teamwork, persistence, and a sheer love for having fun.

Many people have acted as "agents" and "teammates" for me, helping and looking out for my best interests during this process. My former composition director, Jonathan Alexander, was the first to believe in the success of this book. Asking him if I could teach a course on sports rhetoric was a request in academia akin to a Pro-Bowl football player asking if he could call himself "The Torturer" and take up Saturday-night wrestling instead. I wasn't sure he would take me or my idea seriously. Without hesitation, he told me to develop the idea and teach it; shortly afterward, he encouraged me to put my idea into a book. That's where my teammates and agents at Pearson Longman came in, and I owe them thanks as well. My editor, Ginny, went to bat for me (pun intended) many times, and I appreciate her support and encouragement. Thanks also to Rebecca and Stacey for their help, and to my production "coach," Rob.

They say that every athlete needs an inspiration. I owe mine to my teammates and colleagues in English composition at the University of Cincinnati. They work tirelessly to teach a heavy course load and to produce quality scholarship. They allowed me to turn our offices into a locker room, where they listened to me whether I worried that stress would beat me or I gloated that I was at the top of my game. Thanks especially to Joyce, Michele, and Cynthia.

Finally, I owe gratitude to the athletes, teams, and sports organizations that never fail to provide us with controversy, memories, and something to write and talk about.

Playing or Competing: What Do Sports Mean to America?

What comes to mind when you think about sports? Perhaps you think of the sweaty athletes advertising sports drinks on TV. Maybe you envision 3-year-olds stumbling through a soccer game in your local park. You might reminisce about the smells of popcorn and pretzels at the last sporting event you attended. One of the primary reasons for reading, thinking, and writing about sports in a college course is the pervasive nature of sports in American society. In short, sports seem to be everywhere: from the TV, movies, and video games we consider frivolous to the more serious aspects of life such as our schools and our economy. Before we can explore the impact of sports around the world (Chapter 2) and what issues in sports create controversy or debate (Chapters 3–6), we should examine the significance of sports in American culture. Are sports healthy competition or leisurely play? Are they big business or simply entertainment? Are they an outlet for our aggressions and energy or are they addictive and potentially destructive? These questions will be examined in Chapter 1.

The chapter begins with essayist Roger Rosenblatt's analysis of three of America's most popular sports: baseball, football, and basketball. You might be surprised to read his theories about what makes baseball America's national sport. Is baseball more "American" than football or basketball? Rosenblatt claims, "In many odd ways, America is its sports." He recalls the roots of American history, comparing sports to the "wide-open spaces" that drew the first settlers. He writes, "Now every baseball diamond, football field and basketball court is a version of the frontier, with spectators added, and every indoor domed stadium, a high-tech reminder of a time of life and dreams when the sky was the limit." Perhaps more surprising and certainly less dreamy in tone are the criticisms of former athlete John R. Gerdy in his book, *Sports: The All-American Addiction*. Gerdy argues about sports that, "While a little escapism is not harmful, addiction is" and he calls sports "our society's opiate." Can Rosenblatt and Gerdy both be right about sports in American culture?

The remaining readings serve to examine particularly "American" sports and phenomena such as March Madness, the spectacle of NASCAR racing, and the Super Bowl. Do these events help define us as Americans? Should they? It might be helpful to consider how your own view of American sports has changed as you have matured. Perhaps as a child or teenager you read a sports novel by renowned young adult novelist Robert Lipsyte. In his article, "March Madness—A Lot Like Life," Lipsyte compares the NCAA college basketball tournament March Madness to religion and says it fulfills "our yearning for logic and resolution in a format larger than life." Another idea to consider is whether or not we need sports to solidify our identity as a country or culture. As Mary Billard points out in her article, "NASCAR Nirvana," some critics still question whether or not auto racing is even a sport. And yet perhaps no other sport as accurately defines a subculture of America as NASCAR does for the South. Finally, how do we use sports to define who we are, and what do others think of us? The authors of "The Whole World Isn't Watching" place responsibility for the Super Bowl's perceived popularity squarely on two entities: the NFL and the media. But they question: Does anyone else in the world really care?

One thread you might notice running through these selections is the personal tone the authors use, whether the writing appeared in a newspaper or a journal, or is a personal reflection. For example, Rosenblatt analyzes baseball's place in America, but he does so in a narrative tone that sounds nostalgic and personal. The selections on NASCAR and March Madness were originally published in newspapers but both are clearly more than reports. Both authors have firsthand experience with their topics. As you read you can detect a hint of awe in each writer's work. The excerpt from Gerdy's book and the journal article about the Super Bowl each contain biting criticism, perhaps aimed at convincing their audiences of their points. As you read the selections in this chapter, consider how each writer is using personal tone to make you, the reader, think or feel a certain way.

This chapter serves to introduce you to the iconic nature of sports in America. As you read, continue to ask yourself what place sports hold in American culture. You might jot down your current positions *before* reading this chapter, and compare them to your views after considering the readings. Does our emphasis on sports pose a positive or negative image for our country? What evidence does each side have to back up its claim? Are we playing or competing? What do you think?

Reflections: Why We Play the Game
ROGER ROSENBLATT

A journalist, essayist, and television commentator, Roger Rosenblatt has written for Time *magazine,* The New York Times, *and* New Republic, *and has been a frequent contributor for* The NewsHour with Jim Lehrer *on PBS. He has a PhD from Harvard University and has won several awards, including a Peabody, an Emmy, and a George Polk journalism award. Rosenblatt is also the author of numerous books, including* Where We Stand: 30 Reasons for Loving Our Country, *a collection of essays that draws upon nearly 30 years of reporting and commenting on America. The following essay is from the government journal* U.S. Society & Values. *In it, Rosenblatt examines the state of three popular American sports: baseball, football, and basketball. As you read, focus on Rosenblatt's comments regarding baseball, the sport most-often considered America's national pastime. Consider Rosenblatt's arguments and evidence. Why should baseball be America's national sport rather than football or basketball?*

◆

There probably are countries where the people are as crazy about sports as they are in America, but I doubt that there is any place where the meaning and design of the country is so evident in its games. In many odd ways, America is its sports. The free market is an analog of on-the-field competition, apparently wild and woolly yet contained by rules, dependent on the individual's initiative within a corporate (team) structure, at once open and governed. There are no ministries of sports, as in other countries;

every game is a free enterprise partially aided by government, but basically an independent entity that contributes to the national scene like any big business. The fields of play themselves simulate the wide-open spaces that eventually ran out of wide-open spaces, and so the fences came up. Now every baseball diamond, football field and basketball court is a version of the frontier, with spectators added, and every indoor domed stadium, a high-tech reminder of a time of life and dreams when the sky was the limit.

I focus on the three sports of baseball, football, and basketball because they are indigenous to us, invented in America (whatever vague debt baseball may owe the British cricket), and central to the country's enthusiasms. Golf and tennis have their moments; track and field as well. Boxing has fewer and fewer things to cheer about these days, yet even in its heyday, it was less an American sport than a darkly entertaining exercise in universal brutality. But baseball, football, and basketball are ours—derived in unspoken ways from our ambitions and inclinations, reflective of our achievement and our losses, and our souls. They are as good and as bad as we are, and we watch them, consciously or not, as morality plays about our conflicting natures, about the best and worst of us. At heart they are our romances, our brief retrievals of national innocence. Yesterday's old score is tomorrow's illusion of rebirth. When a game is over, we are elated or defeated, and we reluctantly re-enter our less heightened lives, yet always driven by hope, waiting for the next game or for next year.

But from the beginning of a game to its end, America can see itself played out by representatives in cleats or shorts or shoulder pads. Not that such fancy thoughts occur during the action. Part of being an American is to live without too much introspection. It is in the undercurrents of the sports that one feels America, which may be why the attraction of sports is both clear-cut (you win or you lose) and mysterious (you win and you lose).

Of the three principal games, baseball is both the most elegantly designed and the easiest to account for in terms of its appeal. It is a game played within strict borders, and of strict dimensions— a distance so many feet from here to there, a pitcher's mound so many inches high, the weight of the ball, the weight of the bat, the poles that determine in or out, what counts and does not, and so forth. The rules are unbending; indeed, with a very few exceptions, the game's rules have not changed in a hundred years. This is because, unlike basketball, baseball does not depend on the size of the players, but rather on a view of human evolution that says that people do not change that much—certainly not in a hundred years—and therefore they should do what they can within the limits they are given. As the poet Richard Wilbur wrote: "The strength of the genie comes from being in a bottle."

And still, functioning within its limits, first and last, baseball is about the individual. In other sports, the ball does the scoring. In baseball, the person scores. The game was designed to center on Americans in our individual strivings. The runner on first base has a notion to steal second. The first baseman has a notion to slip behind him. The pitcher has a notion to pick him off, but he delivers to the plate where the batter swings to protect the runner who decides to go now, and the second baseman braces himself to make the tag if only the catcher can rise to the occasion and put a low, hard peg on the inside of the bag. One doesn't need to know what these things mean to recognize that they all test everyone's ability to do a specific job, to make a personal decision, and to improvise.

Fans cling to the glory moments of the game's history, especially the heroic names and heroic deeds (records and statistics). America holds dear all its sports heroes because the country does not have the long histories of Europe, Asia, and Africa. Lacking an Alexander the Great or a Charlemagne, it draws its heroic mythology from sports.

We also cherish the game's sublime moments because such memories preserve everybody's youth as part of America's continuing, if a bit strained, need to remain in a perpetual summer. The illusion of the game is that it will go on forever. (Baseball is the only sport in which a team, down by a huge deficit, with but one hitter left, can still win.) In the 1950s, one of the game's greatest players, Willie Mays of the New York Giants, made a legendary catch of a ball hit to the deepest part of one of the largest stadiums, going away from home plate, over his shoulder. It was not only that Willie turned his back and took off, it was the green continent of grass on which he ran and the waiting to see if he would catch up with the ball and the reek of your sweat and of everyone else's who sat like Seurat's pointillist dots in the stadium, in the carved-out bowl of a planet that shines pale in daylight, bright purple and emerald at night.

The game always comes back to the fundamental confrontation of pitcher and batter, with the catcher involved as the only player who faces the field and sees the whole game; he presides as a masked god squatting. The pitcher's role is slyer than the batter's, but the batter's is more human. The pitcher plays offense and defense simultaneously. He labors to tempt and to deceive. The batter cannot know what is coming. He can go down swinging or looking at a strike and be made to appear the fool. Yet he has a bat in his hands. And if all goes well and he can accomplish that most difficult feat in sports by hitting a small, hard sphere traveling at over ninety miles per hour with a heavy rounded stick, well then, fate is thwarted for a moment and the power over life is his. The question ought not to be, "Why do the greatest hitters connect successfully only a third of the time?" It ought to be, "How do they get a hit at all?"

Still, the youth and hope of the game constitute but one half of baseball, and thus one half of its meaning to us. It is the second summer of the baseball season that reveals the game's complete nature. The second summer does not have the blithe optimism of the first half of the season. Each year, from August to the World Series in October, a sense of mortality begins to lower over the game—a suspicion that will deepen by late September to a certain knowledge that something that was bright, lusty, and overflowing with possibility can come to an end.

The beauty of the game is that it traces the arc of American life, of American innocence eliding into experience. Until mid-August, baseball is a boy in shorts whooping it up on the fat grass, afterwards it becomes a leery veteran with a sun-baked neck, whose main concern is to protect the plate. In its second summer, baseball is about fouling off death. Sadaharu Oh, the Babe Ruth of Japanese baseball, wrote an ode to his sport in which he praised the warmth of the sun and foresaw the approaching change to "the light of winter coming."

Small wonder that baseball produces more fine literature than any other sport. American writers—novelists Ernest Hemingway, John Updike, Bernard Malamud, and poet Marianne Moore—have seen the nation of dreams in the game. The country's violation of its dreams lies here too. Like America itself, baseball fought against integration until Jackie Robinson, the first Major League African American, stood up for all that the country wanted to believe. America, too, resisted its own self-proclaimed destiny to be the country of all the people and then, when it did strive to become the country of all the people—black, Asian, Latino, everyone—the place improved. Baseball also improved.

On mute display in baseball is the design of the U.S. Constitution itself. The basic text of the Constitution is the main building, a symmetrical 18th-century structure grounded in the Enlightenment's principles of reason, optimism, order, and a wariness of emotion and passion. The Constitution's architects, all fundamentally British Enlightenment minds, sought to build a house that Americans could live in without toppling it by placing their impulses above their rationality. But the trouble with that original body of laws was that it was too stable, too rigid. Thus, the Founders came up with the Bill of Rights, which in baseball's terms may be seen as the encouragement of individual freedom within hard and fast laws. Baseball is at once classic and romantic. So is America. And both the country and the sport survive by keeping the two impulses in balance.

If baseball represents nearly all the country's qualities in equilibrium, football and basketball show where those qualities may be exaggerated, overemphasized, and frequently distorted. Football and basketball are not beautifully made sports. They are more chaotic, more subject to wild moments. And yet, it should be noted that both are far more popular than baseball, which may suggest that Americans, having established the rules, are always straining to break them.

Football, like baseball, is a game of individual progress within borders. But unlike baseball, individual progress is gained inch by inch, down and dirty. Pain is involved. The individual fullback or halfback who carries the ball endures hit after hit as he moves forward, perhaps no more than a foot at a time. Often he is pushed back. Ten yards seems a short distance yet, as in a war, it often means victory or defeat.

The ground game is operated by the infantry; the throwing game by the air force. Or one may see the game in the air as the function of the "officers" of the team—those who throw and catch—as opposed to the dog-faced linesmen in the trenches, those literally on the line. These analogies to war are hardly a stretch. The spirit of the game, the terminology, the uniforms themselves, capped by protective masks and helmets, invoke military operations. Injuries (casualties) are not exceptions in this sport; they are part of the game.

And yet football reflects our conflicting attitudes toward war. Generally, Americans are extremely reluctant to get into a war, even when our leaders are not. We simply want to win and get out as soon as possible. At the start of World War II, America ranked 27th in armaments among the nations of the world. By the war's end, we were number one, with second place nowhere in sight.

But we only got in to crush gangsters and get it over with. Thus, football is war in its ideal state, war in a box. It lasts four periods. A fifth may be added because of a tie, and ended in "sudden death." But unless something freakish occurs, no warrior really dies.

Not only do the players resemble warriors; the fans go dark with fury. American football fans may not be as lethal as European football (soccer) fans, yet every Sunday fans dress up like ancient Celtic warriors with painted faces and half-naked bodies in midwinter.

Here is no sport for the upper classes. Football was only that in the Ivy League colleges of the 1920s and 1930s. Now, the professional game belongs largely to the working class. It makes a statement for the American who works with his hands, who gains his yardage with great difficulty and at great cost. The game is not without its niceties; it took a sense of invention to come up with a ball whose shape enables it to be both kicked and thrown. But basically this is a game of grunts and bone breakage and battle plans (huddles) that can go wrong. It even has the lack of clarity of war. A play occurs, but it is not official until the referee says so. Flags indicating penalties come late, a play may be nullified, called back, and all the excitement of apparent triumph can be deflated by an exterior judgment, from a different perspective.

Where football shows America essentially, though, is the role of the quarterback. My son Carl, a former sports writer for *The Washington Post*, pointed out to me that unlike any other sport, football depends almost wholly on the ability of a single individual. In other team sports, the absence of a star may be compensated for, but in football the quarterback is everything. He is the American leader, the hero, the general, who cannot be replaced by teamwork. He speaks for individual initiative, and individual authority. And just as the president—the Chief Executive of the land—has more power than those in the other branches of government that are supposed to keep him in check, so the quarterback is the president of the game. Fans worship or deride him with the same emotional energy they give to U.S. presidents.

As for the quarterback himself, he has to be what the American individual must be to succeed—both imaginative and stable—and he must know when to be which. If the plays he orchestrates are too wild, too frequently improvised, he fails. If they are too predictable, he fails. All the nuances of American individualism fall on his shoulders and he both demonstrates and tests the system in which the individual entrepreneur counts for everything and too much.

[margin note:] If people put half as much energy into caring about war as they did into sports

[margin note:] modern day gladiators – not warriors – no purpose

The structure of basketball, the least well-made game of our three, depends almost entirely on the size of the players, therefore on the individual. Over the years, the dimensions of the court have changed because players were getting bigger and taller; lines were changed; rules about dunking the ball changed, and changed back for the same reason. Time periods are different for professionals and collegians, as is the time allowed in which a shot must be taken. Some other rules are different as well. The game of basketball begins and ends with the individual and with human virtuosity. Thus, in a way, it is the most dramatically American sport in its emphasis on freedom.

Integration took far less time in basketball than in the other two major American sports because early on it became the inner city game, and very popular among African Americans. But the pleasure in watching a basketball game derives from the qualities of sport removed from questions of race. Here is a context where literal upward mobility is demonstrated in open competition. Black or white, the best players make the best passes, block the most shots, score the most points.

Simulating other American structures, both corporate and governmental, the game also demonstrates how delicate is the balance between individual and team play. Extraordinary players of the past such as Oscar Robertson, Walt Frazier, and Bill Russell showed that the essence of basketball was teamwork; victory required looking for the player in the best position for a shot, and getting the ball to him. A winning team was a selfless team. In recent years, most professional teams have abandoned that idea in favor of the exceptional talents of an individual, who is sometimes a showboat. Yet it has been proved more often than not that if the individual leaves the rest of the team behind, everybody loses.

The deep appeal of basketball in America lies in the fact that the poorest of kids can make it rich, and that there is a mystery in how he does it. Neither baseball nor football creates the special, jazzed-up excitement of this game in which the human body can be made to do unearthly things, to defy gravity gracefully. A trust in mystery is part of the foolishly beautiful side of the American dream, which actually believes that the impossible is possible.

This belief goes to the heart of sports in America. It begins early in one's life with a game of catch, or tossing a football around, or kids shooting basketballs in a playground. The first time a baseball is hit, the first time a football is thrown with a spiral, the first time a boy or a girl gains the strength to push the basketball high enough into the hoop—these are national rites of passage. In a way, they indicate how one becomes an American whether one was born here or not.

Of course, what is a grand illusion may also be spoiled. The business of sports may detract from its sense of play. The conflicts between rapacious owners and rapacious players may leave fans in the lurch. The fans themselves may behave so monstrously as to poison the game. Professionalism has so dominated organized sports in schools that children are jaded in their views of the games by the time they reach high school. Like sports, America was conceived within a fantasy of human perfection. When that fantasy collides with the realities of human limitations, the disappointment can be embittering.

Still, the fantasy remains—of sports and of nations. America only succeeds in the world, and with itself, when it approaches its own stated ambitions, when it yearns to achieve its purest form. The same is true of its sports. Both enterprises center on an individual rising to the top and raising others up with him, toward a higher equality and a victory for everybody. This is why we play the games.

Questions for Discussion and Writing

1. Rosenblatt claims that in many ways "America is its sports." What does he mean by this statement? He also says that "Part of being an American is to live without too much introspection. It is in the undercurrents of the sports that one feels America, which may be why the attraction of sports is both clear-cut (you win or you lose) and mysterious (you win and you lose)." Is he complimenting or insulting Americans with this language? Do you agree or disagree with his views? How well does he support them?

2. Respond to Rosenblatt's notion that baseball is an "individual" sport. What evidence does he use to support this claim? Isn't baseball a team sport? Can it be both?

3. What qualities make baseball an appropriate national sport for the United States? List some. Do you recognize or enjoy those qualities? Do you identify with them as an American? Are the qualities of football and basketball, then, *un*-American? How does Rosenblatt compare the three sports?

4. Examine the word choice of Rosenblatt's essay. How would you describe the writing? Is this selection an argument, a narrative, an analysis, or something else? Point to specific passages of the selection to support your answer.

5. The end of the essay argues that the heart of American sports begins in child-hood, in rites of passage that Rosenblatt claims "indicate how one becomes an American whether one was born here or not." Does love for a sport make one an American? Write about an experience you have had with sports, whether you were a participant or a spectator, that made you feel more "American" or view that sport as particularly American. Use details to support your analysis.

Sports: The All-American Addiction
JOHN R. GERDY

The son of a high school football coach, an All-American college basketball player drafted into the NBA, and a former associate com-missioner with the NCAA's Southeastern Conference, John R. Gerdy now teaches sports administration and consults with educational institutions. The following excerpt is from his book Sports: The All-American Addiction, *in which he argues that America's love affair with sports has gone beyond a healthy interest or hobby to obsession and addiction. He even compares sports fans to drug addicts. Gerdy begins his book by pointing out the various positive aspects of sports, such as bringing "widely diverse communities together for a common cause," "shattering racial stereotypes," creating heroes and role models, and contributing millions to American business enterprise. This selection questions whether those positive qualities outweigh the negative consequences of addiction.*

━━━━━━━━━ ✦ ━━━━━━━━━

More people are investing more time in watching more sport-ing events. Attendance at sporting events has risen decade after decade even while the number of televised sporting events has skyrocketed. Our emotional investment in sport seems to have increased as well. Our financial investment has never been higher. Athletes are making more money than ever could have been imag-ined twenty years ago. College coaches are earning six-figure contracts simply for allowing their student-athletes to wear a par-ticular brand of sneaker. Cities are offering ever-larger incentive packages to attract professional sports franchises to their commu-nities. Bigger stadiums are being built. College athletic budgets are increasing. Ticket prices are skyrocketing. The influence of organized sport in our culture continues to grow, largely because of our belief that sport is connected to various "higher causes." The advantages of organized sports participation on the athletes and our society generally have become so ingrained in our collective American psyche, that they have become American "truths"—unquestioned and virtually unassailable. To question the validity of these supposed benefits is tantamount to questioning America, motherhood, and apple pie.

Sport's influence in our culture has never been bigger. The resources we lavish upon athletes and the programs that support them have never been greater. Sport has never been more popular.

But is it better? Are the alleged benefits of organized athletics real, or have they been perpetuated to support what has become a large consumer of our nation's resources? Is sports' connection to the various "higher purposes" previously mentioned real?

It is important to ask such questions because if organized sport does, in fact, build character, generate economic growth, bring communities together, contribute in positive ways to educational institutions, improve the health of our populace, and contribute in a dynamic way to our educational institutions, perhaps we should invest more heavily in it. Perhaps we should pump even more money into our high school and college athletic programs. We should start more children in youth sports at even younger ages. We should invest even larger amounts of public tax dollars in professional franchises and encourage year-round participation in organized, highly competitive sports leagues. If these claimed links to higher purposes are real, perhaps we should be watching even more sports on television.

But what if organized sport in America is not doing all of these things? What if we determined that, on balance, when all of the positives and negatives are tallied, organized sport has become more of a negative, than a positive, influence in our society? What if we determine that organized sports' only redeeming value is in the entertainment it provides, that it has no lasting or significant positive link to any of its alleged higher causes? Is sports' entertainment value alone enough to justify our heavy personal and societal investment? To make this determination, we must approach the issue with a clear, open, and honest perspective. Specifically, we must determine exactly what sport represents, the images it projects, the values it promotes, and the behavior it encourages.

Evaluating sports' impact on our society is a difficult challenge. It is difficult because sport undoubtedly has the potential to do all of the things it claims to do. Sport can build character and teach lifelong lessons in discipline, teamwork, and sportsmanship. Sport can bind a community, and it can promote social change. Sport can teach humility and compassion for a competitor. And sport can have a positive impact on our health.

But the question remains, is it doing these things? And, if not, what do we do as individuals and society?

THE ALL-AMERICAN ADDICTION

I know the addiction well. I have spent countless hours at games, watching them on television, or reading about them in newspapers and magazines. I have to willfully resist snapping on the television to check out that night's big game, or to catch a quick sports news update from ESPN. I am drawn to it like a moth to flame.

Sport's lure is powerful; often irresistible. On far too many occasions, I have found myself sitting on the sofa, beer in hand, wasting away the afternoon or evening mindlessly flipping from one sporting event to another. I awake from my sports-induced coma, awash in feelings of guilt that I was not doing something more productive. Periodically, I muster the nerve to fight back. I vow to turn off the television set . . . at the next timeout. Often, when the moment of truth arrives, I cannot raise my arm to do so. Taking comfort in the fact that the game will be decided by the next timeout, I settle in for more. But rarely is the contest decided by the next commercial break. So, I would continue to sit, sometimes all day.

I am not alone. There are lots of us out there. Millions. Perhaps you have been there, too.

We have become addicted to sport; it is our society's opiate. We plan our days, weekends, and even vacations around it. If it is on the television anywhere near us, at home, the local bar, or a restaurant, we invariably turn to watch. We can't even get away from it in the car as we tune to the incessant wail of sports talk radio. And we'll do whatever we need to do to get it, twenty-four hours a day, seven days a week, from Key West to Seattle, Maine to New Mexico.

While a little escapism is not harmful, addiction is. Although not as destructive as an addiction to drugs, educationally, intellectually, and personally, a sports addiction can be very harmful as it lures us into physical inactivity and a mindless stupor.

Like a drug addiction, being a sports fan offers little of long-term substance or meaning. It allows us to escape our problems and ignore the issues we face, and it undermines our attempts to solve them. We invest our effort and emotion in sports stars and teams rather than improving our own lives by reading, writing, learning a new skill or how to play a musical instrument, or simply engaging in some meaningful conversation with a friend or family member. It is not enough to watch one game. We must watch the next and the next. Like a drug addiction, we need to repeat the act again and again and again just to feel normal. And, as with drugs, addiction to sports adversely affects those around us: friends, spouses, and children. "The love of sports can become so consuming that it corrodes all but the strongest unions between husband and wife. When a fan pours all of his emotion into baseball, basketball, or football, there is very little left for his wife, children, career, and community. That is a recipe for marital disaster" (Putnam 1999, 169).[1]

For example, how many thousands of times does conversation come to a standstill the moment a game is turned on? Rather than interacting with a friend or family member, our eyes and attention turn instead to the tube, where we slowly slip into a collective ESPN-induced stupor. Rather than getting involved, sport makes it easy for us to choose to sit idly and watch, television remote in hand. Sport is what we talk about when we want to avoid thinking or talking about anything meaningful or important. Like crack addicts sitting around their pipe in a dream state waiting for their next "hit," we sit in front of our televisions, unresponsive to the world around us, eyes glazed over and minds numbed, totally absorbed in a sports fantasy "trip," waiting for the next big play.

Yet, we don't mind our addiction. In fact, we embrace it. Sport is pure, it is wholesome, it embodies the "American way," showcasing champions and providing us with winners to worship and emulate. We don't mind our addiction to sport because it is the All-American addiction. And because it is the All-American addiction, we don't believe we suffer any consequences from it. But we do. To understand those consequences, we must determine what it is we have become addicted to. In other words, what is sport today? What has it evolved into? What values, images, and behaviors are associated with it? Exactly what is it that we have been mainlining into our minds each and every day?

What Have We Become?

I had never been subject to a "hard frisk." Not one of those cursory checks for a hidden flask on the way into a Rolling Stones or Bruce Springsteen concert, but rather, a thorough pat-down; shoes to chest. The kind of search where you realize "these guys mean business!" Yet, there I was, submitting to one at the door of what was billed as a "sporting event." A security guard explained, "These fans are crazy. They'll throw anything."

I chuckled at the thought of anyone getting worked up over an ECW (Extreme Championship Wrestling) Professional Wrestling match. Professional wrestling is not a *real* sport. It is staged entertainment. Everyone knows it is fake. The winners are predetermined and the idea is to get in as much "wrasslin', dancin', trash talkin', and entertainin'" in the amount of time allotted until the next scheduled television commercial. How can that be considered *real* sport? If I wanted to witness *real* sport I would have gone to an NBA game. Secure in my knowledge that what I was about to witness had nothing to do with sports, I settled into my seat for a night of low-grade entertainment.

But as the evening wore on, it began to dawn on me that what I was watching sure looked like the *real* sporting events I had seen recently. During "player" introductions, there were flashing, glittering, and whirling lights, pounding music, and lots of smoke. Athletes preened, pointed, chest bumped, and "high fived." About every other match, a scantily clad woman accompanied the wrestler to ringside under the guise of being a "manager" or "ring mate."

Somewhere around the third match, it clicked. It wasn't that the ECW looked like a "real" sporting event, but rather, that the last NBA game I watched, not only looked, but felt, strikingly like a professional wrestling event. I couldn't distinguish between the opening introductions of the Chicago Bulls or the grand entrance of former University of Kentucky basketball coach Rick Pitino minutes before tip-off at Rupp Arena and the tag team of Rob Van Dam and the Great Sabu. There was every bit as much preening, pointing, chest bumpin', and high fivin' and every bit as much pomp, pageantry, glitter, and glam. And it looked to me that there wasn't much difference between the ECW's "head cheerleader," the lovely Lady Francine, and the Laker Girls or UNLV's cheerleaders. All were simply women portrayed as sex objects in a sideshow as the men dueled it out in the main event.

The ECW fans in Dayton, Ohio, were every bit as vocal and serious about the fate of the Sandman and the Dudley Boys as those in New York are over that of Allan Houston. After a wrestler leaped off the top turnbuckle, descending fifteen feet onto an opponent who just happened to be sprawled out on a table at ringside, splintering the table and cutting himself, the fans, sweaty and redfaced, burst into a wild-eyed, lung-busting, fist-waving chant of "E-C-W, E-C-W." They could have easily been chanting, "Let's go, Knicks!" The same sweaty red faces and wild-eyed looks I had seen on numerous occasions at Giants Stadium or the Southeastern Conference basketball tournament and the same fists waving and lungs busting. I was not going to be the one to tell those ECW fans that their "sport" wasn't real.

The day where hard frisks become a normal part of entering a real sporting event may not be far off. Some athletes might say they are long overdue as it is not uncommon for fans to throw coins, batteries, and other assorted objects at umpires and opposing players. One of the reasons the Chicago Bulls were disappointed in not being able to wrap up their 1998 championship in Chicago was the fact that they would have to return to play in front of the notoriously rabid Utah Jazz fans. It wasn't the noise that distracted the Bulls, but rather the coins that were apparently thrown at them.

There was a time when the thought of comparing professional wrestling and the NFL, NBA, or major college sporting events was unthinkable. The lines of distinction were simply too clear. Wrestling was staged. Rivalries were created and then hyped. What transpired outside of the ring was every bit a part of the show as what went on in it. It was entertainment, pure and simple. *Real* sports were something entirely different. They were serious. It was the game that mattered. But there is very little difference between today's professional, and increasingly, college sporting events and an ECW or WWF event. In fact, the NBA has gotten so far away from being about sport, that the league does not feel the game is interesting enough to entertain fans without help of an organist or taped snippets of deafening "rev up the fan" music blaring incessantly in the background . . . during play! Even the ECW respects their "sport" enough to turn the music off during the match.

To describe an NBA or NFL game or the Final Four as a "sporting event" is no longer accurate. These events are entertainment extravaganzas, subject to all the promotional and marketing gimmicks of a three ring circus. Even the issue of games being predetermined can be called into question. Concerns regarding game fixing at the college level are increasing. And there is always "league interest" in certain teams advancing into the next round of the playoffs. Do you think NBA and NBC executives breathed a sigh of relief when Michael Jordan and the Chicago Bulls finally put away the Indiana Pacers to move on to the 1998 Finals? Indiana versus Utah? What kind of television ratings would that generate?

Today, sport is packaged, merchandised, and marketed as entertainment. It is more about money, television ratings, advertising rates, and corporate sky boxes than it is about sport. Think it's simply a coincidence that ESPN is the abbreviation for the Entertainment Sports Programming Network? As Dick Vitale might say, "It's showbiz, Baby!"

NOTES

1. Putnam, Douglas T. 1999. *Controversies of the Sports World*. Westport, Conn.: Greenwood Press.

Questions for Discussion and Writing

1. Gerdy is a former athlete and he begins his critique by discussing the positive aspects of sports. As a reader, are you more likely to trust in his opinion or agree with him because of this rhetorical strategy? Why does he place himself among the addicted? What rhetorical purposes does this type of introduction serve?

2. What does Gerdy say to make you suspect that he is not speaking positively about his and America's addiction to sports? Explain your reaction when you discovered that this former athlete was criticizing sports.

3. Gerdy states, "Perhaps you have been there, too" in reference to feeling "addicted" to sports. Have you? Write your own critique or defense of sports' role in your life. How much of your life do sports consume? Do you view your interest in sports as positive or negative? Do you consider yourself "addicted?" Support your answer with examples from your experiences.

4. Does Gerdy compare sports addiction to a physical, emotional, or psychological addiction? How do the three forms of addiction differ? How are they similar? Are the differences and similarities clear in Gerdy's comparison?

5. Write a letter either supporting or disputing Gerdy's thesis. Whether you agree or disagree, support your claims with evidence and examples you see in American sports today.

March Madness—A Lot Like Life
ROBERT LIPSYTE

Robert Lipsyte likes to say he has "two writing lives" and they have "complemented each other." A journalist since 1957, Lipsyte got his break when he covered the 1964 heavyweight boxing championship between heavily favored Sonny Liston and Cassius Clay (who later changed his name to Muhammad Ali). Clay surprised everyone and won the fight, and Lipsyte won the title of boxing reporter at The New York Times. *His interest in boxing led him to write his first best-selling novel for young adults, a classic in young adult sports fiction titled* The Contender. *Several books followed, including the autobiographical* One Fat Summer *and the critically acclaimed 2006 novel* Raiders Night. *Lipsyte has also written several books, both fiction and non-fiction, for adults. His journalistic writing made him a runner-up for a Pulitzer Prize in 1992 and his fiction earned him a lifetime achievement award from the American Library Association in 2001. In this* USA Today *article Lipsyte compares America's Division I college basketball tournament, fondly referred to as March Madness, simultaneously to religion and the cycle of life.*

———————— ◆ ————————

There is a method to March Madness: It's a model for what we'd like our lives to be—an orderly progression through victory and defeat to a final celebration, or at least an unambiguous conclusion.

March Madness, of course, is the sports page tag for the 65-team, 13-city, three-week NCAA men's basketball tournament. (There's a women's tournament, too. More on that later.) The soul and road map of the tournament is "the bracket," a diagram of the matchups that will converge on a final game. From Selection Sunday on March 11 when the 65 teams were announced to the title game on April 2, people throughout America will be following their favorite teams (and the teams they are betting on, which are not always the same).

The followers aren't all college hoop-heads. Something else is going on, and I think it is our yearning for logic and resolution in a format larger than life. This could be the secret behind all religions like sports. After all, what could be more intelligently designed than March Madness?

There are six stages to the schematic bracket, and they can symbolize phases in a life's journey as well as in the tournament. Thus, March Madness becomes a way to chart our existence in a manner that seems to give shape to destiny. The clear lines of the bracket override our feelings of personal and political helplessness, the sense that all is out of control.

Stage one: The 33 games of the first round (which includes an opener in which two teams compete just to get into the first round) represent that early scramble of childhood. The possibilities of life are laid out. Everybody has an equal shot, it seems: If you don't make the cut, it's your own fault. This, of course, is silly, in life or March Madness. Of the 65 teams in the bracket, only 34 are "at-large" teams selected by committee (out of the hundreds of Division I college teams in the country). The others in the bracket are mostly conference champions, and all are rated by order of their chances of winning. In life, as we know, a rich daddy provides a better head start than even Head Start.

In stage two, the 16 games of the second round, the dismissal of losers and the unlucky is well underway. Think of high school where all is competition—for grades, dates, scholarships, the right track to colleges that lead to Wall Street, Broadway, Yankee Stadium, the White House. Such competition is celebrated and satirized in *The Enlightened Bracketologist: The Final Four of Everything*, a new book edited by Mark Reiter and Richard Sandomir that makes 101 tournaments out of such things as red wine, Shakespearean insults, Scrabble words and fruit (peach wins!). Full disclosure: I did the bracket on despicable sports figures.

Stage three: The eight games played by the Sweet 16 teams parallel early working and family life. The future is beginning to take shape, dreams have disappeared and been replaced. That's the subtext of the *American Idol, Dancing with the Stars* and *Survivor* shows. By this time, we have a pretty good idea of who came to win, who came to play and who just showed up. Hero coaches have been designated, and some players are deciding whether they should continue their college careers or go pro.

Stage four, the four games played by the Elite Eight teams, is when reality sets in. The concurrent women's tournament is being played with as much passion but far less attention; after all, the women's professional league, the WNBA, doesn't even play during the traditional basketball season. In a political bracket, here is where the war in Iraq lost favor when the public realized there was no coherent game plan, no way to win.

In stage five, the two games of the Final Four, the chosen ones reach for the gold. They have been tested and found worthy of the mountaintop—the CEOs of the Fortune 500, the top cops, the Teachers of the Year, the Best Doctors, the award-winning actors, writers, scientists. Even vicariously feeling the peak and the pit— the joy in victory, the desolation in defeat—can make this addictive. We will be back next year!

Stage six, the championship game, produces the winner, as well as the lesson we will forget by next year. The ultimate prize is often made possible by a lucky bounce, a ref's bad call, a rival's injury. Just as politics, chicanery, a fluke, can determine the Oscar, the Nobel, the presidency. The second-best slinks off to shame and/or sympathy. It is some sad measure of this society that the "also-rans," the finalists who didn't quite snatch the ring, are often scorned more than those who never made stage one. Is that because most of us never made stage one?

This is why some non-sports religions have a seventh stage, the second chance called reincarnation.

In college basketball, I'd call it April Sanity and bring all the teams back, merge the rosters, choose up new sides, and this time play for fun.

Questions for Discussion and Writing

1. Lipsyte's claims about March Madness are based on the idea that the "madness" actually provides structure. Can these two paradoxical ideas be used to describe the tournament? How about life?

2. Lipsyte uses the rhetorical strategy of comparison to discuss sports in relation to religion and the cycle of life. Do either of the comparisons work for you as a reader? Is one more effective than the other? Is the success of this selection based on how well written these comparisons are? Why or why not?

3. Identify some religious terms that Lipsyte uses in regard to sports. Do the terms work to strengthen the comparison or do they seem like jargon to you?

4. Stages one and two of Lipsyte's March Madness journey of life seem a bit jaded and sarcastic. Why do you think he describes childhood and adolescence in such negative terms? Write about your own life so far in relation to March Madness. Do your impressions differ from Lipsyte's?

5. Despite the ominous tone of most of Lipsyte's comments, the end of the article ends on a high note. Why?

NASCAR Nirvana: R.V.'s, Rock Bands and Jell-O Shots

MARY BILLARD

Can a sport describe a cultural demographic of American citizens? If it can, then surely stock car racing—NASCAR in particular—has historically been the sports definition of Southern culture. As a travel writer, Mary Billard has reported from some exotic places, from the pristine mountains of Aspen, Colorado, to the "City of Water," Venice, Italy. To write "NASCAR Nirvana," Billard spent a weekend at one of NASCAR's famous races, where she experienced the smells—"a combination of gasoline, burning rubber and stale beer"—the sounds of country music and loud engines, and the sights, including a makeshift village of RV's and dozens of American flags. Over the course of a weekend, Billard observed what makes the sport a growing favorite among Americans everywhere, but especially among those who claim its roots in the South. As you read, consider what NASCAR represents in America. The South? Entertainment? By the way, is racing even a sport in your opinion?

◆

First there is the noise. You could call it deafening, but that wouldn't begin to describe the sheer overwhelming force at which it attacks you, drowning out all conversation, boring in on you with an almost physical presence. Then there is the smell, a combination of gasoline, burning rubber and stale beer. And finally there are the surroundings, a makeshift campground about the size of four football fields, home to some 500 trucks, mobile homes and R.V.'s, many separated by nothing more than a portable toilet. Thousands of people mill about, from middle-aged couples clutching "I Got Wrecked on Redneck Hill" T-shirts to florid-faced partygoers downing blackberry and lemon Jell-O shots while a band energetically plays "Sweet Home Alabama."

Sound like fun? Well, Bill Montgomery is having the time of his life.

But then Mr. Montgomery, 52, a manufacturing engineer for a metal stamping company, isn't exactly down in the trenches. On this Saturday evening on Columbus Day weekend, here to witness the running of the U.A.W.-G.M. Quality 500 race, part of the NASCAR Winston Cup series, Mr. Montgomery and his family have set up at a prime spot (the curve of the first turn) at Lowe's Motor Speedway, where they have painstakingly constructed a living room on stilts.

Twice a year, Mr. Montgomery takes three old couches, two love seats and what he calls a few "lamps from hell" out of storage from the basement of his home in Welcome, N.C., an hour away. He hauls his old furniture in a trailer to a camping space in the Lowe's infield, a spot he has reserved since the mid-1980's. There he builds a 46-foot-long platform, seven feet high, rents two Port-o-Johns, hooks up a water heater and arranges the furniture on the platform. Friends supply a Holland Grill and a television set. "We think of it as our time share," Mr. Montgomery says, laughing.

And, in fact, all around him are people who seem equally at home in their unlikely weekend residences. Three brothers—Lawrence, Billy and Luther Bishop—have placed a plywood platform on top of their pickup truck with a handful of molded plastic seats attached to the platform. Then there's a customized school bus modified with steel rails on top.

"It is a different world in the infield," says Jim Visbeck, 38, of Fort Mill, S.C., a salesman for a conveyer belt company. "It's about the freedom. And the friends. And the race. And the drinking."

This racetrack just north of Charlotte, N.C., is one of the largest sports arenas in the Southeast, larger than even the Louisiana Superdome. Last weekend, as this season's points leader, Matt Kenseth, tried to hold off competitors eager to gain ground before the year-end title is decided in November, an estimated 160,000 spectators filled the stands.

But the real action took place in the infield, where another 3,000 people gathered for a two-day tailgate party that began at 6 a.m. on Friday and ended late Sunday morning, when the participants packed up and either headed home or to yet another race the following weekend in Martinsville, Va.

Unlike other sports, say basketball, where the best seats are either courtside or up in luxury skyboxes, racing has a sort of reverse fan ethic. Yes, there are high-priced seats in the grandstand itself and luxury boxes as well. There are even condominium units available if you or your company wants to plunk down $300,000 or more to view the action from on high.

But fans like Mr. Montgomery have nothing but disdain for those who give up the infield for a comfortable, air-conditioned perch well above the track. "It looks like they are running the track in Matchbox cars from up there," he said.

When Lowe's opened in 1960, the infield campgrounds were apportioned on a chaotic first-come-first-served basis. Then about 25 years ago, the raceway began the system of reserved sites for two of its NASCAR race weekends, Memorial Day and Columbus Day. The cost is $100 for a motor home space, $60 for a camping space and $50 for individual infield tickets. The spots have since become family heirlooms.

"People leave spots in the will to pass it down to the next generation," said Scott Cooper, the speedway's senior manager for promotions and media relations. "As long as they renew, it's theirs."

There has been some talk that NASCAR has gone upscale over the years, particularly as some of the fans replaced their pickup trucks with ever more elaborate R.V.'s. And there are signs of change. The NASCAR Winston Cup circuit is replacing R. J. Reynolds Tobacco with Nextel as its title sponsor in 2004; Fox and NBC are paying $2.4 billion over six years for television rights (and, in fact, Saturday's race was telecast during prime time by NBC); and the term "NASCAR dads" has replaced "soccer moms" as the hot political buzzwords.

But the heart of this sport remains in the infield, and the relationships formed there.

On this Saturday afternoon, Joe Hill, 30, of Mount Holly, N.C., is standing by the grill with members of the Bishop family, along with Brent Shires, 26, of Denver, N.C., who has stopped by to visit, bringing his dog, Wiggles, whom he unsuccessfully tries to keep from eating the baked beans that have spilled to the ground.

The Bishops are second-generation infielders. "Daddy used to take us," says Lawrence Bishop, 34, also of Mount Holly. Over the years, the Bishops have clearly perfected the fine art of infield cooking. The picnic table is piled high with pork chops, the grill is ready to go and there's even a kitchen stove.

"I've been coming for 20 years," Mr. Hill explains. "From back when there was a real driver," an allusion to Dale Earnhardt, who died in a crash at the Daytona 500 in 2001. A moment of respectful silence follows. Then Mr. Hill opens the cooler. "Hey, who put all the Bud Light in here?" he says accusingly.

Garbage collectors, security guards, police officers and E.M.S. workers service the ragtag town that resembles nothing so much as a refugee camp, with dirt roads, tarps strung between trucks and worn carpets thrown onto the grass. An enterprising man delivers ice for $1.50 a bag.

Weaving down the narrow dirt road are two young blond women delivering banners for Irwin Industrial Tools, the strains of "Mamas, Don't Let Your Babies Grow Up to Be Cowboys," coming out of their truck's speakers. Soon the banners are everywhere.

On the part of the infield that racegoers have named Redneck Hill, a band called Rhetoric plays to an appreciative, if somewhat inebriated, crowd. (Those Jell-O shots are beginning to kick in.) The band's leader, Randy Pless, a 44-year-old contractor from Spencer, N.C., has been coming here since he was 2 1/2 years old, brought by his father, a rescue squad volunteer who "helped pull Fireball Roberts from the October '63 race," as Mr. Pless proudly explains.

People from all over the infield stream in to hear the band. A seven-foot wall made of camouflage netting has been erected, and illuminated American flag lights frame the opening. Over a rousing chorus of AC/DC's "Dirty Deeds Done Dirt Cheap," Todd Himes, a salesman from Rockwell, N.C., shouts that Redneck Hill, known for the battles that break out between fans over their allegiances to different drivers, has mellowed over the years.

"There were only two or three fights last night," Mr. Himes says.

Space in the infield has been carefully apportioned by raceway officials. There are spots for motor homes and campsites, and an additional area with tight security reserved for the race competitors. But within those designations, it is all about location, location, location. Donna Pfeufer, 55, of Troutman, N.C., has a spot right on the backstretch. "God was good," Mrs. Pfeufer says. "We don't know what we did right!"

Jim Craig, 61, the owner of C&C Boilers in Charlotte, owns an impressive 39-foot American Dream motor home complete with five television sets, including two with flat screens, behind which he pulls a Chevy Suburban.

Mr. Craig sponsors a racecar driven by Jeff Fultz and travels with his family, sometimes including the grandchildren, from raceway to raceway. Still, even Mr. Craig has house envy. He gestures over to the trailer occupied by Jeff Gordon, a star driver, that sits behind the fence in competitor parking. "Two million bucks," Mr. Craig estimates.

Dr. Jay Selle, a retired heart surgeon from Charlotte, watches as his friends, helped by some neighbors, are working on some beautifully constructed scaffolding. One is holding precisely drafted architectural plans. Two satellite dishes are stashed in the corner, waiting to be hooked up to the televisions.

"We are the highest point of the hill," Dr. Selle says with evident satisfaction. "Six spots, all in my name."

At 7:11 p.m. on Saturday, a formation of four fighter jets from the Oceana Naval Air Station in Virginia Beach stream overhead. At exactly 7:20, the green starting flag unfurls. Forty-three cars gun their massive engines and blast off. They average 142.871 miles per hour with top speeds of over 200.

Mr. Montgomery stands with his son, Will, 11, and Will's friend Josh Jones, also 11, on the platform they have constructed, shouting encouragement to their favorite drivers—Mr. Gordon (Josh) and Dale Earnhardt Jr. (Will)—and twisting their heads as the cars whiz by.

Their eyes are shining with excitement, but no one is talking. The noise makes any conversation pointless. A young woman also on the platform shouts something to her companion, but he can't understand her, so they hug instead. In fact, it's impossible to even hear the race announcer from here, so Will is wearing headphones tuned to a scanner that has 200 stations. He can hear the race commentary and can even pick up Mr. Earnhardt talking to his crew chief.

The Montgomerys' platform vibrates for the next 3 hours 30 minutes 24 seconds until the checkered flag comes down.

Tony Stewart wins. The race is over. And Bill Montgomery will be back in May.

Questions for Discussion and Writing

1. How much of Billard's description of what goes on at a typical NASCAR race would you consider reasonable and how much seems stereotypical? Identify words or phrases in her writing that seem either objective or stereotypical to you. Does she use any language that insinuates what her opinion of the NASCAR culture is?

2. This 2003 article mentions some changes that have taken place in NASCAR, and others have surely occurred since then. Consider the demographic audience for NASCAR, the money it takes to run the sport, and the overall image of auto racing in America. Are these changes for the better or would you agree with critics that NASCAR is a "sellout"?

3. Racing fans are known to be self-deprecating (consider the article's mention of "Redneck Hill"). Is that kind of self-aimed rhetoric appropriate or not? Why or why not?

4. Is auto racing still considered a Southern sport in our culture? Why or why not?
5. Watch as many different sports as you can find on television for one week. How many of them seem tied to a particular geographic area of our country? What are they? Write about what makes each a part of a subculture of America.

The Whole World Isn't Watching (But We Thought They Were): The Super Bowl and U.S. Solipsism
CHRISTOPHER R. MARTIN AND JIMMIE L. REEVES

Christopher R. Martin and Jimmie L. Reeves are both communications professors. Martin's interests include journalism criticism and history, while Reeves studies media history and criticism with an emphasis on television analysis. Culture, Sport, Society *(changed to* Sport in Society *in 2004) is an academic journal that covers issues in sociology, social anthropology, political science, and social sciences. Its articles, including this one from 2003, "consider issues associated with sport in societies, cultures and political systems." In the following excerpt from their study, the authors argue that the Super Bowl is not as "super" around the world as Americans might think it is or want it to be. While the Super Bowl is undoubtedly one of America's most revered sporting events, we might be surprised to learn what Martin and Reeves found in their research. As you read, consider many questions, including how many sporting events can boast the largest television audience in America and charge millions of dollars for 30-second commercials. However, do viewers and sports fans in other countries even know when the Super Bowl occurs? Do they care? Before you read this study, you might also look up the word* solipsism.

------------------- ✦ -------------------

A little more than a decade ago, as the symbolic Berlin Wall was coming down [in 1989], political leaders in the United States assured their citizens that a New World Order had come to fruition. This new, international, political arrangement would bring peace, of course, but more important was that it was implicitly an orderly peace—one which would be administered and maintained by the

United States, to the advantage of the United States. In other words, to the winner go the spoils.

Almost as quickly, the New World Order got disorderly. [The first] Gulf War quelled, but did not dislodge Saddam Hussein's regime in Iraq; hundreds of thousands died in Rwanda as warring factions engaged in genocide; Pakistan and India rattled sabers with nuclear tests; and the worst act of terrorism visited U.S. soil, performed by a U.S. citizen [Oklahoma City bombing]. Daily NATO bombings of Serbia (including a few that were unfortunately aimed at the Chinese Embassy in Belgrade) failed to quickly halt ethnic cleansings in Kosovo, nor end the rule of the Serbian leader Slobodan Milosevic. And at a mostly white, upper-middle-class high school in Littleton, Colorado [Columbine], two students turned guns and assorted weaponry on their peers and then themselves, ultimately killing 14 people and seriously injuring many more.

In countless ways U.S. political hegemony has been deflated in this New World Order. [Although the U.S. side of the global economy mostly hums along, the problems of ungovernable international leaders, ineffective military interventions, and chronic internal violence make the U.S.'s favorite chant of 'We're Number One' ring a little hollow in the post-cold war era.] *Thesis*

Into this tableau enters the Super Bowl. Each year, this supremely nationalistic event—the United States' most-watched television program—is marketed to people in the U.S. by the National Football League (NFL) and the mainstream national news media as an international affair. World-wide audiences of nearly one billion are routinely announced in the pre-game hyperbole, and actively promoted during the broadcast. Many reports proclaim, as a public relations official for the NFL told us, that the Super Bowl 'is the greatest one-day sporting event around'.

But, is the Super Bowl the most super and most watched of sporting events in the world? What is the cultural significance of laying claim to being the sporting event with the most television viewers world-wide, especially in the historical conditions of this New World Order? . . .

THE GLOBALIZATION OF THE SUPER BOWL

With the overwhelming dominance of U.S. entertainment content—especially films, television, and music—around the globe, it is no surprise that the National Football League has worked to build a worldwide audience for American football and its premier television event. From the NFL's perspective, it is expanding the market for its product. Don Garber, then senior Vice President of NFL International, explained in 1999: 'We invest in a long-term plan to help the sport grow around the world. The vision is to be a leading global sport. We need to create awareness and encourage involvement.'[26]

But the desire for global dominance of American football extends beyond just the NFL's profit-oriented interests. As an American cultural ritual, it is increasingly relevant (and increasingly common) that the Super Bowl is represented as the greatest and most watched sporting event on the planet. The enormous, *estimated* Super Bowl audience of between 800 million and a billion represents at least two competing ideals. On one hand, the Super Bowl's portrayal in mainstream U.S. news media as the leading international sporting event seems to combat post-cold war fragmentation by emphasizing increasing global unity, via a worldwide, shared Super Bowl experience. On the other, it is significant that this international unity is a unity not focused around World Cup soccer (which is *football* to the majority of the planet), but around *American football*, a U.S.-controlled export. Herein lies the great solipsism of the Super Bowl. To a large extent, Americans (and their mass media) cannot imagine—or do not wish to—the Super Bowl as being anything less than the biggest, 'baddest', and best sporting event in the world.

To imagine the Super Bowl as being this top sporting event is to ignore the counter-evidence of several other major sporting events:

- The estimated audience for the soccer World Cup (held every four years) is more than two billion viewers world-wide for the single-day championship match. In 1998 an estimated cumulative audience of 37 billion people watched some of the 64 games over the month-long event.[27]
- The Cricket World Cup, held every four years (most recently in England in 1999) and involving mostly the countries of the former British Empire, has an estimated two billion viewers world-wide, but receives scant attention in the United States.[28]
- Even the Rugby World Cup, also held every four years (most recently in Wales in 1999), claimed 2.5 billion viewers for its 1995 broadcast from South Africa.[29]

- Canada, perhaps the country outside the U.S. most likely to adopt the Super Bowl as its own favorite sporting event—given Canada's geographic proximity, limited language barriers, and familiarity with the NFL, favors its own sports championship. The Grey Cup, the title game of the Canadian Football League, regularly draws three million viewers, more than the annual broadcasts of the Super Bowl and hockey's Stanley Cup final. Only the Academy Awards generate a larger Canadian television audience each year.[30] . . .

IMAGINING THAT THE U.S. IS THE CENTER OF ATTENTION

Although the Super Bowl holds second-level status among world sporting events, the National Football League and other organizations have actively promoted American football to an international audience at least since the early 1980s. In England in 1982 the then-new Channel 4 joined with the NFL and the U.S. brewing giant Anheuser-Busch to show a weekly edited highlight program of American football. This program (edited versions of a featured game's highlights with flashy graphics and rock and roll music) offered novel programming for Channel 4 and strategic marketing opportunities to develop a British taste for American football and Budweiser beer. (Anheuser-Busch later even established the Budweiser League that organized a competition of local, American-style, football clubs.) Although the size of the television audience for American football in the United Kingdom grew between 1982 and 1990, its popularity peaked in the mid 1980s and leveled off to a little over two million for the average game audience by 1990, leading the British sport researcher Joe Maguire to conclude that, 'while American football may be an emergent sport in English society, it certainly has not achieved dominance.'[36]

The first instance of an international audience for the Super Bowl mentioned in the *NFL Record and Fact Book* on-line is for the year 1985.[37] That Super Bowl, notable for President Reagan doing the game's coin toss shortly after he took his second term oath of office, attracted nearly 116 million viewers in the U.S. The *Record and Fact Book* also notes that, in addition, 'six million people watched the Super Bowl in the United Kingdom and a similar number in Italy.' In that same year the NFL adopted a resolution to begin its series of preseason, international, exhibition games, which would field NFL teams in foreign countries to build interest in American football.

In 1986 the *Record and Fact Book* noted, 'Super Bowl XX was televised to 59 foreign countries and beamed via satellite to the *QE II*. An estimated 300 million Chinese viewed a tape delay of the game in March' (more than a month later). The international broadcast remained at about 60 countries for the next several years; but by the end of the cold war the NFL greatly expanded the Super Bowl's reach. In 1993, according to the *Record and Fact Book*, the game was shown live or taped in 101 countries. However, the data for the numbers of countries and viewers are often wildly reported. For the same 1993 Super Bowl (this one was notable for Michael Jackson's 'Heal the World' halftime performance), the *Los Angeles Times* reported that the NFL estimated 'an audience of more than one billion people in the United States and 86 other countries', *USA Weekend* noted 'an estimated one billion viewers in more than 70 countries', and *Amusement Business* (an industry journal concerned with the halftime program) explained the 'television audience is estimated at 1.3 billion in 86 countries, which is one reason Jackson agreed to participate.'[38]

By 1999 the estimates of audience size were smaller, but the scope of the international coverage had expanded to include more nations and more languages. The NFL reported that:

> Nearly 800 million NFL fans around the world are expected to tune in to watch. International broadcasters will televise the game to at least 180 countries and territories in 24 different languages from Pro Player Stadium: Chinese (Mandarin), Danish, Catalan, Dutch, Norwegian, English, French, German, Italian, Japanese, Russian, and Spanish.
>
> In addition, the game will be broadcast in Arabic, Bulgarian, Cantonese, Flemish, Greek, Hebrew, Hindi, Icelandic, Korean, Portuguese, Romanian, Slovak, Thai, and Turkish. Approximately 90 percent of the international coverage will be through live telecast of Super Bowl XXXIII.
>
> ERA in Taiwan, RDS (Canada), SAT 1 (Austria, Germany, and Switzerland), Sky (United Kingdom), TV-2 (Norway), and TV-2 (Denmark) will be broadcasting on-site for the first time.[39]

On Sunday, 30 January 2000 the *Los Angeles Times* noted that 'the game will be broadcast on 225 television stations, 450 radio stations, and in 180 countries. The cliche about a billion people in China not caring is no longer applicable.'[40] Yet the notion that the entire world pauses to pay homage to the Super Bowl is national mythology, continuously constructed via the NFL and the U.S. mass media. . . .

SUPER BOWL SUNDAY EVERYWHERE

That reports of the Super Bowl's international appeal are always estimated figures is disconcerting. While it is impossible to get an exact count of the viewers—the United States might have the most technically advanced television ratings systems, yet methodological deficiencies are commonly noted—the number of 800 million viewers is never documented in any way by the NFL nor the news media.

We were curious about this and approached the NFL's public relations department. According to one of the NFL's officials, the figure for the 800 million global audience for the Super Bowl is estimated, based on ratings-company figures from the U.S. (Nielsen) and from similar companies in each of the 180 other nations and territories that carried the game.[45] Yet the estimates of the audience always are announced during the pre-game hype, and are never—to the best of our knowledge and research—verified after the game (except for the U.S. numbers). Who could possibly check out these statistics, particularly if the NFL is not forthcoming? (Our NFL source seemed initially surprised that anyone would question the global audience figures, then just recited the same data.) The NFL official did acknowledge that the 800 million means that that number of people tuned in to watch at least a portion of the broadcast, not necessarily the entire one. This, of course, is similar to the American viewing experience; as ratings data indicate, many viewers tune out halfway through the game, particularly if the competition is lopsided.

Although the hyped international audience figures suggest that the whole planet is sharing the same American Super Bowl cultural experience, the time differential (particularly if 90 percent of the international coverage is via a live feed, as the NFL claims) makes the viewing experience quite different. First of all, Super Bowl Sunday in the United States is Super Bowl Monday for the bulk of the world's population. With a kick-off time at approximately 6 p.m., Eastern Time in the U.S. (the time zone shifts, depending on the annual location of the game) on Sunday evening, game time for European viewers ranges from 12 midnight to 2 a.m., Monday morning. Kick-off is 7 a.m. Monday morning in

Beijing, 8 a.m. in Seoul, and 9 a.m. in Brisbane. Thus the Sunday evening weekend party atmosphere that typifies the U.S. experience is awkwardly transplanted to an all-night ordeal in Europe or a Monday morning working day in east Asia and Australia. The Super Bowl's Sunday evening time slot—the evening with the heaviest television viewing in the U.S. each week contributes to the Super Bowl's big viewership. But the Super Bowl's broadcast time in Europe, Asia, and Australia is clearly out of the realm of prime time and is one when few can afford to watch television.

Moreover, while the Super Bowl has free broadcast delivery in the United States, bringing the game to the more than 99 percent of American households that have a television set, in other global markets the program's live distribution often comes only via paid cable or direct broadcast satellite television, both of which have a limited number of subscribers. The global audience is further limited by the fact that significant portions of the world's population are not even served by the cable or satellite signals that carry live feeds of the Super Bowl. For example, ESPN Star Sports, a joint venture between ESPN, Inc. (owned by Disney) and Star TV (owned by the News Corp., Ltd), was the sole carrier of the January 2000 Super Bowl XXXIV game to most Asian nations.[46] In fact, with China, India, Indonesia, Pakistan, Bangladesh, Vietnam, and South Korea among the markets exclusively served by ESPN Star Sports for the Super Bowl broadcast, the company was the provider of the event to a geographic area representing more than three billion people, over half of the world's population. Yet, as of November 1999, ESPN and Star Sports combined to serve fewer than 93 million households in all of its Asian national markets.[47] . . .

CONCLUSION

The fact that the Super Bowl is not the number one television sporting event may speak volumes about America's overestimation of its global might. It is not surprising, then, that soccer (the world's genuine top televised sporting event) remains a sport to ridicule for many people in the U.S. The *Los Angeles Times* in 2000 wryly stated that:

> The NFL estimates that more than 800 million people will watch the Super Bowl. An estimated 1.3 billion people watched the 1998 World Cup soccer final between Brazil and France. Can you remember the final score? Hint: one of the teams probably had 0.[50]

The comment, a typical joke about soccer's low scoring, which presumably makes it boring for the sporting fan, allows American football fans to dismiss soccer as a sport that does not matter. Meanwhile, soccer continues to diffuse into U.S. culture much more quickly than the American football game extends globally.

Ironically, the hope for extending interest in professional American football in global markets requires the sport itself to be flexible—more malleable than the franchise managed closely by the NFL bureaucracy. But the game is likely to become less American and more internationalized if it should succeed in diffusing widely into other cultures, which is the case with the three leading world team sports—soccer, basketball, and volleyball.[51] Thus the traditional mythic elements of NFL football that are so distinctly American are the same elements that prevent the Super Bowl from becoming the most-watched sporting event in the world.

NOTES

26. J. Buckley, 'Football Is Booming around the World' (28 Jan. 1999), http://www.nfl.com/international/990128future.html

27. 'More than Super Bowl; World Cup Worldwide TV Audience', *Financial Post* [Toronto] (1 June 1994), 82. Also see B. Giussani, 'World Cup Sites Target Ticketless Fans', *New York Times on the Web* (12 May 1998), http://www.nytimes.com; see H. Dauncey and G. Hare (eds), *France the 1998 World Cup: the National Impact of a World Sporting Event* (London and Portland, OR: Frank Cass, 1999) for a book-length treatment of the impact of the World Cup.

28. T. Melville, 'A World in Love with Cricket (Except in US)', *Christian Science Monitor* (14 May 1999), 18.

29. International Rugby Board, 'Off the Field' (16 May 1999), http://www.rwc99.com/OffField/OffField.html

30. 'Game Still an Easy Sell for the CBC', *Toronto Star* (21 Nov. 1998).

36. J. Maguire, 'More than a Sporting Touchdown: The Making of American Football in England 1982–1990', *Sociology of Sport Journal*, 7 (1990), 213–37.

37. See *NFL Record and Fact Book*, 'Chronology: 1981–1990', www.nfl.com/randf/chron90.html

38. See R. Rauzi, 'It's so L.A.: Super Bowl Goes Show Biz', *Los Angeles Times* (26 Jan. 1993), F1; T. McNichol, 'Will Michael Finally Touch Down?', *USA Weekend* (31 Jan. 1993), 20; Linda Deckard, 'Halftime Show to Blend High-Tech and Traditional Entities', *Amusement Business* (25 Jan. 1993), 15.

39. 'Super Bowl XXXIII Expected to Be Broadcast in 180 Countries in 24 Languages' (22 Jan. 1999), http://www.nfl.com/tvradio/990122sbskedintl.html

40. Springer, 'Sure, There's a Football Game', 6.

45. Interview with Greg Solomon, NFL Public Relations Office, 14 May 1999.

46. '1999 Country Table: List of Countries where the NFL Can Be Seen', http://www.nfl.com/international/990512countries.html (2001).

47. ESPN Star Sports, 'Corporate Information' (2001); the company broadcast the NFL to China, India, Indonesia, Pakistan, Bangladesh, Vietnam, South Korea, Myanmar, Nepal, Malaysia, Sri Lanka, Cambodia, Hong Kong, Laos, Papua New Guinea, Singapore, Mongolia, Bhutan, Macau, Brunei, the Maldives, and Guam exclusively, and competed with other NFL broadcasters in the Philippines, Taiwan, and Thailand.

50. T. J. Simers, 'The Super Bowl Will Have a Global Audience of about 800 Million, Many of Whom Are Passionate, Some of Whom are Curious; the Others Just Need a Reason to Party', *Los Angeles Times* (30 Jan. 2000), Dl. For U.S. soccer fans, the victory of the U.S. team in the 1999 Women's World Cup was an enormous event, yet the championship did not have the same cultural impact (nor the television ratings) as the Super Bowl.

51. See Wagner, 'Sport in Asia and Africa', 399.

Questions for Discussion and Writing

1. The events mentioned in this article are now history. For example, the authors mention the first Gulf War and the shootings at Columbine High School; since that time, we have seen a second Gulf War and the shootings at Virginia Tech and many other schools. The authors claim that "ungovernable international leaders, ineffective military interventions, and chronic internal violence" diminish America's view of itself as "Number One." Do more recent events serve to reinforce the authors' argument? Why or why not?

2. What does our desire to see the Super Bowl as the world's greatest sporting event say about us as Americans? Write an essay that either critiques Americans' view of ourselves or defends it.

3. Does the Super Bowl's international stature really reaffirm America's political and economic power as the authors suggest? Are the two really related? If you disagree, what evidence would you use to support your counter-argument?

4. What reasons do Martin and Reeves offer as concluding support that the Super Bowl is not, in fact, the greatest sporting event in the world? Evaluate the authors' use of this evidence.

5. What does *solipsism* mean and how does it apply to this topic?

Making Connections: Writing

1. Synthesize the arguments made by Roger Rosenblatt in "Reflections: Why We Play the Game" and John R. Gerdy in *Sports: The All-American Addiction*. Gerdy is a former athlete and an admitted sports fanatic and Rosenblatt is a cultural commentator. Yet it's Rosenblatt who clearly advocates for sports fanaticism in America while Gerdy, surprisingly, criticizes it as "addiction." Compare the arguments, using specific examples and support from each piece.

2. Compare what various authors in this chapter say about particularly "American" sports. What qualities do popular American sports share? Brainstorm a list of those qualities and compare two or more American sports. Use evidence from the reading selections in this chapter to support your comparison.

3. Trace and analyze the development of a major American sporting event as Christopher Martin and Jimmie Reeves do in "The Super Bowl and U.S. Solipsism" and Lipsyte does in "March Madness—A Lot Like Life." You might consider the Rose Bowl in college football; the World Series in major league baseball; the U.S. Open in golf or tennis; or the Kentucky Derby in horse racing. Consider the non-sports aspects of the event such as advertising and television coverage. What makes this event an American cultural phenomenon?

4. Argue the definition of a cultural icon. What athletes, teams, or events are iconic in our culture? What criteria must they meet to become icons?

5. Create a PowerPoint, poster, or other visual presentation that links a particular sport with the cultural stereotypes or images associated with that culture. Consider Mary Billard's observations in "NASCAR Nirvana." NASCAR fans are stereotyped as blue-collar Southerners. Conversely, golf is often associated with white, wealthy businessmen. Are the stereotypes associated with your chosen sport accurate? Are they fair? Do they carry a negative or positive connotation? Write an essay analyzing which images are stereotypes and which ones are accurate depictions of the culture.

6. Analyze a segment of sports advertising. You might consider advertising associated with a particular event as Christopher Martin and Jimmie Reeves do with Super Bowl ads or you might examine a concept such as endorsement or the sports apparel industry.

7. Write a letter to the editor of a major American newspaper arguing what sport America should consider as its national sport. Use evidence from various sources to support your claim.

8. Model the structure of "NASCAR Nirvana." Write as if you are traveling to a major sporting event in America. Note the distinct qualities, traditions, and fans of the sport and try to write without stereotyping.

9. Interview a sibling or friend about an American sporting event. Use the interview as part of your research on the sport's history and why it is so prominent in America.

10. Read the excerpt from John R. Gerdy's book and analyze the level of "addiction" on your own campus. You might want to tour your school's athletic facilities, attend some games, and interview students and staff as evidence for your analysis.

Books Worth Reading

The Best American Sports Writing of the Century edited by David Halberstam and Glenn Stout. Includes the 50 best pieces of sports writing of the twentieth century.

Boys of Winter: The Untold Story of a Coach, a Dream, and the 1980 U.S. Olympic Hockey Team by Wayne Coffey. Chronicles the U.S. team's journey to a gold medal over the heavily favored Soviet team.

The Cruelest Miles: The Heroic Story of Dogs and Men in a Race Against an Epidemic by Gay Salisbury. Chronicles the inspiring story of dog sled teams who captured the nation's attention as they raced through Alaskan wilderness and blizzards to deliver a life-saving serum.

Driving with the Devil: Southern Moonshine, Detroit Wheels, and the Birth of NASCAR by Neal Thompson. Examines the secret but proven connection between stock-car racing and whiskey running, particularly during America's prohibition.

Friday Night Lights: A Town, a Team and a Dream by H. G. Bissinger. Offers a critique of high school and college sports by following a football team in Texas.

Hurricane Season: A Coach, A Team and Their Triumph in the Time of Katrina by Neal Thompson. Follows the head coach and players of an undefeated high school football team torn apart by Hurricane Katrina.

Last Dance: Behind the Scenes at the Final Four by John Feinstein. Author goes behind the scenes at America's most prestigious basketball tournament.

Road Swing: One Fan's Journey into the Soul of American Sports by Steve Rushin. A *Sports Illustrated* writer takes off the day before his 30th birthday on a cross-country quest to examine American sports.

Seabiscuit: An American Legend by Laura Hillenbrand. An unlikely champion, racehorse Seabiscuit wins the hearts of Depression-era Americans.

Sports Wars: Athletes in the Age of Aquarius by David W. Zang. Examines the role sports played in the 1960s culture of Vietnam, disenchantment with government, and counter-culture.

Films Worth Watching

Baseball: A Film by Ken Burns (1994). DVD set captures 18-hour PBS miniseries on America's national pastime.

Dogtown and Z Boys (2001). Documentary on the evolution of American skateboarding featuring Stacy Peralta. Follow this one with Peralta's *Riding Giants* (2004), about surfing culture.

Field of Dreams (1989). Fantasy about baseball's meaning in America; based on W. P. Kinsella's novel *Shoeless Joe.*

Marshall University: Ashes to Glory (2006). Documentary about the 1970 plane crash that killed Marshall's football team, one of the most devastating tragedies in college sports history. Complements the more fictional but equally inspirational *We Are Marshall* (2006).

Nine Innings from Ground Zero (2004). Documentary about the New York Yankees in the 2001 World Series and the relationship between national tragedy and the healing nature of sports.

Sites Worth Surfing

http://www.americanpopularculture.com
Click on the "sports" link for *Americana* magazine's site on sports.

http://sportsillustrated.cnn.com
Home page for *Sports Illustrated* magazine.

http://usa.usembassy.de/sports.htm
Embassy's site on sports in America.

Popular or Political: What Do Sports Mean to the World?

As Americans, we already know what sports mean in our own culture. As we noted in Chapter 1, sports are everywhere in America: on TV, in our movies and video games, in our malls and shopping centers, and in our educational and economic systems. Sometimes we use sports to define us: baseball as our sport of summer; auto racing as our Southern, blue-collar sport; and golf as our sport of choice in the business world. But how much do we know about sports in other cultures? Do all countries have a national sport to define them? Certainly some countries' sports would seem bizarre, bewildering, or even barbaric to us. Is sport a means of both entertainment and competition for other nations as it is for Americans? Are citizens free to choose what sports are popular in their countries as we do? Do foreign governments use sports for political gain or oppression? Many Americans might admit that they haven't even thought about such questions. Should we? Chapter 2 will examine these questions.

This chapter begins with analyses by two distinguished writers: Carl Sagan and Allen Guttmann. Why would the late Dr. Carl Sagan—a renowned scientist who worked with NASA—concern himself with sports? Sagan recognized the social, political, and economic impacts of sports not just in America, but in many world cultures—he calls this idea our "trans-cultural need" for sports. Tracing sports back to pre-classical Greece, Sagan argues that we are all tied together by an ancient "calling." Whether from America, Afghanistan, or an ancient tribe from Africa, we all have a longing for sport because we originated as hunter-gatherer cultures. Likewise, sports historian Allen Guttmann links the nations of our world together by examining the purpose of the Olympic Games. He claims that the Olympics have always been political and created debate, and that sport might not even be the focus of our international Olympic Games. "To witness the spectators' emotions when *their* national representative mounts the victor's podium," Guttmann explains, "when *their* flag is raised, when *their* anthem is played, is to wonder if nationalism—or sport—is not the true religion of the modern world."

Other readings in this chapter examine sports in particular world cultures. Lucian Kim gives us a firsthand view of Afghanistan's national sport in his article, "Buzkashi: An Afghan Tradition Thrives." In "A Cricket Match Bridges a Longtime Gap in Punjab," Somini Sengupta explains how cricket plays a role in healing wounds created decades ago between India and Pakistan. Ernest Hemingway, considered America's foremost literary authority on Spanish sports, explains and perhaps justifies the sport of bullfighting in his 1923 article, "Bullfighting a Tragedy." In addition, according to Jack Curry, America is not the only country in love with baseball. He views the sport from the Cuban perspective in "Passion in Work and at Play." What do these four sports have in common? Other than baseball, none is popular in the United States. More importantly, three of the four sports are probably misunderstood by most Americans. In addition, Curry points out that it's equally difficult for our wealthy and privileged country to understand what baseball means in a society like Cuba's. Kim calls buzkashi "sport reduced to its simplest form, with no contrived side-shows or complicated rules. And, as many things are done in Afghanistan, the seeming chaos of a buzkashi match actually follows a deliberate system that is not always obvious to the foreign observer." Sengupta invites us to examine how a sport can help close the divide caused by years of religious and political upheaval. She reports on the significance of a cricket match between India and Pakistan in a town that was "the epicenter of the bloody 1947 migration: when Sikhs and Hindus fled east into India and Muslims streamed west into the newly created Pakistan." Perhaps the most defensive of a foreign sport, Hemingway writes about his first bullfight: "I suddenly saw what bullfighting is all about. For the bull was absolutely unbelievable. He seemed like some great prehistoric animal, absolutely deadly and absolutely vicious." While baseball is familiar to Americans, playing under a dictatorship is not. "This is how we do it and how we are taught to do it," Cuban players tell Curry, who remarks that they never mention "President Fidel Castro's omnipresence . . . barely addressing the prickly topic of defection." He emphasizes cultural norms in Cuba, observing that Cubans live "a way of life that stresses the whole, not the parts."

The readings in this chapter also serve as varied models of writing, ranging from journalism to historical analysis. It's interesting to note how Kim, Sengupta, Hemingway, and Curry report on buzkashi, cricket, bullfighting, and Cuban baseball, respectively, from firsthand observation. What are the writers' goals? Look for language in the works that seems to defend or criticize the sports, the players, or even the governments. Are the writers objective, supportive, or defensive? Sagan and Guttmann tackle the place of sports in world culture overall and can afford to offer more opinionated analysis. Does their language differ from the less analytical reading selections?

This chapter is intended to introduce you to the idea that there *are* sports outside of the United States and sometimes those sports have different meanings in those cultures than ours do to our culture. As you read, continue to ask yourself what place sports hold in world cultures. Are they meant for popular entertainment or political strength? If you have traveled outside the United States or if you know friends or family from other countries, you might begin by reflecting on what you already know about sports in other cultures. How much do most Americans really know about sports in other cultures? How much do we care? If we really claim to care about our place in this world, shouldn't we think and talk about other cultures? Why or why not?

Game: The Prehistoric Origin of Sports
CARL SAGAN

Noted astronomer Carl Sagan is best known for his writing related to science. His works range from the novel Contact, *which was the basis for the 1997 Robert Zemeckis film starring Jodie Foster, to the nonfiction* Cosmos, *which became the best-selling science book ever published in the English language. In 1978 he won the Pulitzer Prize for his book* The Dragons of Eden: Speculations on the Evolution of Human Intelligence. *Sagan died in 1996, after spending many years as a leader in the U.S. space program and as an advisor to NASA. In his book* Billions and Billions, *which was published posthumously, Sagan applies his knowledge of math, science, and space to everyday life, including questions regarding the future of our environment. Sagan wrote many articles for* Parade *magazine, which is carried by hundreds of Sunday newspapers. Though Sagan was a sports fan, and in particular an enthusiastic New York Yankees fan, he rarely wrote about sport. This article, originally published in a 1987 issue of* Parade, *combines his love for sport with his philosophical and inquisitive nature. By examining society's hunter-gatherer origins, he asks, "Why should we feel compelled to watch people run or hit? Why is this need trans-cultural?"*

✦

We can't help ourselves. On Sunday afternoons and Monday nights in the fall of each year, we abandon everything to watch small moving images of 22 men—running into one another, falling down, picking themselves up and kicking an elongated object made from the skin of an animal. Every now and then, both the players and the sedentary spectators are moved to rapture or despair by the progress of the play. All over America, people (mainly men), transfixed before glass screens, cheer or mutter in unison. Put this way, it sounds stupid. But once you get the hang of it, it's hard to resist, and I speak from experience.

Athletes run, jump, hit, slide, throw, kick, tackle—and there's a thrill in seeing humans do it so well. They wrestle each other to the ground. They're keen on grabbing or clubbing or kicking a fast-moving brown or white thing. In some games, they try to herd the thing toward what's called a "goal"; in other games, the players run away and then return "home." Teamwork is almost everything, and we admire how the parts fit together to make a jubilant whole.

But these are not the skills most of us use to earn our daily bread. Why should we feel compelled to watch people run or hit? Why is this need trans-cultural? (Ancient Egyptians, Persians, Greeks, Romans, Mayans and Aztecs also played ball. "Polo" is Tibetan.)

There are sports stars who make 10 times the annual salary of the President; who are themselves, after retirement, elected to high office. They are national heroes. Why, exactly? There is something here transcending the diversity of political, social and economic systems. Something ancient is calling.

Most major sports are associated with a nation or a city, and they carry with them elements of patriotism and civic pride. Our team represents *us*—where we live, our people—against those other guys from some different place, populated by unfamiliar, maybe hostile people. (True, most of "our" players are not *really* from here. They're mercenaries and with clear conscience regularly defect from opposing cities for suitable emolument: A Pittsburgh Pirate is reformed into a California Angel; a San Diego Padre is raised to a St. Louis Cardinal; a Golden State Warrior is crowned a Sacramento King. Occasionally, a whole team picks up and migrates to another city.)

Competitive sports are symbolic conflicts, thinly disguised. This is hardly a new insight. The Cherokees called their ancient form of lacrosse "the little brother of war." Or here is Max Rafferty, former California Superintendent of Public Instruction, who, after denouncing critics of college football as "kooks, crumbums, commies, hairy loudmouthed beatniks," goes on to state, "Football is war without killing . . . Football players . . . possess a clear, bright, fighting spirit which is America itself." (That's worth mulling over.) An often-quoted sentiment of the late coach Vince Lombardi is that the only thing that counts is winning. Former Washington Redskins' coach George Allen put it this way: "Losing is like death."

Indeed, we talk of winning and losing a war as naturally as we do of winning and losing a game. In a televised U.S. Army recruitment ad, we see the aftermath of an armored warfare exercise in which one tank destroys another; in the tag line, the victorious tank commander says, "When we win, the whole team wins, the whole tank wins—not one person." The connection between sports and combat is made quite clear. Sports fans (the word is short for "fanatics") have been known to commit assault and battery, and sometimes murder, when taunted about a losing team; or when prevented from cheering on a winning team; or when they feel an injustice has been committed by the referees.

The British prime minister was obliged in 1985 to denounce the rowdy, drunken behavior of British soccer fans who attacked an Italian contingent for having the effrontery to root for their own team. Dozens were killed when the stands collapsed. In 1969, after three hard-fought soccer games, Salvadoran tanks crossed the

[handwritten marginal note: So what if someone goes to war but doesn't like football?]

Honduran border, and Salvadoran bombers attacked Honduran ports and military bases. In this "Soccer War," the casualties numbered in the thousands.

Afghani tribesmen played polo with the severed heads of former adversaries. And 600 years ago, in what is now Mexico City, there was a ball court where gorgeously attired nobles watched uniformed teams compete. The captain of the losing team was beheaded, and the skulls of earlier losing captains were displayed on racks—an inducement possibly even more compelling than winning one for the Gipper.

Suppose you're idly flipping the dial on your television set, and you come upon some competition in which you have no particular emotional investment—say off-season volleyball between Burma and Thailand. How do you decide which team to root for? But wait a minute: Why root for either? Why not just enjoy the game? Most of us have trouble with this detached posture. We want to take part in the contest, to feel ourselves a member of a team. The feeling simply sweeps us away, and there we are rooting, "Go, Burma!" Initially, our loyalties may oscillate, first urging on one team and then the other. Sometimes we root for the underdog. Other times, shamefully, we even switch our allegiance from loser to winner as the outcome becomes clear. (When there is a succession of losing seasons, fan loyalties tend to drift elsewhere.) What we are looking for is victory without effort. We want to be swept into something like a small, safe, successful war.

The earliest known organized athletic events date back 3500 years to pre-classical Greece. During the original Olympic Games, an armistice put all wars among Greek city-states on hold. The games were more important than the wars. The men performed nude; no women spectators were allowed. By the eighth century B.C., the Olympic Games consisted of running *(lots* of running), jumping, throwing things (including javelins) and wrestling (sometimes to the death). While none of these events was a team sport, they were clearly central to modern team sports.

They were also central to low-technology hunting. Hunting is traditionally considered a sport, as long as you don't eat what you catch—a proviso much easier for the rich to comply with than the poor. From the earliest pharaohs, hunting has been associated with military aristocracies. Oscar Wilde's aphorism about English fox hunting, "the unspeakable in full pursuit of the uneatable," makes a similar dual point. The forerunners of football, soccer, hockey and kindred sports were so-called "rabble games," recognized as substitutes for hunting—because young men who worked for a living were barred from the hunt.

So, perhaps team sports are not just stylized echoes of ancient wars. Perhaps they also satisfy an almost-forgotten craving for the hunt. Since our passions for sports run so deep and are so broadly distributed, they are likely to be hard-wired into us—not in our brains but in our genes. The 10,000 years since the invention of agriculture is not nearly enough time for such predispositions to have evolved. If we want to understand them, we must go much further back.

The human species is hundreds of thousands of years old. We have led a sedentary existence—based on farming and domestication of animals—for only the last 3 percent of that period, during which is all our history. In the first 97 percent of our tenure on Earth, almost everything that is characteristically human came into being. We can learn something about those times from the few surviving hunter-gatherer communities uncorrupted by civilization.

We wander. With our little ones and all our belongings on our backs, we wander—following the game, seeking the waterholes. We set up camp for a while, then move on. In providing food for the group, the men mainly hunt, the women mainly gather. Meat and potatoes. A typical itinerant band, mainly an extended family of relatives and in-laws, numbers a few dozen; although annually many hundreds of us, with the same language and culture, gather— for religious ceremonies, to trade, to arrange marriages, to tell stories. There are many stories about the hunt.

I'm focusing here on the hunters, who are men. But women have significant social, economic and cultural power. They gather the essential staples—nuts, fruits, tubers, roots—as well as medicinal herbs, hunt small animals and provide strategic intelligence on large animal movements. Men do some gathering as well, and considerable "housework" (even though we have no houses). But hunting—only for food, never for sport—is the lifelong occupation of every able-bodied male.

Preadolescent boys stalk birds and small mammals with bows and arrows. By adulthood they have become experts in weapons-procurement; in stalking, killing and butchering the prey; and in carrying the cuts of meat back to camp. The first successful kill of a large mammal marks a young man's coming of age. In his initiation, ceremonial incisions are made on his chest or arms and an herb is rubbed into the cuts so that, when healed, a patterned tattoo results. It's like campaign ribbons—one look at his chest, and you know something of his combat experience.

From a jumble of hoofprints, we can accurately tell how many animals passed; the species, sexes and ages; whether any are lame; how long since they passed; and how far away they are likely to be. Some young animals can be caught by open-field tackles; others with slingshots or boomerangs, or just by throwing rocks accurately and hard. Animals that have not yet learned to fear man can be approached boldly and clubbed to death. At greater distances, for warier prey, we hurl spears or shoot poisoned arrows. Sometimes we're lucky and, by a carefully coordinated rush, can drive a herd of animals into an ambush or off a cliff.

Teamwork among the hunters is essential. If we are not to frighten the quarry, we must communicate by sign language. For the same reason, we need to have our emotions under control; both fear and exultation are dangerous. We are ambivalent about the prey. We respect the animals, recognize our kinship, identify with them. But if we reflect too closely on their intelligence or devotion to their young, if we feel pity for them, our dedication to the hunt will slacken; we will bring home less food, and again our band may be endangered. We are obliged to put an emotional distance between us and them.

So contemplate this: For a million years, our male ancestors are scampering about, throwing rocks at pigeons, running after baby antelopes and wrestling them to the ground, forming a single line of shouting, running hunters and trying to terrify a herd of startled wart hogs upwind. Imagine that their lives depend on hunting skills and teamwork. And good hunters were also good warriors. Then, after a long while—a few thousand centuries, say—a natural predisposition for both hunting and teamwork will inhabit many newborn boys. Why? Because incompetent or unenthusiastic hunters leave fewer offspring. I don't think how to chip a spearpoint out of stone or how to feather an arrow is in our genes. That's taught or figured out. But a zest for the chase—I bet that *is* hard-wired. Natural selection helped mold our ancestors into superb hunters.

The clearest evidence of the success of the hunter-gatherer lifestyle is the simple fact that it extended to six continents and lasted a million years. After 40,000 generations in which the killing of animals was our hedge against starvation, those inclinations must still be in us. We hunger to put them to use, even vicariously. Team sports provide a way.

Some part of our being longs to join a small band of brothers on a daring and intrepid quest. The traditional manly virtues—taciturnity, resourcefulness, modesty, consistency, deep knowledge of animals, love of the outdoors—were all adaptive behavior in hunter-gatherer times. We still admire these traits, although we've almost forgotten why.

Besides sports, there are few outlets available. In our adolescent males, we can still recognize the young hunter, the aspirant warrior—leaping across apartment rooftops; riding, helmetless, on a motorcycle; making trouble for the winning team at a post-game celebration. In the absence of a steadying hand, those old instincts may go a little askew (although our murder rate is about the same as among the !Kung San, the present-day hunter-gatherer people of Botswana). We try to ensure that any residual zest for killing does not spill over onto humans. We don't always succeed.

I think of how powerful those hunting instincts are, and I worry. I worry that Monday-night football is insufficient outlet for the modern hunter-gatherer, decked out in his overalls or uniform or three-piece suit. I think of that ancient legacy about not expressing our feelings, about keeping an emotional distance from those we kill, and it takes some of the fun out of the game.

Hunter-gatherers generally posed no danger to themselves: because their economies tended to be healthy (many had more free time than we do); because, as nomads, they had few possessions, almost no theft and little envy; because greed and arrogance were considered to be not only social evils but also pretty close to mental illnesses; because women had real political power and tended to be a stabilizing and mitigating influence before the boys started going for their poisoned arrows; and because, when serious crimes were committed—murder, say—the band collectively rendered judgment and punishment. Hunter-gatherers organized egalitarian democracies. They had no chiefs. There was no political or corporate hierarchy to dream of climbing. There was no one to revolt against.

So, if we're stranded a few hundred centuries from when we long to be—if (through no fault of our own) we find ourselves, in an age of nuclear weapons, with Pleistocene emotions but without Pleistocene social safeguards—perhaps we can be excused for a little Monday-night football.

Questions for Discussion and Writing

1. Examine how Sagan supports his theory that our need for sports is based on our hunter-gatherer origins. How much of the support is rooted in some sort of hard evidence and how much comes from Sagan's own knowledge or observations? Which type of evidence is more convincing and why?
2. Everyone has a role in Sagan's analysis of culture: men, women, children, and even prey. How do those roles differ in countries around the world and how might those differences impact or change Sagan's analysis?
3. Why didn't our ancestors hunt for sport? Write your own answer based on your ancestral history. Then consider how the answer might change if you were born and raised in another country or culture.
4. Sagan says that competitive sports are "symbolic conflicts, thinly disguised." What quotations in Sagan's essay support this thesis and why?
5. According to Sagan, how might we exercise our hunter-gatherer tendencies if we didn't have sports? Explain how you arrived at your answer.

The Olympics: A History of the Modern Games
ALLEN GUTTMANN

In a classic case of "the chicken or the egg" argument, many sports experts and scholars have debated which came first: the Olympics or politics. In The Olympics: A History of the Modern Games, *scholar Allen Guttmann claims that the two can't live without each other. A professor of English and American Studies at Amherst College, Guttmann's early scholarly interests were in American history and literature. But while serving a brief teaching stint in Germany, Guttmann says he "visited the Olympic Stadium in Berlin and observed 50,000 Germans screaming their heads off at a soccer match," and he wondered, "What was* that *all about? Why weren't they playing baseball or football?" Now a noted sports historian, Guttmann has since written several books on sports history, including* Women's Sports: A History; Games and Empires: Modern Sports and Cultural Imperialism; *and* From Ritual to Record: The Nature of Modern Sports. *He received the first President's Award for Sports Studies from the International Olympic Committee. In the following excerpts from* The Olympics: A History of the Modern Games, *Guttmann writes as part-scholar, part-journalist, part-debater. In the book, he discusses many "political" instances in Olympic history, including South Africa's refusal to put aside its policy of Apartheid for the Olympic Games, the terrorist attack at the 1972 Olympics in Munich, and the call for a boycott of the 1980 Olympics when the Soviets invaded Afghanistan. He argues early on that "politics . . . has always been a part of the Olympics." Later he examines "The Most Controversial Olympics," the so-called Nazi Olympics of 1936.*

---------------- ◆ ----------------

Whenever the Olympic Games are threatened by political protests or disrupted by acts of terror, as was the case in 1968 and 1972, whenever the games are diminished by massive boycotts, as was the case in 1976, 1980, and 1984, the International Olympic Committee (IOC) and most of the world's sportswriters lament the intrusion of politics into the domain of sports. Politics, however, in the broadest sense of the term, has *always* been a part of the Olympics. The modern games were, in fact, revived to propagate a political message. In the eyes of Pierre de Coubertin and the men who succeeded him as president of the IOC, the political purpose of the games—the reconciliation of warring nations—was more important than the sports. *They* were merely the competitive means to a cooperative end: a world at peace. The games, wrote Coubertin in his *Mémoires Olympiques*, "are not simply world championships, they are the quadrennial festival of universal youth."

The brighter the dream, the darker the despair when the dream is disappointed. The most horrific episode in Olympic history—the ghoulish murder in the middle of the Olympic village of eleven Israeli athletes and officials by Palestinian terrorists—was obviously the antithesis of what Coubertin wanted, but the horror perpetrated in 1972 has to be understood against the background of idealism. The nightmare of nationalistic hatred was the terrorists' answer to the dream of international harmony.

Since most sports spectators are more interested in the athletes and their performances than they are in Olympism as a social movement, the notion that the games are inherently political might seem odd; but a brief consideration of the symbolism of the Olympics is instructive. The interlocked Olympic rings were designed by Coubertin in 1914 as a representation of the five continents and the colors of their many national flags. The Olympic torch, lit at the site of the ancient games and carried by thousands of relay runners from Greece to the host city, is intended to dramatize connection and continuity through time and space. The parade of national teams, beginning with Greece and concluding with the host country, is another symbol of international cooperation. The athletes who stand and recite the Olympic oath do so in the name of thousands of male and female athletes who come together from every portion of the globe. The Olympic hymn is still another statement of peaceful internationalism.

Coubertin's vision of a better world was liberal in the sense of classic nineteenth-century liberalism (which should not be confused with its collectivist twentieth-century variant). Individual liberty was the highest good. Like other prophets of nineteenth-century liberalism, however, Coubertin was torn between a belief in individualism and the conviction that nationality is the indispensable core of individual identity. His internationalism was never cosmopolitan. Although the Olympic Charter proclaims that the games are contests between individuals, not between nations, the IOC created an institutional structure based on national representation: no athlete can compete as an individual; every athlete must be selected by his or her country's national Olympic committee; every athlete—even the otherwise irrepressible Florence Griffith-Joyner—must wear a national uniform; when a victor is honored, a national flag is raised and a national anthem is played. There have been many efforts to replace these symbols of nationalism with the Olympic flag and the Olympic hymn, but they have always failed. When a number of European teams marched behind the Olympic banner in 1980 to protest the Soviet Union's invasion of Afghanistan, there were bitter complaints from nationalistic fans who wanted to see the Union Jack and the Tricoleur.

In other words, the political vision institutionalized in the Olympics has always been inconsistent and contradictory. The danger of rabidly nationalistic partisanship was there from the start. No wonder, then, that the history of the Olympics has been a mixed one in which the glories of individual athletic achievement have been accompanied by frenzies of chauvinism. To witness the spectators' emotions when *their* national representative mounts the victor's podium, when *their* flag is raised, when *their* anthem is played, is to wonder if nationalism—or sport—is not the true religion of the modern world.

It all depends, of course, on how one defines religion. In their beliefs, Coubertin and his followers were liberals in the spirit of

Thomas Jefferson and John Stuart Mill. Deeply suspicious of conventional theistic religions, they promoted Olympism as a substitute for traditional faith. "For me," Coubertin wrote in his *Mémoires Olympiques*, "sport is a religion with church, dogma, ritual." In a radio address delivered in Berlin on August 4, 1935, he repeated his frequently expressed desire that the games be inspired by "religious sentiment transformed and enlarged by the internationalism and democracy that distinguish the modern age." Nearly thirty years later, Coubertin's most dedicated disciple, Avery Brundage, proclaimed to his colleagues on the International Olympic Committee that Olympism is a twentieth-century religion, "a religion with universal appeal which incorporates all the basic values of other religions, a modern, exciting, virile, dynamic religion."

Coubertin and Brundage were quite serious when they touted Olympism as a religion. They realized that, historically, religious differences have caused as much bloodshed as national differences, and they imagined that the Olympic Games might form the nucleus of a modern secular faith based on "good sportsmanship and fair play." To a surprising degree they succeeded. Adherents of every major faith have put aside their religious differences in order to participate, however briefly, in Olympism. The Olympics have actually been far more successful in damping the flames of religious conflict than in controlling the repercussions of political controversy. The one great exception to this generalization occurred when sports, religion, and politics intersected. Attempting to justify the murders committed at the 1972 Games, a Palestinian spokesman averred that the terrorists recognized "that sport is the modern religion of the western world. . . . So we decided to use the Olympics, the most sacred ceremony of this religion, to make the world pay attention to us."

Although Coubertin and his followers were not immune to the racism of their day, their liberalism was—at least theoretically— colorblind. The Olympic Games were also meant to symbolize the irrelevance of race within the world of sports and, ultimately, within the political realm. The removal of racial barriers was a less explicit goal than the elimination of hostilities based on national and religious differences, but interracial harmony has gradually become a major tenet of Olympism. This tenet was especially salient during the long struggle with the South African National Olympic Committee over its refusal to condemn the government's strict policy of apartheid.

Like most nineteenth-century liberals, the aristocratic Coubertin was so enthralled by the notion of individual liberty that he was insufficiently attentive to the constraints of social class. (Karl Marx was definitely *not* one of Coubertin's intellectual mentors.) Although the Frenchman was highly skeptical about the cult of amateurism, he nonetheless embraced it, at least in public, and he seemed unaware that its central purpose was the exclusion of the lower classes from the sports competitions of their "betters." (Amateurism in the late nineteenth century meant the ineligibility of all those who performed *any kind* of manual work, whether or not the work was sports related.) Although more consistently liberal views have prevailed, so that the disadvantages of class have been lessened, the amateur-professional dichotomy still confuses the rule books.

Coubertin's version of liberal individualism was even more inadequate in its narrowly conventional treatment of women. Nonwhite athletes and athletes from working-class families have been disadvantaged, but their road to Olympia has been straighter and smoother than the rocky path female athletes have been forced to traverse. For Coubertin's generation, the socially constructed distinctions of gender seemed to be the dictates of biological inevitability. The games were definitely *not* meant to minimize the differences between men and women. They were never intended, in those days, as a platform for women's rights. The games began as a sports festival for men, and if Coubertin had had his way, women would have remained forever restricted to the role of admiring spectators.

Needless to say, it has taken nearly a century for some of the internal contradictions of Olympism to be understood and partially eliminated (and for other problems, like commercialism and drug abuse, to have arisen). None of the explicit or implicit values of Olympism has ever been perfectly realized. When the German philosopher (and Olympic victor) Hans Lenk attempted to assess the degree to which the goals of Olympism have been reached, he was left with a complicated list of partial successes and partial failures.

Small wonder. The story of the Olympics is a complex narrative. It is comprised of the stellar sports achievements of the world's most gifted athletes competing among themselves as representatives of the strength, swiftness, endurance, grace, and courage of all humankind. It is also comprised of the bitter political conflicts and petty squabbles of men and women groping their way to what we hope may be a better world. The chronologically organized chapters that follow are an attempt to tell this composite story of sports and politics. Although it is quite impossible in a single volume to report on the thousands of contests and the tens of thousands of athletes who have participated from 1896 to 1988, I have tried to comment briefly on some of the most memorable sports achievements. My primary purpose, however, is to demonstrate that the Olympics have, indeed, been what their founders wanted them to be: political. To lament the "intrusion of politics into the world of sports" is naive. To hope that modern sports can contribute significantly to the cause of a more just and humane political order may be equally naive. But Pierre de Coubertin was surely right about one thing: we need our ideals.

THE MOST CONTROVERSIAL OLYMPICS

At the Olympic congress held in Berlin in 1930, the German organizers had worked hard to demonstrate to the International Olympic Committee that Berlin would be the ideal venue for the 1936 Games. As Theodor Lewald, one of Germany's three IOC members, said in what was for him unusually vivid language, "Here [at the Congress] we detonated our bombs." The effort succeeded. At its twenty-ninth session in Barcelona in April 1931, the IOC had been unable to select the site for the 1936 Games, but a subsequent mail ballot produced forty-three votes for Berlin and only sixteen for Barcelona. The choice of Berlin ratified the full reintegration of Germany within the world of international sports. When the IOC's decision was announced on May 13, 1931, Heinrich Brüning was Germany's chancellor and a shaky centrist coalition was in power. When the games were actually held, the National Socialists were in power and Adolf Hitler was chancellor. In fact, Hitler's rule began only six days after the creation, on January 24, 1933, of the Organisationskomitee. This state of affairs was certainly not what the IOC had expected when Berlin was chosen as the site of the games.

Quite apart from any general concern they might have had about nazism, there was reason for committee members to be worried. Although Hitler thought that German boys should learn to box, in order to steel themselves for the rigors of their role as natural rulers, neither he nor his cohorts were advocates of modern sports. Sports were almost unmentioned in *Mein Kampf* and in the pages of the party's newspaper, *Der völkische Beobachter*. The problem in Nazi eyes was that modern sports had developed in England rather than in Germany and they were, at least in principle, universalistic rather than particularistic. Among the most important characteristics of modern sports—in theory if not in practice—is equality: neither race nor religion nor ideology should be a factor in the determination of athletic excellence. Such a notion was, of course, anathema to Nazis dedicated to a primitive belief in the racial supremacy of the "Aryan" people. A Nazi spokesman, Bruno Malitz, condemned modern sports because they were international, "infested" with "Frenchmen, Belgians, Pollacks, and Jew-Niggers" who had been allowed "to start on the tracks, to play on the soccer fields, and to swim in the pools." On August 19, 1932, *Der völkische Beobachter* demanded that the Olympic Games be restricted to white athletes.

The Nazi conception of modern sports was only a little more demented than the attitudes of some of the traditional *Turner*. While the British and the Americans were inventing games like soccer, rugby, basketball, and volleyball, games that quickly spread throughout the world, most *Turner* remained devoted to gymnastics as their nation's sole authentic form of physical exercise. These believers in German gymnastics condemned competition, which is an inherent aspect of sports, and they were appalled by the specialization, rationalization, and quantification that are characteristic of modern sports. The Deutsche Turnerschaft, the largest and most important gymnastics organization, had shunned the first Olympics and had been quite ambivalent about participation in subsequent games. The Nazis were ideologically close to the Deutsche Turnerschaft, whose last leader, Edmund Neuendorff, invited Hitler in 1933 to be the guest of honor at a grand *Turnfest* in Stuttgart. Hitler accepted the invitation and was received by Neuendorff with hysterical declarations of fealty. Massed displays of Teutonic vigor and parades to martial music seemed much more in tune with Nazi ideology than an international sports festival open to Afro-Americans, to Asians, and to Jews. The IOC and the organizing committee braced themselves for Hitler's announcement that he wanted another authentic *Turnfest* in 1936—not some international celebration of human solidarity.

Among the most worried were the president and the secretary of the Organisationskomitee, Theodor Lewald and Carl Diem. The former was the son of a Berlin lawyer and civil servant. A member of the IOC since 1924, Lewald had also served as president of the German National Olympic Committee (and as chairman of the Deutscher Reichsausschuss für Leibesübungen, the closest German equivalent to the Amateur Athletic Union). Although Lewald seemed to typify the austere Prussian tradition of public service, he had good reason to be anxious about his personal safety as well as about the future of the Olympic Games. His father had converted from Judaism to Christianity and *Der völkische Beobachter* had already begun screaming for his dismissal. Diem, the secretary of the organizing committee, was a self-made man with a career in sports journalism and in sports administration. At the age of thirty he was captain of the German team that competed in Stockholm. Despite his lack of formal education, he eventually developed into a remarkable scholar, still known for his comprehensive history of sports (published in 1960) and for many monographs in sports history. In 1920, with support from Lewald, he founded the Deutsche Hochschule für Leibesübungen (German Sports University). Although Diem was sufficiently the child of his times to have been an ardent nationalist throughout the twenties, he was definitely a believer in modern sports and he was able to acknowledge the achievements of athletes from foreign nations. For the German tradition of *Turnen* he had less sympathy. Although Diem was not stigmatized by Jewish forebears, his wife was. It was also held against him that the Deutsche Hochschule für Leibesübungen had several Jews on its faculty. For these sins, Diem was denounced in the Nazi press as a "white Jew."

Given their endangered personal positions and the shrill hostility of many Nazis to sports in general and the Olympics in particular, neither Lewald nor Diem was optimistic about the 1936 Games and both were apprehensive when they were summoned, on March 16, 1933, to meet with Hitler at the chancellory. To their astonishment and relief, Hitler did not order an immediate cessation of preparations but instead gave the two men his tentative approval. He had not suddenly changed his mind and become a convert to Olympism; rather, his propaganda minister, Josef Goebbels, had realized that the games were a splendid opportunity to demonstrate German vitality and organizational expertise. Lewald was forced to resign from his post with the Deutscher Reichsausschuss für Leibesübungen and Diem had to give up his position at the Deutsche Hochschule für Leibesübungen; however, pressure from Comte Henri de Baillet-Latour and the IOC prevented the Nazis from expelling Lewald and Diem from the organizing committee. Thus, Lewald, Diem, and Hitler became uneasy collaborators. On October 5, 1933, Hitler toured the site of the games, inspected the progress of the construction, and became positively lyrical about the prospects for the grandest Olympics ever. Five days later, at the chancellory, he promised the startled Lewald the full financial support of his regime, a sum later set at 20,000,000 Reichsmarks. Lewald and Diem were stunned by their unexpected good fortune. . . .

If the 1936 Summer Games were not the triumph of Olympism that Brundage and Baillet-Latour insisted they were, were they, on the contrary, a propaganda coup for the Nazis? The question is not easily answered. Hitler had told Diem and Lewald that he wanted to impress the world with the magnificence of the games, and the world was impressed. The facilities were monumental. The magnificent Deutsches Stadion that was originally planned for the 1916 Games was expanded to accommodate 110,000 spectators. At the open-air Olympic pool, 18,000 spectators were able to follow the swimming and diving events. The pageantry, which can still be vicariously experienced in Leni Riefenstahl's documentary film *Olympia*, was truly extraordinary. Among Diem's inspired innovations was an enormous iron bell inscribed with the words *"Ich rufe die Jugend der Welt"* (I summon the youth of the world). It was also Diem's idea that a torch be lit at Olympia and carried by a relay of thousands of runners from there to the stadium in Berlin, where it was used to ignite the Olympic flame. Spiridon Louys, the Greek peasant who had won the first marathon in 1896, was invited to Berlin, where he presented Hitler with an olive branch. (In retrospect, the symbolism becomes a tragic irony. Other victors from 1896, like gymnast Alfred Flatow and his cousin Gustav, were murdered in the course of Hitler's monstrous "final solution of the Jewish problem.") . . .

The athletes were impressed not only by the magnificent sports facilities but also by the Olympic village, where every effort was made to secure their comfort. (The second half of Riefenstahl's film begins with a pastoral sequence set in the village.) There were over one hundred buildings to house the athletes, and their national cuisines were served in thirty-eight separate dining halls. While in the village, runners were able to train on a 400-meter track, while swimmers and oarsmen utilized a specially constructed artificial lake. There was no way for the athletes to have anticipated that Captain Wolfgang Fürstner, who had been in charge of the village, was later to be driven to suicide by Nazi persecution.

The strongest evidence for Brundage's claim that the 1936 Summer Olympics were not a propaganda triumph is the fact that Jesse Owens was unquestionably the star of the games. Setting a world record of 10.3 seconds for 100 meters and an Olympic record of 20.7 seconds for 200 meters, he went on to jump an astonishing 8.06 meters and to help set still another world record in the 400-meter relay. In photographs published in the German press during and after the games, Owens appears in a favorable light. On August 7, *The Spectator* (London) commented, "The German spectators, like all others, have fallen under the spell of the American Negro Jesse Owens, who is already the hero of these Games." He was described in the text of one popular publication as the *Wunderathlet of* the games. In Riefenstahl's documentary film, he appears as if he really were an Olympian, a god of sports. A French journalist reviewed the film in an article aptly entitled *"Les Dieux du stade"* (The Gods of the Stadium). In *Olympia* the camera follows Owens as it does no other athlete. When Goebbels, whose propaganda office secretly financed the film, protested that there were too many positive shots of the black American athlete, Riefenstahl appealed to Hitler, who intervened to prevent the cuts ordered by Goebbels. Ironically, no photographs of Owens (or of any of the other black athletes) appeared in the Atlanta *Constitution*, the most liberal of southern U.S. newspapers. . . .

All in all, the United States did well enough in track and field and in diving for American journalists gleefully to claim that the United States had "won" the 1936 Olympics. There was certainly reason to be proud not only of the black athletes but also of Glenn Morris, who won the decathlon, and Helen Stephens, whose time in the 100-meter race (11.5 seconds) was faster than Thomas Burke's had been at the first modern Olympics. It is said that even Hitler was impressed by her "virile beauty." It was easy for the Americans to overlook the aquatic achievements of the Japanese men and Holland's champion swimmer, Hendrika Mastenbroek (three gold medals and one silver). How many readers, sitting over breakfast and scanning the local paper, realized that the Egyptians were superb in weight lifting, the Swedes and Hungarians in wrestling, the Italians in fencing, the French in cycling, and the Germans in just about everything? In fact, the Germans won thirty-three events, came in second in twenty-six, and finished third in another thirty. *The Spectator* for August 21 contained that journal's quadrennial vintage of sour grapes: "When to win the Olympic Games becomes an object of British, as it has German, policy, we shall really have reached the stage of senility, the true decadence."

If most of the world's sports fans were but dimly aware of German athletic superiority, it was not the fault of the government-controlled media. In addition to pre-Olympic newsletters and other publications, there was television transmission to twenty-five TV halls and shortwave radio broadcasts that reached some forty countries. Commentators from twenty-two countries sent the message. Finally, in 1938, Riefenstahl's *Olympia* was released with English and French as well as German narration. The Nazi propaganda apparatus made much of the mostly favorable press coverage of the games and exploited to the utmost the aged, infirm Coubertin's remarks (his last public pronouncement) that these "grandiose" games, organized with "Hitlerian strength and discipline," had "magnificently served the Olympic ideal."

Questions for Discussion and Writing

1. Guttmann claims that the terrorist attack at the 1972 Olympics in Munich was meant to deliberately upset the "international harmony" of the Olympic Games. To believe that claim, must we see the Olympics as political in nature? Do you see the Olympics as political or not? Explain your reasoning.

2. How effective is Guttmann's explanation of Olympic symbols such as the rings and torch in furthering his claim that the Olympics are by nature political?

3. Look at the way Guttmann organizes the beginning of his book. Why do you think he writes about nationalism first, then religion, and then discussions of racism, social class, and gender?

4. According to Guttmann and many other historians, much of the reason Hitler allowed the 1936 Olympics to go on in Germany had to do with propaganda. How did Hitler use the 1936 Olympics to make Germany "look good"? Research the use of propaganda by the Nazi party and write an analysis that includes an examination of Olympic propaganda.

5. Analyze the final quotation from the excerpt where Pierre de Coubertin, the first president of the International Olympic Committee, says the 1936 Olympics were organized with "Hitlerian strength and discipline" and had "magnificently served the Olympic ideal." Think about the quotation in light of Guttmann's remarks about Olympic ideals from the introduction. Is Coubertin praising Adolf Hitler with his comment? What is Guttmann's opinion of Coubertin's statement and of the Nazi propaganda machine?

Buzkashi: An Afghan Tradition Thrives

LUCIAN KIM

The work of prolific writer Lucian Kim has appeared in publications ranging from The Independent (London) *to* The Moscow Times *to* The Boston Globe. *He has traveled throughout the world, notably to Germany, Afghanistan, Hungary, and Russia. Kim earned a graduate degree in journalism from the University of California-Berkeley and also studied at Central European University. In 1996 he earned a fellowship with the Human Rights Center and worked in the press office of the International Criminal Tribunal for the former Yugoslavia in The Hague, Netherlands. In September 2001 he wrote a special article for* The Christian Science Monitor, *an international daily newspaper, describing the outpouring of European sympathy following the 9/11 attacks on America. Though owned by a church organization, the* Monitor *is not a religious newspaper. While most daily newspapers rely on wire services like the Associated Press for international coverage,* The Christian Science Monitor *sends writers all over the world for firsthand coverage. It's obvious from reading Kim's article, which appeared in the* Monitor, *that he had a front-row seat to watch buzkashi, Afghanistan's national sport. As you read, look for phrases Kim uses to link the centuries-old sport to the culture of this war-torn country.*

---------------- ✦ ----------------

The dozens of turbaned horsemen on their prancing steeds assemble on a dusty field on the outskirts of this city in northern Afghanistan. Despite their shouts and cracking whips, however, the riders' intent is peaceful. As they do on most Friday afternoons after prayer, the horsemen have gathered for a friendly match of buzkashi, or goat grabbing.

Across northern Afghanistan, as well as in neighboring Central Asian states, this winter sport has been an enduring pastime for centuries. The object of the game is for a member of two competing teams to pick up the carcass of a decapitated calf or goat from the ground, carry it around a flag, and return it to a circle in front of the judges.

It is not surprising that a game that prizes courage, horsemanship, and brute strength would be one of the most popular forms of public entertainment here.

Buzkashi is sport reduced to its simplest form, with no contrived side-shows or complicated rules. And, as many things are done in Afghanistan, the seeming chaos of a buzkashi match actually follows a deliberate system that is not always obvious to the foreign observer.

During Taliban rule, many of the top players fled their villages or fought with the Northern Alliance. Others left the country. But now the pros are trickling back. Teams from local villages play each other. Sometimes matches are held to celebrate a wedding or the birth of a son; other times tournaments take place in which thousands of horsemen participate.

At the start of a round, the master riders, known as chapandaz, bunch up in a tangle of men and horses. Players in the midst of the fray stoop down from their mounts—whip in mouth—and try to grab the carcass, which can weigh up to 150 pounds. Suddenly, one rider breaks from the crowd, dragging the calf as he gallops across the field with his rivals in hot pursuit. Opposing riders use their whips to urge on their horses and to hit the rider with the carcass in order to steal it.

Admission is free to the couple of thousand men and boys who have come to cheer on the riders. Armed men futilely try to hold back the throngs by swinging their Kalashnikovs. Often the bystanders become unwilling participants in the game, as the riders charge headlong toward the sidelines, causing the crowd to scatter.

During the match, one chapandaz falls headfirst over his horse, but jumps back on his mount and continues the pursuit. At one point, a motorcycle with a little girl clinging to the back speeds across the field. Nobody seems to mind the three mounted U.S. soldiers, dressed in desert fatigues, who ride with the mass of horsemen.

As the lead horseman with the calf disappears over an embankment and across the road behind the field, a medical student named Baryalai offers a running commentary: "It's not like a football game where there's out-of-bounds," he says. "Because horses are also taking part in this game, it's allowed."

For the owners of the horses, possessing buzkashi champions is a matter of prestige. For the chapandaz, too, glory comes before money. Here, corporate sponsorship is not a foreign idea. At this match, a trading company put up the prize money: about $12.

After the game, Amir Zoyer sits on the field and pulls off his long, pointy riding boots. The 40-year buzkashi veteran is also a local fighter. Once out of his boots, he clambers into a pickup truck, bristling with rocket-propelled grenades, and roars off.

Questions for Discussion and Writing

1. Kim leads the article with several juxtapositions: "cracking whips" and "peaceful," "prancing steeds" and "prayer," "friendly match" and "goat grabbing." What purpose do these seemingly opposite phrases serve in describing this foreign sport for readers?

2. After reading the description of buzkashi, what is your initial impression of the sport? What does it have in common with sports you are familiar with? What is unfamiliar about it? What surprises or shocks you about this sport?

3. Buzkashi seems to serve a higher purpose in Afghanistan than simply being a game or sport. What examples does Kim offer to prove this point?

4. Kim writes much of the article in "travel log" fashion, as if he were there watching a game and reporting what he sees. Examine some of the parts where his descriptions and observations are particularly effective and discuss why.

5. Write your own description of a sport that might seem foreign to most of your classmates. Include references to traditions or elements of the sport that help explain the culture to your class. What does the sport mean to the citizens of its country? What can it tell us about their culture?

A Cricket Match Bridges a Longtime Gap in Punjab
SOMINI SENGUPTA

A longtime reporter for The New York Times, *Somini Sengupta has written extensively about India-Pakistan affairs. Born in Calcutta, India, Sengupta lived in Canada for a short time but spent most of her childhood in California. She graduated from the University of California-Berkeley in 1988 and went on to write for the* Los Angeles Times *and* Newsday *before joining* The New York Times. *In 2005 Sengupta became the first South Asian American to hold the position of New Delhi bureau chief at the* Times. *She has a George Polk Award for foreign reporting and has been recognized by the South Asian*

Journalists Association. The following article recounts one of Sengupta's trips to India and Pakistan in 2005 and was published in The New York Times. *The sport called cricket has a long history in India, Pakistan, and neighboring countries. Similar to American baseball, cricket is a team sport that involves a bat and ball. Also like baseball, cricket is recognized as the national sport for many countries. Cricket matches between India and Pakistan temporarily ceased in 1947, when independence from British rule divided India in two; Hindus claimed India and Muslims moved to the newly created Pakistan. In recent years the countries have attempted to resume playing cricket together but political and governmental differences still exist.*

———————— ✦ ————————

After a half-century of fratricide, three wars and a nuclear buildup, now comes another battle between Asia's blood rivals: the India versus Pakistan cricket match.

Except here, high up in the bleachers of the Mohali cricket stadium, under a gorgeous blue sky on Friday, Sameer Dua of India and Muhammad Amjad of Pakistan sit side by side waving flags, showering each other with typically subcontinental accolades.

Mr. Dua, 35, and Mr. Amjad, 32, both textile industry men, met at a business conference last December in Bombay and hit it off. Mr. Dua visited Pakistan for the first time in January. Mr. Amjad and his extended family of six came to India this week to watch cricket.

"The kind of hospitality that was extended to me was unbelievable," Mr. Dua recalled of his visit to Lahore in January.

"He has given us five times what we gave him," Mr. Amjad gushed back.

"No, no, it's not like that," Mr. Dua said with a grin and patted Mr. Amjad's leg. After the cricket match, Mr. Dua planned to take Mr. Amjad's family home to Delhi and then to see the Taj Mahal.

As luck would have it, the two men shared more than cricket and textiles. Mr. Dua's grandfather had fled the newly created Pakistan— in fact, a village not too far from Lahore, where Mr. Amjad's family lives—when the subcontinent was violently partitioned in 1947, prompting one of the largest migrations in human history. Some 12 million people crossed the new border.

As India and Pakistan faced off here in Mohali, in the heart of a divided Punjab Province, for the first test match of a six-week long cricket series, Indians and Pakistanis greeted each other with a mixture of intense curiosity, apprehension, guilt, affection, longing, hope.

Spectators wandered around the stadium here with an Indian flag painted on one cheek and a Pakistani flag on the other. On the streets nearby, sari shops announced discounts for "our friends from Pakistan." Local families took perfect strangers into their homes and refused to take any money. Inside Indian living rooms, Pakistanis traded stories about weddings and children, the quality of the roads, the price of chickens and motorbikes.

Amid the enthusiasm, ordinary Indians and Pakistanis uttered the unthinkable. "There is no difference between us," said Naveed Ahmed, of Bahalwalnagar, in the Pakistani Punjab. It was his first time in India.

Adding an explicitly political flavor to the game, President Pervez Musharraf of Pakistan is expected to attend a match during the series, most likely on April 2 in the Indian city of Kochi.

Last year's cricket match took the Indian team to Pakistan, prompting what people from both countries recall as an effusion of hospitality and grace. "We even applauded the defeat of our own team," recalled Senator Mushahid Hussein of Pakistan.

If partition and cricket were among the principal gifts the British Raj bequeathed to their former subjects on the subcontinent, there was no better place to kick off the India versus Pakistan cricket series than here in Punjab, the epicenter of the bloody 1947 migration: when Sikhs and Hindus fled east into India and Muslims streamed west into the newly created Pakistan. At the cricket match, it was impossible not to find Indians and Pakistanis who carried stories of that time.

For Rajinder Singh, the match offered an occasion to pay what he considered a 50-year-old family debt. His father, a Sikh, was a teenager when their village, Rangpur, now in the Pakistani part of Punjab, broke out in a spasm of sectarian violence. One night, during the worst bloodletting, some neighbors hid them in their car and ferried them to where an Indian Army truck could take Hindus and Sikhs across the border. His family survived.

Settling in what became the Indian side of Punjab, the Singhs named every family enterprise in memory of their native village: Rangpuri Finance, Rangpuri Autos, Rangpuri Handloom. This week, Mr. Singh and his wife, Jaswinder Kaur, to repay their onetime neighbors' kindness, went to where the buses unloaded hundreds of Pakistani cricket fans and brought home an extended family of six young Pakistanis, roughly the same age as their own two sons.

"This was a wish in our hearts, that these people would come as our guests," said Mr. Singh, 45.

"We feel now we have generations-old friendship," said Ayaz Mahmood, 29, one of his Pakistani guests.

Every evening this week, the Indians and the Pakistanis have been drinking together in the Singhs' living room ("I take a hard drink, they take a soft drink," Mr. Singh explained with a nod to his well-stocked bar). Every morning for breakfast, a stream of inquisitive friends have poured in "just to see the Pakistanis," is how he put it.

"As the German people have broken the German wall, we too want to break the Punjab wall," Mr. Singh said. "This is one body, one heart, one language."

Indian officials said that nearly 4,000 Pakistanis were given limited nine-day visas for the test matches. More than a fourth of them also sought permission to visit other tourist sites in India.

Amritsar is the only place that Mateen Azeem's grandparents urged him to visit. They had fled Amritsar in 1947 and settled in Lahore. "They said, 'You must have a few sips of water from Amritsar,'" Mr. Azeem, 30, recalled. He planned to on his way back home.

The Indian prime minister, Manmohan Singh, was himself born in what is now Pakistan. The Pakistani president, General Musharraf, was born in New Delhi.

The cricket series comes at a time when the topsy-turvy relations between the two countries are at a crucial moment. Peace talks have recently yielded agreement on a bus route that would allow Indians and Pakistanis to travel between the two capitals of disputed Kashmir. A new dispute over water rights has been referred to the World Bank for an independent opinion.

Here on the ground, cricket opened people's eyes. A Pakistani teenager admitted to being apprehensive about how the Indians would treat him; all through school, he said, he had learned they were his enemies.

Some things, they learned, were different. Women could walk around more easily without their brothers in India. Cold beer was served during the afternoon tea break. The Pakistanis were horrified by Indian driving standards. "They don't have any traffic sense," said Ali Ahmed, a grain dealer from Pakistani Punjab.

Motorcycles, skin bleaching creams and the price of a rickshaw ride all were found by the Pakistanis to be cheaper here than at home. Saris were half the price.

At Roop Saree Center in a Chandigarh shopping strip, Karamjit Singh and Shaista Tahir sat inspecting a pile of saris. Their families had met when they were living in Tanzania more than 20 years ago. Mrs. Tahir's family had returned to Lahore, and Mrs. Singh's to Chandigarh. They hadn't seen each other since.

As it turned out, Mrs. Singh was born in present-day Pakistan and, until partition, shuttled between family homes in Lahore and Amritsar. In 1947, when Mrs. Singh was 8, the family fled to the Indian side of Punjab. This week, she took her Lahori guests to the Golf Club for lunch, then to see a movie, and on Friday, for an afternoon of shopping. "It's nonstop catching up on things, late-night chatting," she said of their week together.

The women picked over piles of saris. A red paisley print was rejected. An ice-blue chiffon was selected.

The sari shop owner, V.K. Sachdeva, was himself eager to welcome his Pakistani customers and was offering cut-rate prices during the test matches.

It paid to be gracious. This week alone, Mr. Sachdeva said he had done hundreds of thousands of rupees worth of business.

But there was also this other fact. "We belong to Pakistan," he said. His parents fled a village in what is now the Pakistani side of Punjab.

Questions for Discussion and Writing

1. Sengupta begins the article by comparing a cricket match to "fratricide, three wars and a nuclear buildup." As a reader, do you find the comparison shocking or unnatural? Does your reaction make the introduction effective? Why or why not?

2. Dua and Amjad seem like good friends. How were they able to overcome the differences in their countries? Did cricket contribute to their peacemaking or not? Explain your answer.

3. Sengupta waits until the middle of the article to explain the root of the problems between India and Pakistan. Should she have outlined the 1947 migration earlier in the piece? Why or why not? What other writing strategies does Sengupta use to illustrate the seriousness of the divide between India and Pakistan?

4. Sengupta offers the personal story of Rajinder Singh and his family. She also points out that India's prime minister at the time was born in what is now

Pakistan while the Pakistani president was born in a major city in India. What do these types of personal narratives add to an article about two warring countries?

5. This article was published in 2005. Conduct some research to see what the current status is on India-Pakistan relations. As you research the situation, ask yourself the question: Can a sport heal wounds created when two nations despise each other? How powerful can a sport be?

Bullfighting a Tragedy
ERNEST HEMINGWAY

The late Ernest Hemingway is undeniably one of American litera-ture's most renowned authors. His books include classics such as For Whom the Bell Tolls, The Old Man and the Sea, *and* A Farewell to Arms. *He is the winner of both a Pulitzer Prize and a Nobel Prize. Aside from his writing, Hemingway was also an avid athlete and out-doorsman. He lived life on the edge—marrying several times, leaving the United States to live in France, and earning the reputation as a heavy drinker—and he liked his sports equally as edgy. Much of his early journalism appeared in the newspaper the* Toronto Star. *In his articles, he wrote about sports like hunting, big-game fishing, fist fighting, boxing, and bullfighting. Hemingway's travels often led him to write as well. His big-game safari, for example, prompted him to write* The Green Hills of Africa. *Hemingway also loved Spain and considered its national sport, bullfighting, to be more about cere-mony than sport. One of his most famous works is* Death in the Afternoon, *his firsthand experience and defense of the sport. In the following excerpt, from his 1923* Toronto Star *article "Bullfighting a Tragedy," Hemingway argues that bullfighting is not a sport. How-ever, he doesn't use the word* tragedy *in the way we are accustomed to, as in something awful that has happened. How does he mean that bullfighting is a tragedy?*

———————— ✦ ————————

It was spring in Paris and everything looked just a little too beau-tiful. Mike and I decided to go to Spain. Strater drew us a fine map of Spain on the back of a menu of the Strix restaurant. On the same menu he wrote the name of a restaurant in Madrid where the specialty is young suckling pig roasted, the name of the pensione on the Via San Jerónimo where the bullfighters live, and sketched a plan showing where the Grecos are hung in the Prado.

Fully equipped with this menu and our old clothes, we started for Spain. Our objective—to see bullfights.

We left Paris one morning and got off the train at Madrid the next noon. We saw our first bullfight at 4:30 that afternoon. It took about two hours to get tickets. We finally got them from scalpers for twenty-five pesetas apiece. The bullring was entirely sold out. We had barrera seats. These, the scalper explained in Spanish and broken French, were the first row of the ringside, directly under the royal box, and immediately opposite where the bulls would come out.

We asked him if he didn't have any less distinguished seats for somewhere around twelve pesetas, but he was sold out. So we paid the fifty pesetas for the two tickets, and with the tickets in our pockets sat out on the sidewalk in front of a big café near the Puerta del Sol. It was very exciting, sitting out in front of a café your first day in Spain with a ticket in your pocket that meant that rain or shine you were going to see a bullfight in an hour and a half. . . .

Every seat in the amphitheater was full. The arena was cleared. Then on the far side of the arena out of the crowd, four heralds in medieval costume stood up and blew a blast on their trumpets. The band crashed out, and from the entrance on the far side of the ring four horsemen in black velvet with ruffs around their necks rode out into the white glare of the arena. The people on the sunny side were baking in the heat and fanning themselves. The whole sol side was a flicker of fans.

Behind the four horsemen came the procession of the bullfighters. They had been all formed in ranks in the entranceway ready to march out, and as the music started they came. In the front rank walked the three espadas, or toreros, who would have charge of the killing of the six bulls of the afternoon. . . .

The bullfighters march in across the sand to the president's box. They march with easy professional stride, swinging along, not in the least theatrical except for their clothes. They all have the easy grace and slight slouch of the professional athlete. From their faces they might be major league ball players. They salute the president's box and then spread out along the barrera, exchanging their heavy brocaded capes for the fighting capes that have been laid along the red fence by the attendants.

We leaned forward over the barrera. Just below us the three matadors of the afternoon were leaning against the fence talking. One lighted a cigarette. He was a short, clear-skinned gypsy, Gitanillo, in a wonderful gold brocaded jacket, his short pigtail sticking out under his black cocked hat.

"He's not very fancy," a young man in a straw hat, with obviously American shoes, who sat on my left, said.

"But he sure knows bulls, that boy. He's a great killer."

"You're an American, aren't you?" asked Mike.

"Sure," the boy grinned."But I know this gang. That's Gitanillo. You want to watch him. The kid with the chubby face is Chicuelo. They say he doesn't really like bullfighting, but the town's crazy about him. The one next to him is Villalta. He's the great one."

I had noticed Villalta. He was straight as a lance and walked like a young wolf. He was talking and smiling at a friend who leaned over the barrera. Upon his tanned cheekbone was a big patch of gauze held on with adhesive tape.

"He got gored last week at Málaga," said the American.

The American, whom later we were to learn to know and love as the Gin Bottle King, because of a great feat of arms performed at an early hour of the morning with a container of Mr. Gordon's celebrated product as his sole weapon in one of the four most dangerous situations I have ever seen, said: "The show's going to begin." . . .

The crowd had been shouting and yelling. Now it was dead silent. The man with the key stepped toward an iron-barred, low, red door and unlocked the great sliding bar. The door swung open. The man hid behind it. Inside it was dark.

Then, ducking his head as he came up out of the dark pen, a bull came into the arena. He came out all in a rush, big, black and white, weighing over a ton, and moving with a soft gallop. Just as he came out the sun seemed to dazzle him for an instant. He stood as though he were frozen, his great crest of muscle up, firmly planted, his eyes looking around, his horns pointed forward, black and white and sharp as porcupine quills. Then he charged. And as he charged, I suddenly saw what bullfighting is all about.

For the bull was absolutely unbelievable. He seemed like some great prehistoric animal, absolutely deadly and absolutely vicious. And he was silent. He charged silently and with a soft, galloping rush. When he turned he turned on his four feet like a cat. When he charged the first thing that caught his eye was the picador on one of the wretched horses. The picador dug his spurs into the horse and they galloped away. The bull came on in his rush, refused to be shaken off, and in full gallop crashed into the animal from the side, ignored the horse, drove one of his horns high into the thigh of the picador, and tore him, saddle and all, off the horse's back.

The bull went on without pausing to worry the picador lying on the ground. The next picador was sitting on his horse braced to receive the shock of the charge, his lance ready. The bull hit him sideways on, and horse and rider went high up in the air in a kicking mass and fell across the bull's back. As they came down the bull charged into them. The dough-faced kid, Chicuelo, vaulted over the fence, ran toward the bull and flapped his cape into the bull's face. The bull charged the cape and Chicuelo dodged backward and had the bull clear in the arena.

Without an instant's hesitation, the bull charged Chicuelo. The kid stood his ground, simply swung back on his heels and floated his cape like a ballet dancer's skirt into the bull's face as he passed.

"Ole!"—pronounced Oh-Lay!—roared the crowd.

The bull whirled and charged again. Without moving, Chicuelo repeated the performance. His legs rigid, just withdrawing his body from the rush of the bull's horns and floating the cape out with that beautiful swing.

Again the crowd roared. The Kid did this seven times. Each time the bull missed him by inches. Each time he gave the bull a free shot at him. Each time the crowd roared. Then he flopped the cape once at the bull at the finish of a pass, swung it around behind him and walked away from the bull to the barrera.

"He's the boy with the cape all right," said the Gin Bottle King. "That swing he did with the cape's called a veronica."

The chubby-faced Kid who did not like bullfighting and had just done the seven wonderful veronicas was standing against the fence just below us. His face glistened with sweat in the sun but was almost expressionless. His eyes were looking out across the arena where the bull was standing making up his mind to charge a picador. He was studying the bull because a few minutes later it would be his duty to kill him, and once he went out with his thin, red-hilted sword and his piece of red cloth to kill the bull in the final set it would be him or the bull. There are no drawn battles in bullfighting. . . .

I am not going to apologize for bullfighting. It is a survival of the days of the Roman Colosseum. But it does need some explanation.

Bullfighting is not a sport. It was never supposed to be. It is a tragedy. A very great tragedy. The tragedy is the death of the bull. It is played in three definite acts. . . .

At any rate bullfighting is not a sport. It is a tragedy, and it symbolizes the struggle between man and the beasts. There are usually six bulls to a fight. A fight is called a corrida de toros. Fighting bulls are bred like racehorses, some of the oldest breeding establishments being several hundred years old. A good bull is worth about $2,000. They are bred for speed, strength and viciousness. In other words a good fighting bull is an absolutely incorrigible bad bull. . . .

The three absolute acts of the tragedy are first the entry of the bull when the picadors receive the shock of his attacks and attempt to protect their horses with their lances. Then the horses go out and the second act is the planting of the banderillos. This is one of the most interesting and difficult parts but among the easiest for a new bullfight fan to appreciate in technique. The banderillos are three-foot, gaily colored darts with a small fishhook prong in the end. The man who is going to plant them walks out into the arena alone with the bull. He lifts the banderillos at arm's length and points them toward the bull. Then he calls "Toro! Toro!" The bull charges and the banderillero rises to his toes, bends in a curve forward and, just as the bull is about to hit him, drops the darts into the bull's hump just back of his horns. . . .

Last is the death of the bull, which is in the hands of the matador who has had charge of the bull since his first attack. Each matador has two bulls in the afternoon. The death of the bull is most formal and can only be brought about in one way, directly from the front by the matador, who must receive the bull in full charge and kill him with a sword thrust between the shoulders just back of the neck and between the horns. Before killing the bull he must first do a series of passes with the muleta, a piece of red cloth about the size of a large napkin. With the muleta, the torero must show his complete mastery of the bull, must make the bull miss him again and again by inches, before he is allowed to kill him. It is in this phase that most of the fatal accidents occur.

The word "toreador" is obsolete Spanish and is never used. The torero is usually called an espada, or swordsman. He must be proficient in all three acts of the fight. In the first he uses the cape and does veronicas and protects the picadors by taking the bull out and away from them when they are spilled to the ground. In the second act he plants the banderillos. In the third act he masters the bull with the muleta and kills him.

Few toreros excel in all three departments. Some, like young Chicuelo, are unapproachable in their capework. Others like the late Joselito are wonderful banderilleros. Only a few are great killers.

Questions for Discussion and Writing

1. Hemingway is well-known for his descriptive, yet simple writing. Identify several descriptive passages that employ clear, concise language. Is the description as effective in simple language as it would be if written more dramatically? Explain your answer.

2. Aside from the obvious (his clothing and accent, for example), what makes Hemingway stand out as an American commenting on bullfighting? What does he write or how does he write it to give himself away as a foreigner at the bullfight?

3. What do you find foreign, shocking, surprising, or just different about bull-fighting compared to most American sports? Use specific passages from the selection to support your reactions.

4. What is Hemingway's thesis? Does he make his main idea clear in one place in his writing or does he weave the thesis throughout the piece?

5. What is Hemingway's opinion of bullfighting? What does he write to convince you or make it clear what his opinion is? Or is his selection too objective to know his opinion?

Passion in Work and at Play
JACK CURRY

Jack Curry graduated from Fordham University in 1986. He began writing for The New York Times *in 1987, covered the New York Yankees from 1991 to 1997, and became the newspaper's national baseball correspondent in 1998. He has also covered college basketball and football. Curry regularly appears on New York radio programs and nationally on ESPN and other networks. Curry co-authored Yankees player Derek Jeter's autobiography,* The Life You Imagine: Life Lessons for Achieving Your Dreams. *In the following article from* The New York Times, *Curry praises the Cuban national baseball team for their hard work and passion for the game. As you read, consider how much you need to know about the Cuban government in order to fully understand Curry's view of the team.*

---------------- ✦ ----------------

The most fascinating and mysterious team participating in the World Baseball Classic sometimes practices at a field hockey stadium on a worn artificial surface while using a dozen smudged baseballs. No one removes the field hockey nets at each end of the field. The players easily work around them.

They are outfitted in a collage of red, blue and white pants, jerseys and caps. None of the 30 players preparing for what they feel is a historic tournament are dressed identically. Naturally, these resilient players do not measure themselves on sartorial style.

This is Cuba's national baseball team, and the no-frills approach defines them. A three-hour workout Saturday morning was spirited, intense and resourceful. This is how we do it and how we are taught to do it, the players said, while never mentioning President Fidel Castro's omnipresence and barely addressing the prickly topic of defection.

"The Cuban team plays for the love of baseball," said Eduardo Paret, a 33-year-old shortstop and the team's captain. "On this team, we don't have stars. The team is the star."

A tightly controlled glimpse into the usually closed world of the Cubans during two workouts showed them to be a disciplined group—extremely serious about competing but with a playful side. The Cubans worked so hard and relentlessly that some of their frenetic drills looked as if they were being performed by slick-moving robots. Hit, run, throw, game over, repeat.

During the sessions, not a cup of water was visible for the players to consume. No towels were seen in 79-degree weather. Yet the players teased one another as if they were frisky teenagers and wrestled on the damp turf afterward, conditioned to a way of life that stresses the whole, not the parts.

"Our players, when they play, don't think, I'm going to break my hand," Higinio Velez, the manager, said. "Because the player that has money sometimes thinks, What happens if I break my hand?"

The inference was obvious. The references to playing for the love of the game, not for the money, to playing for the team, not for the individual, flowed freely from the typically cautious Cubans.

Cuba won the gold medal at the Athens Olympics in 2004 and also won baseball's World Cup in 2005. So the Cubans are eager to prove themselves in the 16-team World Baseball Classic when they play Wednesday against Panama in San Juan, P.R.

From Nelson Rivas, a taxi driver who bet his friend a case of beer that Cuba would win it all, to Felipe Perez Roque, the foreign minister, who predicted that "people in Cuba will not work" for the next two weeks, the Cubans want to declare, once and for all, that they play baseball better than anyone else in the world.

"We want to play the United States, and we want to win," Pedro Luis Lazo, a 32-year-old pitcher, said. "Because we are big like the United States."

Lazo's voice rose as he used "grande" to describe Cuba in comparison with the United States. He has a bubbly personality and strolled into the Havana Club restaurant in San Antonio de los Banos, about 20 miles southwest of Havana, with a cigar that was almost as long as a windshield wiper.

After Lazo hugged Olga Lopez and shook hands with Tony Diaz, officials from the National Institute of Sports, Physical Education and Recreation who coordinated the interviews, he squeezed his 242-pound frame behind a small table. The institute governs athletic competition in Cuba and selects players for national and international teams.

With Diaz translating for all of the Cubans, Lazo called the United States players professionals and the Cubans amateurs. He said that the United States had solid players, but he quickly added that the Cubans were good, too.

In Cuba, most players make an average of $20 a month, receive better housing than the typical worker and may receive a car from the government. Still, when Lazo was asked about the United States, a country less than 100 miles away, where a player like Alex Rodriguez makes $25.2 million a year, he compared himself to Rodriguez in only one way: They both want to play in the countries where they live now.

"I would prefer to stay in Cuba," Lazo said. "I would prefer to be with my people."

Yulieski Gourriel, 21, an infielder who carries himself with the swagger of Derek Jeter and who could be the next Rodriguez, also parlayed a question about that big salary to express his devotion to Cuba.

"We are different," Gourriel said. "Here, we play for the love of the game. There, they play for the money."

But showing that he had a sense of humor and a better sense of baseball knowledge, Gourriel added a final thought on Rodriguez and the Yankees: "They pay him good because he's a good player."

Lazo was bold to address questions about defection directly. No Cuban has defected from an international tournament since Jose Contreras did so in 2002.

But Joe Kehoskie, an agent who has represented Cuban defectors since 1998, said he knew of several players who would like to defect. Kehoskie estimated that more than 40, none as renowned as Contreras, had defected in the past three years.

Of the 30 players on Cuba's roster, 21 were on the 24-man roster for the World Cup less than a year ago. Kehoskie speculated that the young pitchers Danny Betancourt, who was dazzling in the Athens Olympics, and Frank Montieth were excluded from the Classic because they were viewed as threats to defect.

Like Lazo, Michel Enriquez dismissed the defection question by saying home was sweet to him.

"I respect Alex Rodriguez, and I like his play," said Enriquez, 27, a third baseman who is batting .448 in Cuba's current National Series season. "But we love our people. We help 11 million people because baseball is the first sport here."

Paret sidestepped a question about the possibility of defection by saying the United States would "have a party" if Cuba were to win the tournament because Americans like Cubans. Gourriel seemed to scratch his ear nervously as soon as he heard the names Contreras and Orlando Hernandez, who each defected. Players here are not supposed to discuss that delicate subject.

"In the Classic final, if it's the United States and Cuba, then the winner is the best," Gourriel ultimately said.

On Saturday at the Antonio Maceo field hockey stadium in Santiago de las Vegas, about a 20-minute drive south from Havana, some fans peeked between slender openings in the cinderblock walls for a long-distance look at their favorite players. Even from 150 feet away, they could see that the Cubans, as always, were sweating.

On nearly every inch of the turf, some kind of intense drill was under way. A coach positioned himself about 20 feet from the infielders and smashed one-hop rockets toward them, surely making them wish they had worn goalie pads. The session forced the infielders to be alert, smart and fearless, nice traits for any player.

Another coach tested the outfielders by hitting shots that made them run—really run—to have even a chance of getting a glove on the ball. When the outfielders practiced throwing to the plate, any catcher who was not taking the throw simulated a play at home as a base runner. The lumbering catchers did this while still in full gear.

"Nobody thinks, 'I'm a star,'" Velez, the manager, said. "The star is the team. Everyone plays. The star is the victory."

Velez discussed his team, which is considered the fourth or fifth strongest in the tournament, for about 10 minutes and did not mention one player. Not Paret, who is hitting .365 this season. Not Gourriel, who has 17 homers in 66 games. Not Osmani Urrutia, who is batting .447 and may hit over .400 for the fifth time in six years.

After the morning practice, the Cubans traveled to their headquarters at the Las Yagrundas hotel in San Antonio de los Banos; it is about an hour southwest of Havana and about an hour from activities that could tempt the players. Velez said he liked it that way. He instructed a reporter to interview players there, not at the stadium, because it would be more "tranquilo" for them.

The trip from the field to the secluded hotel is along a two-lane highway that can feature memorable sights. A man in a horse and carriage puttered along in the right lane and appeared unconcerned that he was heading toward oncoming traffic. About a mile later, two trucks had stopped to tend to their cargo—four missiles that would not fit into a two-car garage.

The Cubans love baseball and love to put on a show, so they often combine the two at practice. Five infielders stood about 15 feet from one another in a tight circle. They threw a ball from one player to the next, whipping it hard and off the turf to strengthen their reflexes. It was baseball roulette, if the roulette ball never stayed in one numbered slot.

Then the players added a second ball. The game grew tougher, but they adapted. The ball moved faster and faster. There was laughing, shouting. At one point, the players made 29 transfers without a drop or even a bobble.

If the Cubans did not have a second workout in six hours at Estadio Latinoamericano in Havana, they might have continued the draining drill for an hour. Instead, they stopped after 15 minutes, then sat down and stretched. Without uttering a word, Velez soon walked to the bus. Everyone else followed. The team followed.

Questions for Discussion and Writing

1. Though he calls them "typically cautious," Curry says that references to "playing for the team . . . flowed freely" among Cuban players he spoke to. How do Cuban players' views on team versus individuality differ from American players' views? Which style is more effective in a sport like baseball? What do the differing views say about the two countries?

2. Curry is American. Yet comparisons between Cubans and Americans are woven throughout his writing. Do most of the comparisons place America in a positive or negative light? Is Curry trying to make an argument or take a side through his writing or does he remain objective? Support your answer with specific examples from the article.

3. Curry quotes several players, especially toward the end of the article. Examine the quotations as a whole. What message are they sending collectively? Does Curry balance similar quotations with the opposite view?

4. Defection is a topic that is off-limits to Cuban players. Yet as a reporter, Curry must address the issue in the article. How does he discuss defection without putting players in a bad position? Are his strategies effective or not?

5. Search for and find the Web site for the World Baseball Classic. What textual and visual elements make the site look "American"? Which elements give the site more of an international flavor? Why would baseball fans from countries other than America want to read the Web site?

Making Connections: Writing

1. According to Carl Sagan, we need sports, whether we participate in them or not. He says we will root for a team even if we have no stake in the outcome. Respond to Sagan's claim. Do you need sports? Would you root for a team from another country just because it was the only thing on TV? Keep in mind Allen Guttmann's assertions as you write.

2. Lucian Kim discusses buzkashi as Afghanistan's national sport, Somini Sengupta says cricket is the national sport for many countries, and baseball seems to be the national sport for both America and Cuba. Research the idea of a "national sport." What makes a sport a "national" sport? What does a national sport say about its country's culture? Analyze a national sport that might be unfamiliar to you.

3. Allen Guttmann wonders if nationalism or sport might be "the true religion of the modern world." Which is the case in America? Does this "religion" differ in other countries? Watch footage of the Olympics, available online, and keep a log of instances of nationalism you see. Write your analysis of the footage. You might use Carl Sagan's essay to support or oppose your observations.

4. Attend a sporting event and keep a journal of patriotic messages or traditions you see. Before you go, re-read what each selection says about patriotism and how particular sports are patriotic in their home countries. How do sports and patriotism relate? Is patriotism different from nationalism? Explain.

5. Many of the writers in this chapter take on different roles in the same selection: journalist, observer, American, scholar, debater, and historian, for example. Choose one of the selections and analyze the writer's role. Use specific examples from the selection to explain why the writer is serving a particular role.

6. Interview someone—perhaps an exchange student or a friend who has traveled internationally—about a sporting event in another country. Compare that event with a similar American sporting event. Think about the atmosphere, fan behavior, and the importance of the event in that culture.

7. Lucian Kim, Somini Sengupta, and Ernest Hemingway are describing foreign sports as outsiders. Attend a sporting event that is more closely associated with another culture than with American culture. You might watch a karate tournament, for example, or a Latin dance competition. Why might a foreigner—particularly an American—feel like an outsider? Write an essay that describes your reactions to the traditions of the sport and others' reactions to you as an outsider.

8. Compare the "image" that national sports convey about different countries. Write about a country with a national sport that might reflect negatively on its culture—such as buzkashi in Afghanistan or bullfighting in Spain—and a country with a national sport that might reflect positively on its culture, such as baseball in Cuba.

9. Using Carl Sagan's essay as a model, choose a sport and write your own essay entitled "Game: The Prehistoric Origin of (Baseball, Volleyball, or any sport of your choice)." Dissect the elements of your sport and analyze why it remains popular and what impact our ancestors might have had on its development.

10. Defend a sport that seems uncomfortable for Americans as Ernest Hemingway does for bullfighting. Make sure to thoroughly explain the sport and its origins. Argue why it is still relevant in contemporary culture.

Books Worth Reading

Barefoot Runner: The Life of Marathon Champion Abebe Bikila by Paul Rambali. Tells the story of Ethiopia's Bikila, the first African athlete to win an Olympic gold medal—and he did so barefoot.

Beyond a Boundary by C. L. R. James. Part memoir, part tribute to the sport of cricket, this book shows how sport can transcend politics and international conflict.

Big Game, Small World by Alexander Wolff. *Sports Illustrated* basketball writer argues that the international popularity of basketball began when Lithuania nearly beat the United States in the 2000 Olympics.

Buzkashi: Game and Power in Afghanistan by G. Whitney Azoy. Examines the sport that has become a metaphor for Afghanistan's aggressive and chaotic culture.

Death in the Afternoon by Ernest Hemingway. Considered one of the best books about bullfighting; argues that bullfighting is more than sport.

Emerald Fairways and Foam-Flecked Seas: A Golfer's Pilgrimage to the Courses of Ireland by James W. Finegan. Provides a tour of Ireland's great courses via historical information and eloquent storytelling.

Fever Pitch by Nick Hornby. Humorous autobiography that nonetheless contains serious analysis of the soccer obsession in Great Britain.

How Soccer Explains the World: An Unlikely Theory of Globalization by Franklin Foer. Argues that soccer is more than a sport; it is a symbol for social class and political ideology around the world.

Pitching Around Fidel: A Journey into the Heart of Cuban Sports by S. L. Price. *Sports Illustrated* writer describes the state of sports in Cuba through interviews, investigative reporting, and personal observations.

Sports: The First Five Millennia by Allen Guttmann. Traces sports from ancient Egypt to the modern age to examine how sports shape world cultures.

Films Worth Watching

Lagaan (2001). People of a small village bet their future on a cricket game against their British rulers.

Munich (2005). Fictional account based on the Israeli government's quest to avenge the deaths of their athletes killed by terrorists in the 1972 Olympics. Complemented by the documentary *One Day in September* (1999), which uses video and news footage to re-create the scene.

Viva Baseball! (2005). A look at influential Latin American baseball players.

Sites Worth Surfing

http://www.olympic.org
Official Web site of the International Olympic Committee.

http://www.fifa.com
The Fédération Internationale de Football Association (FIFA), ruling body of football (soccer) and the World Cup.

http://isca-web.org/english
Site of the International Sport and Culture Association, an advocacy organization for youth sports around the world.

http://edition.cnn.com/SPORT/
CNN International's site on world sports, written completely in English.

Offensive or on the Defense: What Role Does Violence Play in Sports?

People who do not like, watch, or participate in sports cite many reasons: Sports are too commercialized, sports are entertainment enterprises more than athletic competition, athletes are paid too much, and the list goes on. Ask many critics of sports and they will tell you that a primary reason for their dislike is the real or perceived violence in sports. Certainly there are sports that are not considered violent, such as running, swimming, and golf. Other sports are considered violent by some but not by others: martial arts and hunting, for example. Some sports are dangerous to the point that they can be perceived as violent when something tragic happens; these include auto racing, rock or mountain climbing, and bull riding. Sports that are most often accused of exhibiting or even encouraging blatant violence include football, hockey, lacrosse, boxing, wrestling, and rugby. Even mainstream sports such as baseball and basketball have the occasional brawl among players, placing them in the violent category, at least temporarily.

Is violence necessary in sports? Is it necessary only in particular sports? Most people would probably agree that violence associated with individual decisions, such as punching an opponent or starting a fight on the basketball court, is not appropriate. But what about the violence that is *part* of the sport? How hard should football players tackle? How should spectators react when a race car slams violently into a concrete wall and spins several times? And is violence more acceptable when it's associated with sports like martial arts, which uses it for self-defense, or when providing food is the purpose as with hunting and fishing? Chapter 3 examines these questions.

The reading selections in this chapter cover five sports often perceived as "violent" by society. Two of them—football and hockey—are mainstream American sports. One—boxing—is not as popular as it once was but has a very long history in the United States. The other two—mixed martial arts and mountain climbing—might be unfamiliar to some Americans right now but probably won't be in the next decade. Interest in mixed martial arts (or MMA, sometimes known as ultimate fighting or cage boxing) has skyrocketed in recent years, and mountain climbing expeditions and summit ascents continue to gain popularity among extreme sports enthusiasts.

Sports that are—or are perceived as—violent share a common criticism: There is the likelihood that athletes will be injured. John H. Kerr, writing for the journal *Aggression and Violent Behavior*, dissects an incident in the National Hockey League that left a player with severe head and spinal injuries. Kerr invites readers to ask if there is a difference between sanctioned violence—that which is part of the sport—and unsanctioned violence, which crosses the boundary of the sport's rules. Likewise, William C. Rhoden, in his article, "In NFL, Violence Sells, But at What Cost?" admits that violence is part of professional football's allure, but questions the cost to players who suffer multiple concussions. He calls professional football players "latter-day gladiators . . . who rent their bodies for use in a violent sport." Joyce Carol Oates, in her famous book *On Boxing*, does her best to defend the violence in boxing: "To the untrained eye most boxing matches appear not merely savage but mad," she writes. "As the eye becomes trained, however, the spectator begins to see the complex patterns that underlie the 'madness'; what seems to be merely confusing action is understood to be coherent and intelligent, frequently inspired."

While Rhoden and Oates make strong arguments in their writing about football and boxing, the messages from the reading selections on mixed martial arts and mountain climbing are more subtle. Both authors question how the sports are changing as they develop and become more popular. Richard Ryan, a noted combat trainer, questions the tactics of the "new" form of mixed martial arts, better known as ultimate fighting. While he admits that MMA is more akin to pure combat than similar martial arts sports, he asks where the "budo (warrior ways)" is in MMA. He writes, "Respect, honor, integrity and humility make the martial arts more than just a collection of fighting." By focusing on the good in martial arts he subtlely criticizes the negative. Reporter Peter Fimrite spent a weekend with tourists at Half Dome, an 8,842-foot granite mountain crest in Yosemite National Park, to witness firsthand why mountain climbing might be viewed as a violent sport. "The last 400 feet of the grueling 8.6-mile climb to the summit of the world-famous peak was like a holiday scene at a Disneyland ride—a long line and few thrills," he writes. He describes the hodge-podge of people attempting the climb, ranging from "city kids in baggy basketball garb" to "flabby tourists and the elderly," pointing out that "The weekend menagerie at the top of Half Dome is a problem that many people believe is turning one of the world's signature hikes into a flirtation with death."

For some of you, this chapter might be the most difficult to read. Most of you will have predetermined opinions before you read any of the selections. The readings in this chapter all present arguments or opinions. As you read, consider not only the issue of whether or not violence has a place in sports, but how well the writers of these pieces convince you of their points. Sports and culture writers have either defended or criticized violence in sports for decades. Ultimately, though, it's up to each athlete and spectator to decide. How much violence is necessary? What's considered too violent? What violence is used for defensive purposes? What type of violence offends you?

Examining the Bertuzzi-Moore NHL Ice Hockey Incident: Crossing the Line Between Sanctioned and Unsanctioned Violence in Sport

JOHN H. KERR

John H. Kerr is a professor of sport psychology, specializing in aggression and violence in sport. His research has been published in The Sport Psychologist, European Review of Applied Psychology, *and* Psychology of Sport and Exercise. *He is the author of scholarly books and textbooks, including* Rethinking Aggression and Violence in Sport, *and* Experiencing Sport: Reversal Theory. *The following article appeared in the journal* Aggression and Violent Behavior *in 2006. This journal examines issues of violence ranging from family and domestic violence to the physiological basis for aggression. Kerr's article examines the 2004 incident when one professional hockey player attacked another, resulting in severe head and spinal injuries to the victim. Though Kerr explains the incident well, much more has been written about it. You might research what happened and the various responses from fans, media, and athletes. In his research, Kerr tries to differentiate between acceptable and unacceptable—referred to as sanctioned and unsanctioned—violence in hockey.*

———————— ✦ ————————

On occasion, violent incidents in sport occur and, if the athletes involved are performing in sports with national or international prominence, hit the headlines in the news media. When such incidents take place, they often revive debate about the acceptability of aggressive and violent behavior in sport. However, given the generally aggressive and violent nature of play in contact sports like North American ice hockey, it can sometimes be difficult to separate permissible, legitimate, or sanctioned acts during play from those that are impermissible, illegitimate, or unsanctioned. Such an incident occurred on March 8, 2004 in a National Hockey League (NHL) ice hockey game between Todd Bertuzzi of the Vancouver Canucks and Steve Moore of the Colorado Avalanche. The present paper examines the Bertuzzi–Moore incident in detail and attempts to clarify why, even in a sport where "fist-fighting" is considered to be part of the game by players, coaches, and officials, this particular act crossed the line between sanctioned and unsanctioned violence in sport.

There are few competitive sports which do not involve aggression in some form or other, however mild. Even in lawn bowls, players can play "aggressively" and try to knock opponents' bowls away from the "jack" and, in racket sports, play can be seen as aggressive when players deliberately serve towards an opponent's body. Yet, in team sports with high levels of physical contact, like ice hockey and the various forms of football (e.g., rugby, American, Australian rules), certain aggressive and violent acts are encouraged and have a special status within games (e.g., Russell, 1993). The special status afforded to aggressive and violent acts in team contact sports, which distinguishes them from similar acts outside the context of these sports, has been described by Kerr (1997, pp. 115–116): "In general, aggression can be seen as unprovoked hostility or attacks on another person which are not sanctioned by society. However, in the sports context, the aggression is provoked in the sense that two opposing teams have willingly agreed to compete against each other. Aggression in team contact sports is intrinsic and sanctioned, provided the plays remain permissible within the boundaries of certain rules, which act as a kind of contract in the pursuit of aggression (and violence) between consenting adults."

At this point, it should be stated that the term "violence" is considered the most extreme form of aggression and is used within the sports context of the present paper in two ways: to mean either (a) a violent act such as a violent collision or tackle or (b) in the negative sense to mean physical force aimed at hurting or injuring an opponent (Atyeo, 1979; J.H. Kerr, 2004). In addition, the descriptors "sanctioned" and "unsanctioned" are preferred in the present paper to other terms, like "permissible/impermissible", "legitimate/illegitimate", or "legal/illegal", because they are considered to be the most suitable terms for encompassing both the rules of the game and any "unwritten rules" or player norms that come into effect during games (J.H. Kerr, 2004). A further consideration is the special status given to fighting in North American ice hockey (e.g., Colburn, 1985). Although it is considered an act of unsanctioned violence in sports like rugby, American football, and Australian rules football, and has been severely punished in recent years, fist-fighting still retains a special status within North American, and especially NHL, ice hockey. Indeed, it could be said to be sanctioned, as it is freely engaged in by many players, used as a tactic by coaches, expected by fans, and tolerated by officials and administrators: "How much blood has to be spilled, how many athletes need to be hospitalised, before the league does what other rough sports such as rugby, football and soccer have done? In those games a player who attacks another is immediately ejected, not sent to the penalty box for two minutes" (Remove the fighting, 2004).

Given the special nature of aggression and violence within team contact sports and the special status given to fighting in North American ice hockey, why did the Bertuzzi–Moore incident become so controversial and receive such widespread attention? The next section describes the background to the incident, the details of what happened in the incident itself, and the aftermath.

FEBRUARY 16, 2004

Playing a National Hockey League ice hockey game in Colorado, the Vancouver Canucks team defeated the Colorado Avalanche team 1–0. During the game, rookie Colorado player Steve Moore hit Vancouver player Markus Naslund with a dangerous shoulder hit to the head. Naslund was knocked unconscious and missed the next three games with a grade 2 concussion. Moore was not penalized by match referees. The Canucks reportedly promised revenge. Brad May, a Vancouver player, indicated that there was a "bounty" on Moore: "It's going to be fun when we get him" (G. Kerr, 2004a, March 11) and Bertuzzi, his teammate said, "We play them twice more, and hopefully they'll keep him [in the lineup]" (MacIntyre, 2004).

THE INCIDENT

The violent incident took place when Colorado were leading 8–2; with just over 11 min to play in the third quarter, Todd Bertuzzi, a 6′30″, 245 lb power forward playing for Vancouver, followed Colorado player Moore up and down the ice, then skating up from behind him, grabbed his jersey with his left hand, and swung a vicious gloved right-handed "sucker" punch to the side of Moore's head. Both players went down and Bertuzzi appeared to attempt to land another blow, as he drove Moore face first into the ice. After players and match officials broke up the fracas, Moore lay in a pool of blood on the ice while being attended to by medical staff. About 10 min later, Moore was strapped to a stretcher and taken to Vancouver General Hospital. He was reported as being conscious when he left GM Place. It was later confirmed that Moore had suffered a fracture to the C3 and C4 vertebrae at the base of his neck, a concussion, and various cuts to his face. Moore may have been unconscious before he hit the ice. After the incident, Bertuzzi was given a match suspension and took no further part in the game. He was escorted from the ice by a linesman (MacIntyre, 2004).

RESPONSES TO THE INCIDENT

The incident received widespread and universal condemnation from the newspaper and television media. It was shown repeatedly in slow motion on newscasts throughout North America and some other parts of the world. Even the Prime Minister of Canada, Paul Martin, told professional hockey "to clean up its act" (Pap, 2004).

On March 10, Bertuzzi, accompanied by his wife and Vancouver's general manager, made a public apology at a news conference at Vancouver's GM Place arena. He was tearful as [he] made his statement and eventually broke down, could not continue, and the group left the room. He stated: "These comments are for Steve. Steve, I just want to apologize for what happened out there. I had no intention of hurting you, I feel awful for what transpired. To Steve's family, I am sorry you had to go through this. I am so sorry about what happened out there. I am relieved to hear that Steve is going to have a full recovery. It means a lot to me to hear that is going to happen, I want to apologize to Mr. Burke, McCaw (team owner John) and the Vancouver Canucks organization and to my teammates. To the fans of hockey and the fans of Vancouver. To kids who watch the game, I am truly sorry. I don't play the game that way and I am not a mean-spirited person, and I am sorry for what happened" (Kerr & Wharnsby, 2004, p. 1).

The NHL suspended Bertuzzi on March 12 for the final 13 games of the regular season and all of the Stanley Cup playoffs and he had to apply for reinstatement for the 2004–2005 season. In addition, from his annual salary of Can$6.8 million, Bertuzzi had to forfeit at least Can$501,926.23 to the NHL players' emergency fund. The NHL also fined Vancouver US$250,000 for failing to prevent the atmosphere that may have led to the incident (G. Kerr, 2004b, March 11). In addition, without Bertuzzi, Vancouver did not reach the Stanley Cup playoffs and he was not considered for a place in the Canadian team for World Cup of Hockey in September 2004, which Canada won. On June 24 2004, after a 4-month investigation, Bertuzzi was finally charged with assault by the criminal justice branch of the attorney general's office. Before charging Bertuzzi, prosecutors needed to decide if there was a substantial likelihood of conviction and, if so, if it was in the public interest to do so (Bertuzzi charged, 2004). On August 26, he pleaded not guilty in a Vancouver provincial court hearing and his trial was set for January 17, 2005 (Hall, 2004). Bertuzzi could have faced a jail sentence of 18 months, if tried in a provincial court, or up to 10 years in jail if tried in the British Columbia Supreme Court (Bertuzzi charged, 2004).

Vancouver players denied that there had been any "bounty" on Steve Moore. Centre Brenden Morrison was reported as saying,

"No, there was no bounty. I've never heard of a bounty in the NHL. When the incident happened . . . emotions run high. You say things you don't mean" (MacIntyre, 2004).

It might have been expected that this incident and the serious injury to Moore would have reduced the incidence of unsanctioned acts of violence. However, just 2 weeks later, Mark Messier of the New York Rangers was given a two-game suspension for "pitchforking" Martin Strbak of the Pittsburgh Penguins in the groin with his hockey stick. Also, Toronto Maple Leafs player Wade Belak received an eight-game suspension for swinging his stick and hitting Colorado Avalanche player Ossi Vaananen on the head.

DECONSTRUCTING THE INCIDENT

There were fights earlier in the March 8 Vancouver–Colorado game, one of which involved Moore, but they received little attention. Why, therefore, was Bertuzzi's punch and follow-up considered to be in a different category to the previous fights? To understand this, a more detailed examination of the special status afforded to fist-fighting and the difference between sanctioned and unsanctioned acts in NHL ice hockey is necessary.

Colburn (1985, 1989) has pointed out that, when fist-fights occur, there are certain "conventions" to which players usually adhere. Initially, players square up to each other, then the player who feels he has been wronged will drop his stick and throw off his gloves in a challenge to his opponent. The opponent can then either drop his stick and gloves and the two will engage in a fist-fight, or he can skate away, refusing the challenge to fight. As the players are wearing protective pads and helmets and are trying to maintain their balance on the ice while swinging punches, rarely does anyone get seriously hurt. Damage, when it occurs, is mostly limited to black eyes and split lips. Under players' rules, fist-fighting in hockey is considered a form of sanctioned violence that is different to other unsanctioned violent acts, like striking an opponent with a hockey stick. It works as a form of social control that has a moderating effect on other potentially serious unsanctioned violent acts between players (Colburn, 1985; Smith, 1983). Fist-fighting, often said to be "part of the game", is an attempt to establish or re-establish respect and honor between the opposing players involved (Colburn, 1985; Smith, 1983).

This type of open challenge and resultant fist-fight are generally sanctioned among players and condoned by officials; there are other types of fighting that are not (Colburn, 1985). These are fundamentally different in character to the spontaneous fist-fights that occur between willing opponents and generally involve premeditated, vindictive, unsanctioned violent acts. Bertuzzi's violent attack on Moore falls into this latter category. As Florida NHL player Olli Jokinen stated: "But there has always been a code in hockey. If you play dirty, you have got to pay the price. You go and you drop your gloves and have a fair fight. That's enough. What Bertuzzi did is not part of the game" (Naylor, 2004).

There is a line between sanctioned and unsanctioned violence, even in NHL ice hockey, and on this occasion Bertuzzi crossed that line. Still, if the circumstances had been slightly different (e.g., the players had been facing each other, or better still facing each other with gloves off, or had Moore not been so severely injured), Bertuzzi might well have escaped punishment and subsequent prosecution. However, according to Maki (2004), this incident will have a lasting effect on Bertuzzi and how people perceive him as a player: "At 6 foot 3 and 245 pounds, he is the National Hockey League's most intimidating force, a wide body of strength and skill. He may not be a mean spirited person, but he has played a mean game. His legal hits have injured people. He's tormented opponents with his elbows and his stickwork and his comments have crawled under even the thickest skin. You push yourself to the limits, at the very edge of the rulebook, and sometimes you can't help yourself. You cross over. You make a bad decision and you never look the same again" (Maki, 2004).

Without considering the extent of Moore's injuries, several aspects of Bertuzzi's punching help to clearly place it in the category of unsanctioned violence. First, Bertuzzi skated up behind Moore and attacked him from behind. The punch would appear to have been pre-meditated and caught Moore unawares. Second, as the two players went down, Bertuzzi landed another punch. Third, he drove Moore face first into the ice. These are the specific features of the incident that brought such a negative response from observers, gained such wide media notoriety, and brought it to the attention of the police and public prosecutors in Vancouver.

DOES NHL HOCKEY NEED TO CHANGE AND, IF SO, WHAT NEEDS TO BE DONE?

In the furore that arose after the Bertuzzi–Moore incident, the whole game of ice hockey in North America came under the microscope and many interested parties advocated a move away from the violence which has come to be associated with the game. Among these people was Ken Dryden, a former goalie for the Montreal Canadians from 1971 to 1979, the author of *The Game* (Dryden, 1983), a classic book on ice hockey. In a recent newspaper article, Dryden (2004) described the changes that have occurred in North American ice hockey over the years and how they have affected modern play. In addition, he called for a re-examination of the whole game, which he thought could then result in constructive changes. Dryden's (2004) comments reflect the insight that can only come from having played and maintained a deep interest in the game and are relevant here.

According to Dryden (2004), the size and speed of the NHL players has increased from an average 175 lb and 5 ft 10¾ in. in 1952 to 204 lb and 6 ft 1 in. in 2003, and the time players spend on the ice has decreased from about 2 min to just 40 s. Being on the ice for 2 min meant that players had to conserve energy and playing styles involved playing in bursts. Nowadays, playing style has been altered by the shorter time, with players skating at their maximum when on the ice. The result of the increased size of players and increased skating speed is that, when players do collide, the forces involved put the players at a much greater risk of injury. Not only has the risk of injury increased per each individual game, but when considered over an 82-game season, plus four rounds of Stanley Cup playoffs, the level of risk is dangerously further increased. The changes Dryden (2004) described have made a major impact on the sanctioned violent bodychecks and hits that characterize NHL ice hockey.

He also went on to examine some of the developments with regard to previously unsanctioned violent acts, which have made them more or less acceptable (sanctioned) in modern NHL ice hockey. Dryden (2004, p. A19) claimed that contemporary players now carry out hits from behind, hits to the head, use high sticks, and perpetrate cheap shots against opponents because of the pressure of opportunity brought about by the faster game: "As a checker, if you are 10 feet away from a puck carrier, you can't hook or slash him. You can't high stick him, either. And you can't do much damage to him if you are moving at him at cruising pace and not a sprint. But with today's shorter shifts that allow you to move faster, to get closer, it's different. Now you have the opportunity. Now you can hook and slash and high-stick your [opponent] and smash him into the boards. So now you do" (Dryden, 2004, p. A19).

There are grey areas, which exist between sanctioned and unsanctioned acts, and they may well be even larger in NHL ice hockey than in other team contact sports. "Finishing your check" in ice hockey is a good example of this. It is the equivalent of a late tackle or hit in other team contact sports and in these sports is duly penalized as an unsanctioned violent play: "'Finishing your check' is so familiar a phrase that it seems that it must have been a part of the original game. It wasn't. It means, as a checker, going after the puck carrier so that even if he makes a pass, you keep going and run into him, too late to stop the pass, but not too late to stop him continuing up the ice with the play. This is allowed. Indeed it is a strategy coaches insist upon. Yet if a player is hit before a pass gets to him, this is interference, and everyone agrees. Worse, 'finishing your check' rewards the player who is too slow to reach the puck carrier in time, and penalizes the puck carrier who is quick enough to make the pass ahead of the checker. Worse, it puts in physical danger the puck carrier who has to deal with a checker coming at him at high speed, and the checker who has to deal with a puck carrier with his stick raised to protect himself. Or worse, it encourages teammates of the puck carrier to take protection into their own hands and 'obstruct'. All this happened because coaches decided it was a good thing for players to go hard at the puck carrier, and referees got tired of reminding them it wasn't" (Dryden, 2004, p. A19).

If Dryden (2004) is correct, some small changes over the years have led to a kind of 'normalization' of several unsanctioned plays so that they have almost become sanctioned violent acts. Dryden's comments appear to be supported by medical evidence, which has shown that, since helmets were introduced, reckless checking and hitting has increased considerably. And, more recently, when face shields were introduced, incidents of high sticking and elbows to the head also increased. Paradoxically, the introduction of safety measures led to an increase in foul play and some injuries. However, like Dryden (2004), medical experts also noted that referees were not penalizing high hits to the head and face as often as they used to (Smart hockey: More safety more fun, 2002).

Dryden (2004) is clear about some of the changes which would make a difference in North American ice hockey. He argues for hits to the head and hits from behind, which have brought danger to the game, to be penalized properly. He also argues for the tactic of finishing your check to be eliminated and to have it again classified as interference or obstruction. This would mean that players would have to go in fast enough to make the body check, but slow enough to avoid it if necessary when the puck had already been passed. However, many coaches and managers in NHL ice hockey do not appear to share Dryden's opinions and, for example, the then Vancouver Canucks manager Brian Burke, who was involved in the aftermath of the Bertuzzi–Moore incident, came out strongly against the views expressed by Dryden (Morris, 2004).

Dryden's suggestions would actually bring ice hockey more into line with other team contact sports where hits to the head (high tackles) and finishing your check (late tackles or hits) are severely penalized by match officials. Acts of unsanctioned violence have become much less common because of game officials' zero tolerance approach and the use of post-game video analysis, which has meant that unsanctioned acts of violence not seen by match officials can be punished after the fact by adjudication panels (Heads, 1992; Hutchins & Philips, 1997; Kerr, 1999; J.H. Kerr, 2004). One wonders what would happen to NHL ice hockey if they took on board the changes suggested by Dryden and other changes, which have been effective in several other team contact sports. What would happen if fist-fighting was eliminated, as it has been from the World Cup of Hockey involving international teams? A probable outcome would be that NHL ice hockey play would be improved in much the same way as play in other team contact games has been improved in recent years. If similar changes occurred and unsanctioned violence was eliminated from ice hockey, the players would still be able to achieve the pleasure and satisfaction that they desire from sanctioned violent plays, and to engage in games which are more skilful, more physically demanding in terms of energy requirements, and more attractive to players and spectators alike. Such changes might mean that NHL enforcers would become redundant as their fighting skills would no longer be required, and coaches and teams could not afford to carry their often poorer skating and stick handling skills.

REFERENCES

1. Atyeo D., Blood and guts: Violence in sports, (1979), Cassell Australia, Melbourne.
2. Bertuzzi charged with assault, *The Japan Times*, (2004, June 26), p. 24.
3. Colburn K., Honor, ritual and violence in ice hockey, *Canadian Journal of Sociology*, Volume: 10, (1985), pp. 153–170.
4. Colburn K., Deviance and legitimacy in ice hockey: A microstructural theory of violence, Kelly D.H., (Ed.) *Deviant behavior*, (1989), St. Martin's Press, New York.
5. Dryden K., The game, (1983), Wiley, Toronto.
6. Dryden K., Saving the game, *Globe and Mail*, (2004, March 27), p. A19.
7. Hall N., Bertuzzi pleads not guilty, *Vancouver Sun*, (2004, August 27), p. A1.
8. Heads I., True blue: The story of NSW rugby league, (1992), Ironbark Press, Randwick, NSW.
9. Hutchins B., Philips M.G., Selling permissible violence: The commodification of Australian rugby league 1970–1995, *International Review for the Sociology of Sport*, Volume: 32, (1997), pp. 161–172.
10. Kerr G., A sombre scene unfolds, *Globe and Mail*, (2004, March 11), p. S2. [Kerr 2004a].
11. Kerr G., Canucks fuming over fine, *Globe and Mail*, (2004, March 11), p. A1. [Kerr 2004b].
12. Kerr G., Wharnsby T., Bertuzzi says he's sorry, *Globe and Mail*, (2004, March 11), p. A1.
13. Kerr J.H., Rethinking aggression and violence in sport, (2004), Routledge, London. [Kerr 2004c].
14. Kerr J.H., Motivation and emotion in sport: Reversal theory, (1997), Psychology Press, Hove, England.
15. Kerr J.H., The role of aggression and violence in sport: A rejoinder to the ISSP position stand, *The Sport Psychologist*, Volume: 13, (1999), pp. 83–88.
16. MacIntyre I., There was no bounty, *Vancouver Sun*, (2004, March 12), p. H3.
17. Maki A., When a 'hellraiser' grows up, *Globe and Mail*, (2004, March 11), p. S1.
18. Morris J., Burke assails Dryden over call for reform, *Globe and Mail*, (2004, March 27), p. S2.

19. Naylor D., NHL players say payback isn't about to go away, *Globe and Mail*, (2004, March 12), p. S3.

20. Pap E., Martin to NHL: 'Clean up your act', *Vancouver Sun*, (2004, March 12), p. 1.

21. Remove the fighting from the NHL's ice, *Globe and Mail*, (2004, March 11), p. A16.

22. Russell G.W., The social psychology of sport, (1993), Springer-Verlag, New York.

23. Smart hockey: More safety more fun, *Presented by TD Waterhouse, Think First Canada and the TSN television channel*, (2002, January).

24. Smith M.D., Violence and sport, (1983), Butterworth, Toronto.

Questions for Discussion and Writing

1. Kerr makes a distinction—as does the title of this journal—between aggression and violence. What is the difference between the two? How do they relate? Along the same lines, how would you have defined "permissible" or "sanctioned" violence prior to reading this article? Has your definition changed after reading the piece? Why or why not?

2. Read Kerr's definition of aggression in the second paragraph. Summarize what he's trying to say. Is he merely defining the parameters of acceptable aggression in sport vs. in society or is he advocating for acceptable aggression in sport? How can you tell? Then look at Kerr's definition of violence in the next paragraph. Is the former form of violence—a collision or tackle—less violent than the latter form—"physical force aimed at hurting or injuring an opponent"?

3. How would you characterize Kerr's article as a piece of writing? Is it most similar to an analytical essay, a research essay, or a persuasive essay? What characteristics make it most like that type of essay?

4. Examine the organization of Kerr's article. This excerpt provides the introduction, responses to the incident, a deconstruction of the incident, and a discussion of what needs to change in hockey. In the full article there were also sections on the legal ramifications against Bertuzzi and the psychological reasons why players are violent. How does Kerr's organization help or hinder his goal for the article? Does the organization support Kerr's thesis? Explain your analysis.

5. Kerr cites K. Colburn's explanation of fist-fighting as a "social control" with unwritten rules by players. Is this type of violence unnecessary in sports or is it acceptable to society because it is acceptable to the players? Write an argument in which you take a position on the necessity of "acceptable" violence in sports.

In NFL, Violence Sells, But at What Cost?

WILLIAM C. RHODEN

Before joining The New York Times, *William C. Rhoden wrote for the* Baltimore Sun *and* Ebony *magazine. He is also a former sports information director at Morgan State University in Baltimore. Rhoden is a frequent guest on the ESPN show* The Sports Reporters. *His books have drawn even more attention than his articles in the* Times. *In* Third and a Mile: The Trials and Triumphs of the Black Quarterback, *Rhoden chronicles the struggle for African-American players to break into a traditionally white position in football: quarterback. Even more controversial, as is probably obvious in the title, is* Forty Million Dollar Slaves: The Rise, Fall, and Redemption of the Black Athlete, *which traces the beginnings of black athletes from nineteenth-century boxing rings to today's fields and arenas. In this book, Rhoden argues that black athletes are still "enslaved" by team owners and managers who exploit their talent to make money. In the following article, from the* Times, *Rhoden claims that the number of concussions football players suffer has created the sport's most urgent crisis. Ironically, as a defensive back in college, it was Rhoden's job to tackle quarterbacks.*

◆

By the time I reached him late Thursday afternoon, Gene Upshaw had already read the article in The New York Times about Andre Waters, the Philadelphia Eagles safety who committed suicide in November [2006] after years of battling depression. One neuropathologist said the condition might have been related to the concussions that Waters sustained as a professional football player.

Upshaw, speaking from his office in Washington, said he had known Waters.

"I just got him into an N.F.L. Europe internship where he could coach, because he was coaching at some small university," said Upshaw, [then] the head of the N.F.L. Players Association. "When we heard about it, it was one of those things where you couldn't believe it."

Upshaw sounded annoyed by the buzz created by the article. "I think everyone is getting a little riled up because this guy's out there trying to sell this damn book," he said. Upshaw was referring to Chris Nowinski, author of "Head Games: Football's Concussion Crisis."

Nowinski's book offers an eye-opening look into an N.F.L. quagmire, and I think that Upshaw, in his heart of hearts, knows Nowinski is doing more than trying to sell books. He's shedding light on one of the N.F.L.'s most persistently haunting safety issues.

Upshaw represents 1,500 latter-day gladiators known as professional football players who rent their bodies for use in a violent sport. Few come out unscathed, and many will not know the real damage to their minds and bodies until years after they retire. Waters might or might not have been a casualty of mild traumatic brain injury, but there is enough evidence to scare the daylights out of anyone who played the game, especially in the N.F.L., for any length of time.

"We all get alarmed when we see something like this," Upshaw said, referring to the article about Waters. "But it's not like we've been just sitting on our hands. That's what's being implied here, that no one is looking at this, that no one's studying this, that no one cares about this. If that was true, I'm irresponsible and I haven't been doing my job, and neither has the N.F.L."

His job, of course, in partnership with the N.F.L., is facilitating violence; it's been a job well done.

What can you do about concussions in a sport whose popularity is rooted in violent collisions?

Bizarre as it sounds, boxing has an effective method of dealing with concussions: A fighter who sustains one is not allowed to fight for at least a month. In contrast, a football player who sustains a concussion can return to the game.

A football player who sustains a concussion should not return to the game in which the injury occurred and should be held out for at least one game, perhaps more, depending on the severity of the concussion.

Upshaw doesn't seem to like the idea. "The last thing that we want to do and the N.F.L. wants to do, and it's the last thing I want to do as a union, is to mandate something that's not medically proven," he said. "That's why we have doctors."

Every N.F.L. team puts its players through a baseline neurological test. When a player sustains a concussion or head injury, the team retests the athlete to make sure he is back to normal, or near normal, before allowing him to play. During a game last month, the Jets' Laveranues Coles sustained a mild concussion. He was allowed to play in the same game. He also played the next week.

Coles's situation gets to the heart of the concussion problem. In a league driven by ferocious competition, a league in which the athletes have virtually no job security, players must be protected from themselves.

Coles could have said, and probably should have said, that he wouldn't play. Even when the Jets cleared Coles to play, if he wasn't feeling right, he should have gotten a second opinion and opted out.

"Players are going to always say they're fine because they want to play," Upshaw said. "They did it when I was playing and they do it now."

Upshaw knows better than anyone that players will always go back on the field, healthy or not, concussion or not.

"They're protected as well as they can be," said Dr. Thomas Mayer, the union's medical adviser. "But this is a warrior mentality, this is a warrior sport." Football is a violent and often brutal game. Players love it; fans love it; so do the news media. We hype it, we celebrate it, we promote it. There will be plays during this weekend's postseason games when a receiver is reduced to jelly or a quarterback is crushed by a blindside tackle. Thanks to high-definition television, the violence is so clear and graphic you can practically see the brain shifting in a player's cranium.

Once upon a time, when players fought for their rights, Upshaw was like the good shepherd. He watched over the flock and went to extraordinary lengths to fight for even that one lamb who went astray. But the flock has grown, and the stakes are higher. Everything, violence included, has become corporate-minded.

I've read the new commissioner's statements and sifted through the doctor's studies. But the life and tragic death of Andre Waters is the only thing that resonates, the only thing that's truly real.

Upshaw must get back to being the good shepherd. Even one lost lamb is one too many.

Questions for Discussion and Writing

1. Rhoden has been one of *The New York Times'* most prolific sportswriters so he has certainly covered his share of football games and issues. He calls

football players "latter-day gladiators" who "rent their bodies for use in a violent sport." Judging from those words, do you think Rhoden is still a football fan? What other words or phrases does he use to give you hints regarding his current opinion of the sport? If he is a fan, how do you account for the unflattering word choices?

2. Much of Rhoden's article is a conversation between himself and Gene Upshaw, the head of the NFL Players Association at the time this article was written. What is the tone of Rhoden's comments about Upshaw? How does he use Upshaw's quotations to reflect his own opinions of Upshaw?

3. Using boxing as an example, Rhoden proposes an idea for solving the concussion problem in football. Why do you think his suggestion hasn't been adopted?

4. Upshaw and football players see playing football as their job. Interview someone with a dangerous or "violent" job. Write about the employee's view on danger or violence in the workplace. Would this employee ignore a serious ailment or injury and return to work? Does the employee love the job too much to find a safer profession?

5. Rhoden uses a writing technique called "framing" to begin and end his article. Read the lead and conclusion again and explain what you think it means to "frame" writing. In this case, is the framing effective? Why or why not?

On Boxing
JOYCE CAROL OATES

Prolific writer Joyce Carol Oates often uses her modest, middle-class upbringing and the hardships of American life as the subjects of her work. She wanted to become a writer from an early age; as a teenager she won both a scholarship from Syracuse University and the Mademoiselle *fiction contest. Aside from writing, Oates' other profession has been teaching, most notably in the creative writing program at Princeton University. Her works are diverse, ranging from novels and short stories to poetry and drama to works for children and young adults. She is the recipient of a National Book Award and her work is anthologized in numerous textbooks for college students. The following excerpt is from one of Oates' most famous and most controversial books,* On Boxing. *The book is based on a number of articles Oates wrote for* The New York Times Magazine *and the* Ontario Review *and reads like a very long essay. It might seem surprising that*

*a literary "heavyweight" like Oates would be a fan of what some think
is America's most brutal sport. But Oates has been a fan since childhood, following the footsteps of her father, who took her to Golden
Gloves matches and subscribed to* The Ring, *a prominent boxing
magazine. If you are intrigued by Oates' comparison of boxing with
the Roman gladiatorial sport in this excerpt, you should read what
she has to say about boxing and film, violence, and women. What
seems to draw Oates to the sport of boxing?*

——————————— ✦ ———————————

No American sport or activity has been so consistently and so
passionately under attack as boxing, for "moral" as well as
other reasons. And no American sport evokes so ambivalent a response in its defenders: when asked the familiar question "How
can you watch . . . ?" the boxing *aficionado* really has no answer.
He can talk about boxing only with others like himself.

In December 1984 the American Medical Association passed a
resolution calling for the abolition of boxing on the principle that
while other sports involve as much, or even more, risk to life and
health—the most dangerous sports being football, auto racing,
hang gliding, mountain climbing, and ice hockey, with boxing in
about seventh place—boxing is the only sport in which the objective is to cause injury: the brain is the target, the knockout the goal.
In one study it was estimated that 87 percent of boxers suffer some
degree of brain damage in their lifetimes, no matter the relative
success of their careers. And there is the risk of serious eye injury
as well. Equally disturbing, though less plausible, is sociological
evidence that media attention focused on boxing has an immediate effect upon the homicide rate of the country. (According to sociologists David P. Phillips and John E. Hensley, the rate rises by
an average of 12 percent in the days following a highly publicized
fight, for the hypothetical reason that the fight "heavily rewards
one person for inflicting violence on another and is at the opposite
end of a continuum from a successfully prosecuted murder trial,
which heavily punishes one person for inflicting physical violence
on another.") Doubtful as these findings are in a culture in which
television and movie violence has become routine fare, even for
young children, it does seem likely that boxing as a phenomenon
sui generis stimulates rather than resolves certain emotions. If
boxing is akin to classic tragedy in its imitation of action and of

life it cannot provide the *katharsis* of pity and terror of which Aristotle spoke. . . .

Between 1945 and 1985 at least three hundred seventy boxers have died in the United States of injuries directly attributed to boxing. In addition to the infamous Griffith-Paret fight there have been a number of others given wide publicity: Sugar Ray Robinson killed a young boxer named Jimmy Doyle in 1947, for instance, while defending his welterweight title; Sugar Ramos won the featherweight title in 1963 by knocking out the champion Davey Moore, who never regained consciousness; Ray Mancini killed the South Korean Duk Koo-Kim in 1982; former featherweight champion Barry McGuigan killed the Nigerian "Young Ali" in 1983. After the death of Duk Koo-Kim the World Boxing Council shortened title bouts to twelve rounds. (The World Boxing Association retains fifteen. In the era of marathon fights, however—1892 to 1915—men often fought as many as one hundred rounds; the record is one hundred ten, in 1893, over a stupefying seven-hour period. The last scheduled forty-five-round championship fight was between the black title-holder Jack Johnson and his White Hope successor Willard in 1915: the match went twenty-six rounds beneath a blazing sun in Havana, Cuba, before Johnson collapsed.)

To say that the rate of death and injury in the ring is not extraordinary set beside the rates of other sports is to misread the nature of the criticism brought to bear against boxing (and not against other sports). Clearly, boxing's very image is repulsive to many people because it cannot be assimilated into what we wish to know about civilized man. In a technological society possessed of incalculably refined methods of mass destruction (consider how many times over both the United States and the Soviet Union have vaporized each other in fantasy) boxing's display of direct and unmitigated and seemingly natural aggression is too explicit to be tolerated.

Which returns us to the paradox of boxing: its obsessive appeal for many who find in it not only a spectacle involving sensational feats of physical skill but an emotional experience impossible to convey in words; an art form, as I've suggested, with no natural analogue in the arts. Of course it is primitive, too, as birth, death, and erotic love might be said to be primitive, and forces our reluctant acknowledgment that the most profound experiences of our lives are physical events—though we believe ourselves to be, and surely are, essentially spiritual beings. . . .

Consider the history of gladiatorial combat as the Romans practiced it, or caused it to be practiced, from approximately 265 B.C. to its abolishment by Theodoric in A.D. 500. In the ancient world, among part-civilized nations, it was customary after a battle to sacrifice prisoners of war in honor of commanders who had been killed. It also became customary to sacrifice slaves at the funerals of all persons of importance. But then—for what reason?—for amusement, or for the sake of "sport"?—the condemned slaves were given arms and urged to defend themselves by killing the men who were ordered to kill them. Out of this evolution of brute sacrifice into something approaching a recognizable sporting contest the notorious phenomenon of Roman gladitorial combat—death as mass amusement—gradually arose. Surely there is nothing quite like it in world history.

At first the contests were performed at the funeral pyre or near the sepulcher, but, with the passage of time, as interest in the fighting detached itself from its ostensibly religious context, matches were moved to the Forum, then to the Circus and amphitheaters. Contractors emerged to train the slaves, men of rank and political importance began to keep "families" of gladiators, upcoming fights were promoted and advertised as sporting contests are today, shows lasting as long as three days increased in number and popularity. Not the mere sacrifice of helpless individuals but the "sport" of the contest excited spectators, for, though the instinct to fight and to kill is surely qualified by one's personal courage, the instinct to watch others fight and kill is evidently inborn. When the boxing fan shouts, "Kill him! Kill him!" he is betraying no peculiar individual pathology or quirk but asserting his common humanity and his kinship, however distant, with the thousands upon thousands of spectators who crowded into the Roman amphitheaters to see gladiators fight to the death. That such contests for mass amusement endured not for a few years or even decades but for centuries should arrest our attention. . . .

The origins of gladiatorial boxing are specifically Greek. According to tradition a ruler named Thesus (circa 900 B.C.) was entertained by the spectacle of two matched fighters, seated, facing each other, hammering each other to death with their fists. Eventually the men fought on their feet and covered their fists with leather thongs; then with leather thongs covered with sharp metal spikes—the cestus. A ring of some kind, probably a circle, became a neutral space to which an injured boxer might temporarily retreat.

When the Romans cultivated the sport it became extremely popular: one legendary cestus-champion was said to have killed 1,425 opponents. Winning gladiators were widely celebrated as "kings of athletes" and heroes for all. By confirming in the public arena the bloody mortality of other men they established for themselves, as champions always do, a kind of immortality.

So it happens that the wealthier and more advanced a society, the more fanatic its interest in certain kinds of sport. Civilization's trajectory is to curve back upon itself—naturally? helplessly?—like the mythical snake biting its own tail and to take up with passion the outward signs and gestures of "savagery." While it is plausible that emotionally effete men and women may require ever more extreme experiences to arouse them, it is perhaps the case too that the desire is not merely to *mimic* but, magically, to *be* brute, primitive, instinctive, and therefore innocent. One might then be a person for whom the contest is not mere self-destructive play but life itself; and the world, not in spectacular and irrevocable decline, but new, fresh, vital, terrifying and exhilarating by turns, a place of wonders. It is the lost ancestral self that is sought, however futilely. Like those dream-remnants of childhood that year by year continue to elude us but are never abandoned, still less despised, for that reason.

Roman gladiatorial combat was abolished under the Christian emperors Constantine and Theodoric, and its practice discontinued forever. Boxing as we know it in the United States derives solely from English bare-knuckle prizefighting of the eighteenth century and from an entirely different conception of sport.

The first recorded account of a bare-knuckle fight in England— between "a gentleman's footman and a butcher"—is dated 1681 and appeared in a publication called the *London Protestant Mercury*. This species of fight, in which maiming and death were not the point, was known as a "Prize Fight" or the "Prize Ring," and was public entertainment of an itinerant nature, frequently attached to village fairs. The Prize Ring was a movable space created by spectators who formed a loose circle by holding a length of rope; the Prize Fight was a voluntary contest between two men, usually a "champion" and a "challenger," unrefereed but governed by rudimentary rules of fair play. The challenge to fight was put to a crowd by a fighter and his accomplices and if any man wanted to accept he tossed his hat into the ring—hence the political expression with its overtone of bellicosity—and the fight was on. Bets were commonly placed on which man would knock the other down first or draw "first blood." Foul play was actively discouraged by the crowd; the fighters shook hands after the fight. "The Noble Art," as prize-fighting was called, began as a low-life species of entertainment but was in time enthusiastically supported by sporting members of the aristocracy and the upper classes.

England's earliest bare-knuckle champion was a man named James Figg who won the honor in 1719. The last of the bare-knuckle champions was the American heavyweight John L. Sullivan whose career—from approximately 1882 to 1892—overlapped both bare-knuckle fighting and gloved boxing as established under the rules of the Marquis of Queensberry which are observed, with some elaboration, to the present time. The most significant changes were two: the introduction of leather gloves (mainly to protect the hand, not the face—a man's knuckles are easily broken) and the third man in the ring, the referee, whose privilege it is to stop the fight at his own discretion, if he thinks a boxer has no chance of winning or cannot defend himself against his opponent. With the introduction of the referee the crudeness of "The Noble Art" passes over into the relative sophistication of boxing.

The "third man in the ring," usually anonymous so far as the crowd is concerned, appears to many observers no more than an observer himself, even an intruder; a ghostly presence as fluid in motion and quick-footed as the boxers themselves (indeed, he is frequently an ex-boxer). But so central to the drama of boxing is the referee that the spectacle of two men fighting each other un-supervised in an elevated ring would seem hellish, if not obscene—life rather than art. The referee makes boxing possible.

The referee is our intermediary in the fight. He is our moral conscience extracted from us as spectators so that, for the dura-tion of the fight, "conscience" need not be a factor in our experi-ence; nor need it be a factor in the boxers' behavior. (Asked if boxers are ever sorry for having hurt their opponents, Carmen Basilio replied: "Sorry? Are you kidding? Boxers are never sorry.") Which is not to say that boxers are always and forever without conscience: all boxers are different, and behave differ-ently at different times. But there are occasions when a boxer who is trapped in the ropes and unable to fall to the canvas while being struck repeatedly is in danger of being killed unless the ref-eree intervenes—the attacking boxer has been trained not to stop his attack while his opponent is still technically standing. In the rapidly escalating intensity of the fight only the referee remains neutral and objective.

Though the referee's role is highly demanding and it has been estimated that there are perhaps no more than a dozen really skilled referees in the world, it seems necessary in the drama of the fight that the referee himself possesses no dramatic identity: referees' names are rarely remembered after a fight except by seasoned boxing fans. Yet, paradoxically, the referee's participation is crucial. He cannot control what happens in the ring but he can control to a degree *that* it happens—he is responsible for the fight if not for the individual fighters' performances. In a match in which boxing skills and not merely fighting are predominant the referee's role can be merely functional, but in a fiercely contested match it is of incalculable importance. The referee holds the power of life and death at certain times since his decision to terminate a fight, or to allow it to continue, can determine a boxer's fate. (One should know that a well-aimed punch with a heavyweight's full weight behind it can have the equivalent force of ten thousand pounds—a blow that must be absorbed by the brain in its jelly sac.) In the infamous Benny Paret-Emile Griffith fight of March 1962 the referee Ruby Goldstein was said to have stood paralyzed as Griffith trapped Paret in the ropes, striking him as many as eighteen times in the head. (Paret died ten days later.) Boxers are trained not to quit. If knocked down, they try to get up to continue the fight, even if they can hardly defend themselves. The primary rule of the ring—to defend oneself at all times—is both a parody and a distillation of life. . . .

To the untrained eye most boxing matches appear not merely savage but mad. As the eye becomes trained, however, the spectator begins to see the complex patterns that underlie the "madness"; what seems to be merely confusing action is understood to be coherent and intelligent, frequently inspired. Even the spectator who dislikes violence in principle can come to admire highly skillful boxing—to admire it beyond all "sane" proportions. A brilliant boxing match, quicksilver in its motions, transpiring far more rapidly than the mind can absorb, can have the power that Emily Dickinson attributed to great poetry: you know it's great when it takes the top of your head off. (The physical imagery Dickinson employs is peculiarly apt in this context.)

This early impression—that boxing is "mad," or mimics the actions of madness—seems to me no less valid, however, for being, by degrees, substantially modified. It is never erased, never entirely forgotten or overcome; it simply sinks beneath the threshold of consciousness, as the most terrifying and heartrending of our lives' experiences sink beneath the level of consciousness by way of familiarity or deliberate suppression. So one knows, but does not (consciously) know, certain intransigent facts about the human condition. One does not (consciously) know, but one *knows*. All boxing fans, however accustomed to the sport, however many decades have been invested in their obsession, know that boxing is sheerly madness, for all its occasional beauty. That knowledge is our common bond and sometimes—dare it be uttered?—our common shame.

To watch boxing closely, and seriously, is to risk moments of what might be called animal panic—a sense not only that something very ugly is happening but that, by watching it, one is an accomplice. This awareness, or revelation, or weakness, or hairline split in one's cuticle of a self can come at any instant, unanticipated and unbidden; though of course it tends to sweep over the viewer when he is watching a really violent match. I feel it as vertigo—breathlessness—a repugnance beyond language: a sheerly physical loathing. That it is also, or even primarily, self-loathing goes without saying.

For boxing really isn't metaphor, it is the thing in itself. And my predilection for watching matches on tape, when the outcomes are known, doesn't alter the fact that, as the matches occurred, they occurred in the present tense, and for one time only. The rest is subterfuge—the intellectual's uneasy "control" of his material. . . .

At such times one thinks: What is happening? why are we here? what does this mean? can't this be stopped? My terror at seeing Floyd Patterson battered into insensibility by Sonny Liston was not assuaged by my rational understanding that the event had taken place long ago and that, in fact, Patterson is in fine health at the present time, training an adopted son to box. (Liston of course has been dead for years—he died of a heroin overdose, aged thirty-eight, in "suspicious" circumstances.) More justified, perhaps, was my sickened sense that boxing is, simply, wrong, a mistake, an outlaw activity for some reason under the protectorate of the law, when, a few weeks ago in March 1986, I sat in the midst of a suddenly very quiet closed-circuit television audience in a suburban Trenton hall watching bantamweight Richie Sandoval as he lay flat and unmoving on his back . . . very likely dead of a savage beating the referee had not, for some reason, stopped in time. My conviction was that anything was preferable to boxing, anything was preferable to seeing another minute of it, for instance standing outside in the parking lot for the remainder of the evening and staring at the stained asphalt . . .

A friend who is a sportswriter was horrified by the same fight. In a letter he spoke of his intermittent disgust for the sport he has been watching most of his life, and writing about for years: "It's all a bit like bad love—putting up with the pain, waiting for the sequel to the last good moment. And like bad love, there comes the point of being worn out, when the reward of the good moment doesn't seem worth all the trouble . . ."

Yet we don't give up on boxing, it isn't that easy. Perhaps it's like tasting blood. Or, more discreetly put, love commingled with hate is more powerful than love. Or hate.

Questions for Discussion and Writing

1. Oates defends boxing in a number of places in her book. Identify areas from this excerpt where she defends the sport. What evidence does she offer readers? How much of the defense is based on her own opinions rather than evidence? Which is more effective?

2. Make a list of sports you consider violent and briefly explain why you see each one that way. Compare your list to Oates'. Do you agree with her? Why or why not?

3. Oates says that gladiatorial sports were moved from religious sites to the Forum, then to the circus or amphitheaters. What do those moves in venue tell us about this sport?

4. Oates says prizefighting was originally a "low-life species" of entertainment but it caught on with aristocracy. Why? Consider her comments at the end of the excerpt as well. Why is boxing appealing to so many people?

5. Examine the structure of Oates' writing. What rhetorical features categorize the writing in the essay genre? Why?

Where Is the Budo in Mixed Martial Arts?

RICHARD RYAN

Martial arts master Richard Ryan founded Dynamic Combat™, a "reality-based combative martial art system designed for the real world." Ryan and his instructors provide martial arts, defensive tactics, self-protection, crime prevention, security, and weapons training for law enforcement agencies, police academies, SWAT and special operations teams, and qualified civilians. Part of the training involves preparing students to face worst-case scenarios on the streets and sudden death encounters against attackers. But the instruction also teaches the legal and moral aspects of the use of force. Though not a writer by profession, Ryan has had work published in Tactical Knives, Sweat Magazine, *and several times in* Black Belt *magazine. Some of his other articles are "The Realities of Violence," "The Morality of Fighting," and "Violence, Passivity and the Warrior's Mind." He is the owner and publisher of Real Combat Online's* RCO Magazine, *a publication about reality-based fighting. In this article from the June 2007 issue of* Black Belt, *Ryan criticizes the increasingly popular sport of mixed martial arts, or ultimate fighting.*

——————————————— ✦ ———————————————

Viewing the Ultimate Fighting Championship and its clones sometimes leaves me feeling empty. As a lifelong martial artist, I enjoy all forms of full-contact competition, especially its newest manifestation, no-holds-barred fighting. Now called "mixed martial arts," it's much closer to real combat than its predecessors. It's been instrumental in proving certain theories about combat—especially the idea that simple is better.

Gone are the head kicks and other showy techniques that are better suited for movies and television. In their stead are the simple basics of combat: jab, cross, hook, uppercut, elbows, knees and low kicks. In place of the referee-controlled "clinch and break" is the more realistic grappling and ground game that shows the reality of combat, and that is as it should be. This is Darwinian evolution at work. It provides validity for the effectiveness of MMA training as opposed to single-discipline, traditional systems. Matt Hughes proved this point convincingly against the man who started it all: Royce Gracie. Today, as in years past, the best in the martial sports tend to be the most versatile, proving that adaptability to the unpredictability of combat is a key component of victory.

But beyond the harsh realities of the cage, something's missing. Where's the budo (warrior ways) in MMA? Despite the glamour that TV coverage bestows, despite the marketing slogans and unapologetic hype, the values we grew up with are getting lost in the mix as MMA's priorities morph into those that govern pro wrestling. There's more punk attitude and less respect, the last bastion between organized competition and common street brawling.

Respect, honor, integrity and humility make the martial arts more than just a collection of fighting skills. Unfortunately, they seem to be in short supply with many of the athletes in MMA. There are exceptions—guys like Frank Shamrock, Rich Franklin and Hughes, who conduct themselves with honor—but there are many more who lack the budo spirit. Frequently we see real and contrived rivalries designed to stir up spectator passions and a thirst for violence or revenge—just like in pro wrestling. MMA cards are adopting a predictable scenario: Two athletes promote their fight by proclaiming how they will demolish each other. Respect and honor are nowhere to be found. Only after the bout (usually with one fighter bruised and bloodied) do they express a modicum of respect. This spawns gangster martial artists whose objective isn't sportsmanship but a path to money, girls and glory that's traveled with no regrets and no regard for others.

This would be fine if MMA were only sports entertainment, but it's not. For many, it defines the martial arts today, and that's the problem. The martial arts are far more than what's seen in the cage or ring. To allow the arts to be defined by MMA alone is like saying all cars are the same. It simply isn't true.

My real question is, What message is this sport sending to people, especially children? Is it OK to taunt and curse a rival, telling him that you'll kill him in an event that's supposed to present fair competition? Is it acceptable to disrespect others if you can back it up with your fists? The behavior of these athletes teaches our children that respect is only begrudgingly earned after a bloody beating. Where are the values the arts were founded on? Don't we have some degree of responsibility to teach our children how to conduct themselves in sport as well as in life?

I know that the promoters are simply running their businesses. I know that the people in charge of these events hold them for profit and that, intentionally or otherwise, they're just following what worked for their predecessors. It's also true that combat sports have a long history of public rivalry, the whole good guy/bad guy thing. These realities I can live with. But nobody seems to be making an effort to inject values into the game. In some ways, the public is responsible. People in business market what sells, and obviously there's a demand for the gangster attitude coupled with blood and violence.

I know it's possible to practice and teach real martial arts while retaining traditional values. NHB [no holds barred] fighting doesn't need to come with bad behavior. Some of its best teachers impart much more than lessons in how to beat someone up. I've met numerous instructors around the world who make sure that integrity, respect and honor are part of the martial arts experience. Maybe someday these qualities will be paid more than lip service by the organizations that profit from the action and excitement of earnest competition. Maybe someday they'll require honorable behavior in their rivalries. Muhammad Ali enjoyed a career that spanned decades, and he always exhibited the utmost class. I hope that as MMA grows in popularity, we don't forget the values that make the martial arts more than just a way of fighting.

Questions for Discussion and Writing

1. Ryan refers to two fighters, Matt Hughes and Royce Gracie. Research more about the two. Find information on current popular fighters as well. Choose one and write a profile that includes what type of fighter the man is and how he is perceived by fans and fellow athletes.

2. Ryan calls attitude and respect "the last bastion between organized competition and common street brawling." How should sport fighting differ from street fighting? Does this statement contradict Ryan's earlier comparison of mixed martial arts (MMA) to other fighting sports? Why or why not?

3. Consider the audience Ryan is writing to. The article appeared in *Black Belt* magazine and on Ryan's Web site for his combat training organization. Research these audiences. Analyze Ryan's comments to these audiences: Is he "preaching to the choir," so to speak, or is he trying to convince others to agree with him? Use specific examples from the text to support your analysis.

4. Ryan seems more concerned about what fighting sports teach children than most commentators on violent sports. Should children be taught about fighting sports at all? Ryan points out the negative lessons that fighting sports teach children. What are the positive lessons?

5. Though Ryan has published a number of articles, he is not a writer by profession. Evaluate his article. How well does he make his argument? How well does he use evidence to support his points? Are there any particularly well-written phrases or paragraphs? Descriptions?

Danger on the Dome
PETER FIMRITE

With so many natural resources surrounding San Francisco, including Yosemite National Park, Muir Woods' famous California redwood forest, and the bay, it's no surprise that reporter Peter Fimrite has covered a number of stories related to the outdoors or extreme elements. He has written for the San Francisco Chronicle *about a diver who died while spearfishing, a group of divers who rescued several whales from crab traps, and the death of James Kim in December 2006. San Francisco's Kim made national news when he became lost hiking through the mountains of Oregon in an effort to find help for his family; their car was stranded during a snow storm. Kim was found dead in a creek but his wife and two young daughters were rescued. Fimrite's writing has won awards, including a Best of the West journalism award for his stories on Kim's tragedy and Hearst Honors for his contribution to the* Chronicle's *coverage of a 2006 heat wave. This article, about the danger of inexperienced climbers attempting to summit Yosemite's Half Dome, mirrors some concerns documented in many other articles about mountain climbing. In fact, one disaster on the sport's most famous and grueling mountain, Mount Everest, began as an article by Jon Krakauer for* Outside *magazine and resulted in the best-selling book* Into Thin Air. *As you read, consider the similarities and differences between "violence" and "danger." When can danger, such as bad weather or inexperienced athletes, turn a sport violent?*

———————— ✦ ————————

Scores of sweating hikers lugging backpacks and water bottles hung onto the cable handrails on the slope leading to the top of Half Dome, waiting for their turn to move.

"Let's go, let's go, let's go!" yelled one frustrated man, but the crowd on the cables didn't budge. It was midday on a Saturday, and the sun was beating down on the tired hikers, who were stalled in midclimb.

The last 400 feet of the grueling 8.6-mile climb to the summit of the world-famous peak was like a holiday scene at a Disneyland ride—a long line and a few thrills.

It was typical of a weekend summer day at the 8,842-foot top of Half Dome. Hikers wearing tennis shoes and sandals, city kids in baggy basketball garb, children, flabby tourists and the elderly were clambering around on the slick granite, where three people have tumbled to their death within the past year—one of them just a few weeks ago.

The weekend menagerie at the top of Half Dome is a problem that many people believe is turning one of the world's signature hikes into a flirtation with death. Yosemite National Park officials acknowledge that the crowds are sometimes excessive but say there are no obvious solutions.

On this particular Saturday, two women panicked while trying to climb the cables and had to be helped down. A man suffering from dehydration was assisted down by a ranger, and a frightened, sobbing young boy was being urged on to the top by his father.

To bypass the crowd, one young man wearing Converse All Stars high tops began pulling himself up the 45- to 50-degree slope on the outside of the cables.

"I can't wear boots," replied the man after someone inside the cables questioned his sanity. "I get all clumsy in boots."

Some of the hikers had heard of the recent deaths on Half Dome, but few appeared to be concerned.

"Accidents happen," said Scott Mutch, 51, of Alta Loma (San Bernardino County), who climbed to the top with his 13-year-old son, Thomas, and 20 others in his Boy Scout troop. "You're in God's hands."

The trail to the summit of Half Dome is perhaps the most famous and scenic day hike in the United States. It gains 4,733 feet in elevation as it winds past two immense waterfalls, climbs steep switchbacks and teeters along 400 rock steps on a cliff to the backside of Half Dome. There, the final push up slippery smooth granite awaits, with only the cable handrails to prevent a slide into thin air.

The top of the climb scares plenty of people off the mountain. The immense summit looms above as hikers approach it; the people on the cables look like ants clinging to a vertical slope.

"Oh s —," said one hiker when he first glimpsed the dome. "You have to climb that?"

But the crowds keep coming. The number of weekend and holiday hikers on Half Dome has increased 30 percent since the mid-1990s, and concerns are mounting about frequent bottlenecks on the summit cables.

"I'm really surprised at the amount of people and the age groups that made it here," said Brian Floyd, 34, of Fresno as he waited at the bottom of the cables with dozens of others. "I've seen little kids and elderly people."

Blake Chapman of the West Marin hamlet of Woodacre said the cables, the crowd and his decision to wear Teva sandals instead of hiking boots had combined to make things very difficult.

"I'll never do this again, and I want to know whose idea it was," Chapman said only half-jokingly as he stood gasping with his friends on the top, his cowboy hat slightly askew. "I turned 61 yesterday, and this isn't a gift."

Some believe the bottleneck was at least partially responsible for the June 16 [2007] death of Hirofumi Nohara. The 37-year-old Japanese citizen lost his footing three-quarters of the way up the cables and slid off the side of Half Dome in front of dozens of horrified witnesses.

There was a 45-minute wait to ascend the cables at the time, and climbers going up and down were jostling past one another, according to witnesses.

It was the third fatal fall from the cables within the past year, but the crowds were clearly not a factor in the other two deaths, which occurred during off-peak months.

On April 19 [2007], Jennie Bettles, a 43-year-old businesswoman from Oakland, fell to her death while trying to descend during wet weather. Emily Sandall, 25, of New Mexico, died Nov. 10, 2006, after slipping on the wet granite. In both cases, the handrail supports and wooden foot planks had been taken out, and the cables were lying flat on the granite, standard practice during the off-season.

Last October, Scott Clancy of Fresno fell when he slipped on the wet granite and lost his hold on the cables, but his pants caught on something before he could plummet off the cliff, and he was saved.

The incidents have prompted calls for Yosemite to make the cables safer, either by regulating who goes up, requiring safety harnesses or adding a third cable. Park officials say no significant change can be made without a great deal of study, public hearings and evidence that spending the money would make the climb safer.

"We've only had the one fatality where other factors like bad weather didn't play a part, so there's no pattern," said ranger Adrienne Freeman, a park spokeswoman.

An average of about 12 people die in Yosemite each year, but the three people who died within the past year were the only ones to simply slip off the rocks at Half Dome in decades, Freeman said. Other deaths have been blamed on heart attacks, lightning strikes and parachute accidents.

In fact, more people have died being swept over Vernal and Nevada falls on the Mist Trail leading up to Half Dome. Drownings in the Merced River next to the trail also outnumber fatal falls from the iconic hunk of rock.

Still, it takes only one climb up the cables on a weekend to see what concerns people.

Planks are spaced about 12 feet apart underneath the cables, and on most weekend afternoons two people are standing on each one. The gridlock is especially hard on the unfortunate folks stranded on the steepest 50-yard section of the route, where getting caught between planks means holding onto the cables for dear life while trying to find a crack in which to wedge one's feet.

This is the spot where people regularly freeze up.

"I had vertigo," said Shea Keane, 31, of Vacaville, who climbed the cables with five friends. "Everything in my body was shaking. I felt like I was going to vomit."

Jen Zuzak, 34, of Berkeley, was so dizzy she had to sit down on one of the planks halfway up. She made it, she said, only because others on the cables encouraged her to continue.

Amal Mehta, 7, of San Jose, had a stunned look as he descended from the top with help from his father, Huzefa, and a climbing harness.

"I wasn't scared," he said, but his father quickly shot back, "Yes you were. I was scared."

"OK," Amal conceded. "A little bit."

As the logjam increased on the cables that Saturday, so did the chatter, mostly out of necessity as people negotiated which side to pass on while moving from plank to plank.

At one point a dropped water bottle bounced on the granite with a loud bop-bop. The hillside went silent as the hikers listened to it bounce and skitter for several hundred feet before going over a ledge into space.

"What surprises me is the lack of concern for safety," said Alan Henderson, a 40-year-old native of Scotland, who wore a harness and clipped himself onto the cable using metal hooks. "There are people up here with just tennis shoes. If you slip, you are a goner."

The colossal, rounded backside of Half Dome is not exactly vertical, but scaling it unaided would be impossible for anyone who is not an experienced rock climber. The summit was considered totally inaccessible until Oct. 12, 1875, when George Anderson drilled his way to the top, fastening his rope to iron eyebolts.

A few days later, Sally Dutcher became the first woman to climb Half Dome, using Anderson's fixed ropes. She was wearing a long dress, according to historians.

In 1919, the Sierra Club installed the steel cables. Scaling them has become almost a rite of passage for Yosemite visitors from around the world.

Royal Robbins, a legend among climbers and part of the team that made the first ascent of Half Dome's 2,000-foot northwest face in 1957, once descended the back side of the rock next to the cables without using his hands.

"One can, if you are careful, stick to that particular surface with good rubber," Robbins said this week of his gravity-defying feat on June 24, 1961.

It is perhaps because of stories like that, and a general impression that scaling Half Dome is not overly difficult, that so many people come ill-prepared for the rigors of the climb.

There are signs about the dangers along the trail. But there are almost always people at the top who have run out of water, are too exhausted to continue, lack proper footwear or are simply paralyzed with fear.

Every year, people have to be taken out by helicopter, rescue workers say.

"We are seeing a change in the pattern of visitor behavior up there," Freeman said. "What this tells us is that we have to start asking some questions. Are more people driving to Yosemite in the morning and trying to climb Half Dome in a day? Are people coming prepared? Are they acclimated? Are they rushing because of time limitations?"

Next year, Yosemite plans to start collecting data on the various impacts, including crowding, on the Merced River corridor, which includes Half Dome and the trail leading to it. That could lead to new policies, but any major changes would have to be accompanied by legislation. That could very well face opposition from environmental groups, climbers, naturalists or wilderness advocates, Freeman said.

In the meantime, park visitors will have to get up extremely early or endure the crowds if they want a transcendent view from the top of Half Dome of the cathedral of nature that is Yosemite Valley.

"I'm not real big on heights," said Shelly Jones, a 28-year-old geography teacher from Virginia, as she looked out wide-eyed from the peak. "But this is about the biggest rush I've ever had."

Questions for Discussion and Writing

1. Would you automatically think of mountain or rock climbing as a dangerous or violent sport? What does Fimrite say to indicate that it is violent in nature? Does he support his thesis effectively?

2. Fimrite spent a weekend with climbers at Half Dome and wrote this article based on firsthand experience. However, he also uses several quotations, primarily from participants, to support his story. How well does he use quotations to support his own experience? Point out specific examples that are effective or ineffective.

3. Aside from quotations, what other types of support or evidence does Fimrite use in his writing? Identify examples and discuss their effectiveness.

4. Examine the tone of Fimrite's article. Is it objective or opinionated? Though he is reporting for a newspaper he is also writing from personal experience. Should that distinction give him more editorial freedom?

5. Evaluate the paragraph structure of Fimrite's story. Though the article is lengthy by newspaper standards, the paragraphs are rather brief. Do the paragraphs seem clear and to-the-point or choppy to you as the reader? What impact do the short paragraphs have on the overall structure of Fimrite's article?

Making Connections: Writing

1. What are the consequences of violence in sports, whether intended or not? Research and write a report that summarizes what has happened to athletes after violent incidents. John H. Kerr discusses Todd Bertuzzi in hockey, for example. Joyce Carol Oates names boxers who have killed other boxers in the ring. Report on the status of these athletes and what, if any, changes have occurred in the sports.

2. Write an annotated bibliography of expert sources on a particular violent sport or incident. John H. Kerr quotes many experts in his journal article, including former hockey player Ken Dryden, and psychologists and other experts on violence. Compile your own list of experts.

3. Many of the writers in this chapter use vivid words and phrases related to violence to make their points. Choose some of the words and phrases and analyze their meaning and placement in the selections. Are they used to make an argument, to add drama, or to appeal to you as the reader?

4. Write a letter to the editor that places blame for the escalation and acceptance of violence in sports. William C. Rhoden and Richard Ryan blame several parties for violence in football and mixed martial arts, respectively. Who or what would you blame and why?

5. Both Joyce Carol Oates and William C. Rhoden mention gladiator combat. Trace the history of gladiator fighting and relate it to the status of current fighting sports.

6. Write a position essay on violence as entertainment. Several of the writers in this chapter question the difference between entertainment and sport. If sport is not entertainment, then is violence acceptable? What about violence in other areas of culture such as television and music?

7. Research changes that violent or dangerous sports have made in recent history. Some sports have improved equipment to protect athletes, for example. With more amateurs attempting extreme sports such as mountain climbing, some venues are restricting their access to trained athletes. Are sports actively seeking ways to become less violent or dangerous?

8. Most, though not all, violent sports are played predominantly by men. But Joyce Carol Oates does refer to female boxers and we know that females participate in hockey, football, mixed martial arts, and mountain climbing. Interview a female athlete who plays a sport considered "violent." Does her reaction to violence differ from a male's reaction? Is she criticized or perceived as "manly" for participating in a violent sport?

9. Review a movie about a violent sport. (See the recommendations at the end of the chapter for ideas.) Is the violence necessary to the film or is it too dramatic? What's the difference between a fictional work with violence such as *Fight Club* and a nonfiction documentary such as *Murderball*?

10. Using William C. Rhoden's article as a model, write a response to an athlete or coach who participates in a violent sport. Argue with the subject as Rhoden does with Gene Upshaw if you like, or side with the subject.

Books Worth Reading

Among the Thugs by Bill Buford. Chronicles the author's travels throughout Britain with supporters of the Liverpool Football Club, famous for their violent behavior at games.

The Code: The Unwritten Rules of Fighting and Retaliation in the NHL by Ross Bernstein. Explores the history of fighting in hockey games.

Combat Sports in the Ancient World: Competition, Violence, and Culture by Michael B. Poliakoff. Describes and analyzes boxing, wrestling, stick-fighting, and other violent games in ancient Greece, Rome, and the Near East.

Fight Club by Chuck Palahniuk (fiction). A group of disillusioned men form a club to beat each other senseless.

Gimp: When Life Deals You a Crappy Hand, You Can Fold—Or You Can Play by Mark Zupan with Tim Swanson. Narrative tells of author's life from the drunk-driving accident that paralyzed him to his championships in quad rugby and starring role in the documentary *Murderball.*

Head Games: Football's Concussion Crisis from the NFL to Youth Leagues by Chris Nowinski. Former Harvard football player, wrestler, and victim of a severe head injury investigates the growing problem of concussions in violent sports, particularly football.

In Defense of Hunting: Yesterday and Today by James A. Swan. Nature writer and environmentalist defends the primal need to hunt.

Into Thin Air: A Personal Account of the Mount Everest Disaster by Jon Krakauer. True account of the violent storm that killed numerous climbers on the world's highest peak.

On Boxing by Joyce Carol Oates. A collection of essays on what the author admits is—and sometimes defends as—a brutal sport.

Punch! Why Women Participate in Violent Sports by Jennifer Lawler. The tae kwon do black belt mixes scholarly research and interviews with women in hockey, boxing, martial arts, football, and rugby to answer the question.

Films Worth Watching

Any Given Sunday (1999). Behind-the-scenes look at modern professional football.

Fight Club (1999). Based on the book by the same name; about "normal" men who form a group to vent their aggression.

Gladiator (2000). Fictional inside look at the life of a Roman gladiator.

Million Dollar Baby (2004). A female boxer is seriously injured by a violent blow and her manager must make a difficult decision.

Murderball (2005). Documentary about quadriplegics who play full-contact rugby in wheelchairs.

Ring of Fire: The Emile Griffith Story (2005). Documentary of a boxer who accidentally killed his opponent in the ring.

Rollerball (2002). Not nearly as good as the 1975 original; takes a futuristic look at a violent sport called rollerball.

Sites Worth Surfing

http://www.broadstreetbully.com
Billed as "All hockey. All Fights. All the time" for its video collection of
hockey fights. Not for the feint of heart. Also see
http://hockeyfights.com/

http://www.thering-online.com/
The official magazine of boxing since 1922.

http://www.quadrugby.com/toc.htm
The home of the United States Quad Rugby Association.

http://www.everestnews.com/
Site for mountain climbing enthusiasts; tracks number of deaths on
Mount Everest.

Discrimination or Opportunity: What Role Does Race Play in Sports?

We often think of racial issues only in terms of black and white. To be sure, sports have been fraught with black-white controversy. African-American baseball players were made to play in a separate system—the Negro League—for many years. Some sports are still played primarily by white athletes. And there has long been a debate over whether or not African-American athletes are "better suited" for particular sports—consider the phrase "white men can't jump" in relation to basketball, for example. But issues of race and sports extend past the boundaries of black-white relations. Did you know that golfer Lee Trevino's nickname was Super-Mex even though he's Texan, not Mexican? Or that when Arturo Moreno bought the Anaheim (Ca.) Angels in 2003 he became the first Hispanic to own a major U.S. sports team? Or that, while figure skater Michelle Kwan became a millionaire from endorsements, her predecessor and gold medalist Kristi Yamaguchi struggled to get endorsements because of her Japanese descent? Do sports provide minorities with more opportunities than other segments of our society such as business or education? Or does discrimination still place a barrier in front of athletes? Chapter 4 examines these questions.

The chapter begins with two opposing pieces on the same issue: the use of Native American team names and mascots. As you read, make note of two elements of the writing: the audience and purpose of each piece and the way one responds to the other. Most Americans are familiar with *Sports Illustrated*, which published S. L. Price's article "The Indian Wars." The general readership magazine is one of the most prominent publications in the country. Does that prominence make the publication more responsible for what it prints?

Are more readers likely to believe what they read simply because they trust *Sports Illustrated?* In contrast, the authors of the article "Of Polls and Race Prejudice," which appeared in the *Journal of Sport & Social Issues*, were writing for a very different audience. The authors criticize several elements of the *Sports Illustrated* article. It might be interesting to read "The Indian Wars" first, then read "Of Polls and Race Prejudice," and then read "The Indian Wars" again to see if your opinions or reactions have changed. You might also ask yourself what the purpose of each article was to begin with and how those purposes might influence you as a reader.

As you read the next few selections, consider whether all racial rhetoric is necessarily negative in nature. For example, "Latino Players Can Revive Baseball in America" by Tim Wendel for *USA Today* and "Joe Louis' Biggest Knockout" by Dave Kindred for *Sporting News* might seem more positive in tone compared to the selections on Native American mascots. Wendel praises the achievements of Latino baseball players and their positive impact on American baseball, and Kindred calls Joe Louis' defeat of German boxer Max Schmeling during the Nazi era the second most significant event in sports history. Yet both of these stories include references to racism. How do Wendel and Kindred manage to turn racial issues around and use rhetoric to show the positive results of these situations?

Finally, Tamara Nopper's "Asian America's Response to Shaquille O'Neal Riddled with Racial-Sexual Anxiety" and Jere Longman's "Debate on Women at Augusta Catches Woods Off Balance" help provide insight into a cultural phenomenon: members of a particular racial group criticizing members of "their own." Nopper was prompted to write her essay after an incident when basketball player Shaquille O'Neal, himself a prominent African American, made what were perceived by many as racist remarks toward fellow player Yao Ming, who is from China. Though she certainly doesn't dismiss O'Neal's words as acceptable, she turns the table on her own race, Asian Americans, to show how their reactions constitute "reverse racism." Longman reports for *The New York Times* on golfer Tiger Woods' reactions to the possibility of allowing women into the all-male Augusta National Golf Club, home to golf's most prestigious tournament, the Masters. With parents of mixed ethnic descent, Woods has been hailed by some as the spokesperson for multi-racial causes. He has endured criticism for not claiming to be strongly one race or another, preferring instead to call himself "Cablinasian," short for Caucasian, Black, Indian, and Asian.

Many black activists have expressed disappointment in Woods' reluctance to speak out against any form of discrimination, including that against women. As Longman says, "They view Mr. Woods, whose father is African-American and whose mother is Thai, as essentially condoning discrimination and, in the process, turning his back on more than a half-century tradition of high-profile black athletes who used their celebrity status to advocate for civil rights." Longman goes on to quote those who oppose and support Woods.

The issues discussed in these selections are controversial and might tempt you to forget to examine the writing in this chapter. For example, "The Indian Wars" and "Of Polls and Race Prejudice," though about the same topic, are based on two very different styles of writing. Price's *Sports Illustrated* article is clear and well-organized, yet lacks the depth that the authors of the academic journal article would have preferred. Using that weakness as the basis of their criticism, they write an effective rebuttal to Price's claims. You must decide as a reader whether their rebuttal is reasonable or whether Price fulfilled his journalistic duties based on the publication in which the article appeared.

This chapter serves to introduce you to the varied issues of race in sports and the various ways that writers tackle this controversial and emotional topic. As you read, continue to ask yourself what role race plays in sports. Is sports history—recent as well as long ago—reflective more of negative racial consequences such as discrimination or positive contributions and opportunities? Where does the future of race in sports seem to be headed? Where do your opinions and experiences fit in?

The Indian Wars

S. L. PRICE

A senior writer at Sports Illustrated *since 1994, S. L. Price has become known as an expert on sports in Florida and Cuba. Prior to working at* Sports Illustrated *he wrote for the* Miami Herald. *In 2000 he published his first book,* Pitching Around Fidel: A Journey into the Heart of Cuban Sports, *in which he uncovers how Cuba's athletes and teams are impacted by their government's regime. He moved his family to Europe for a year to write the travelogue* Far Afield: A Sportswriting

Odyssey. Not only did Price follow several European athletes, he also got a taste of what it's like to be American in Europe in an era of terrorism. His articles for Sports Illustrated *have been anthologized in several collections of sportswriting, including the magazine's own* 50 Years of Great Writing. *Price has written several stories about situations with racial undertones, including the rape case that pitted a black woman against white lacrosse players from Duke University, a profile of Japanese baseball player Ichiro Suzuki, and a piece as thought-provoking as its title, "Whatever Happened to the White Athlete?" The following article, from* Sports Illustrated, *garnered quite a bit of attention, including the rebuttal that follows from a scholarly journal. The issue of naming teams and mascots after Native American tribes and traditions has not disappeared. What impact do you think Price's article has had on the controversy?*

———————————— ✦ ————————————

Solve this word problem: Billy Mills, the former runner who won the gold medal in the 10,000 meters at the 1964 Olympics, is on a commercial airliner hurtling somewhere over the U.S. It is August 2001. Because Mills's father and mother were three-quarters and one-quarter Native American, respectively, he grew up being called half-breed until that was no longer socially acceptable. As sensibilities shifted over the years, he heard a variety of words and phrases describing his ethnic background, from Indian to Sioux to Native American to the one with which he is most comfortable, the age-old name of his tribal nation: Lakota.

Mills is sitting in first class. A flight attendant—the words *steward* and *stewardess* are frowned upon today—checks on him every so often. The man is African-American, the preferred designation for his racial background; before that, society called him *black* or *colored* or *Negro*. The man is friendly, doing his job. Each time he addresses Mills, he calls him Chief. Mills doesn't know if the flight attendant realizes that he is Lakota. Maybe he calls everyone Chief. Maybe he means it as a compliment. Mills motions him over.

"I want to tell you something," Mills says. The man leans in. "I'm Native American, and you calling me Chief, it turns my stomach. It'd be very similar to somebody calling you Nigger."

The flight attendant looks at Mills. He says, "Calling you Chief doesn't bother *me* . . . Chief."

Who is right and who wrong? Whose feelings take precedence? Most important, who gets to decide what we call one another?

If you've figured out an answer, don't celebrate yet. The above confrontation is only a warmup for sport's thorniest word problem: the use of Native American names (and mascots that represent them) by high school, college and professional teams. For more than 30 years the debate has been raging over whether names such as Redskins, Braves, Chiefs and Indians honor or defile Native Americans, whether clownish figures like the Cleveland Indians' Chief Wahoo have any place in today's racially sensitive climate and whether the sight of thousands of non-Native Americans doing the tomahawk chop at Atlanta's Turner Field is mindless fun or mass bigotry. It's an argument that, because it mixes mere sports with the sensitivities of a people who were nearly exterminated, seems both trivial and profound—and it's further complicated by the fact that for three out of four Native Americans, even a nickname such as Redskins, which many whites consider racist, isn't objectionable.

Indeed, some Native Americans—even those who purportedly object to Indian team nicknames—wear Washington Redskins paraphernalia with pride. Two such men showed up in late January at Augustana College in Sioux Falls, S.Dak., for a conference on race relations. "They were speaking against the Indian nicknames, but they were wearing Redskins sweatshirts, and one had on a Redskins cap," says Betty Ann Gross, a member of the Sisseton-Wahpeton Sioux tribe. "No one asked them about it. They looked pretty militant."

Gross's own case illustrates how slippery the issue can be. She grew up on a reservation in South Dakota and went to Sisseton High, a public school on the reservation whose teams are called the Redmen. Gross, 49, can't recall a time when people on the reservation weren't arguing about the team name, evenly divided between those who were proud of it and those who were ashamed. Gross recently completed a study that led the South Dakota state government to change the names of 38 places and landmarks around the state, yet she has mixed feelings on the sports issue. She wants Indian mascots and the tomahawk chop discarded, but she has no problem with team names like the Fighting Sioux (University of North Dakota) or even the Redskins. "There's a lot of division," Gross says. "We're confused, and if we're confused, you guys should be really confused."

Indeed, a recent SI poll suggests that although Native American activists are virtually united in opposition to the use of Indian nicknames and mascots, the Native American population sees the issue far differently. Asked if high school and college teams should stop using Indian nicknames, 81% of Native American respondents said no. As for pro sports, 83% of Native American respondents said teams should not stop using Indian nicknames, mascots, characters and symbols. Opinion is far more divided on reservations, yet a majority (67%) there said the usage by pro teams should not cease, while 32% said it should.

"I take the middle ground," says Leigh J. Kuwanwisiwma, 51, director of the Hopi Cultural Preservation Office in Kykotsmovi, Ariz., and an avid devotee of the Atlanta Braves. "I don't see anything wrong with Indian nicknames as long as they're not meant to be derogatory. Some tribal schools on Arizona reservations use *Indians* as a nickname themselves. The Phoenix Indian High School's newspaper is *The Redskin*. I don't mind the tomahawk chop. It's all in good fun. This is sports, after all. In my living room, I'll be watching a Braves game and occasionally do the chop."

Native American activists dismiss such opinion as misguided ("There are happy campers on every plantation," says Suzan Harjo, president of the Morning Star Institute, an Indian-rights organization based in Washington, D.C.) or as evidence that Native Americans' self-esteem has fallen so low that they don't even know when they're being insulted. American Indians—unlike, say, the Irish Catholics who founded Notre Dame and named its teams the Fighting Irish—had no hand in creating most of the teams that use their names; their identities were plucked from them wholesale and used for frivolous purposes, like firing up fans at ball games.

"This is no honor," says Michael Yellow Bird, an associate professor of social work at Arizona State. "We lost our land, we lost our languages, we lost our children. Proportionately speaking, indigenous peoples [in the U.S.] are incarcerated more than any other group, we have more racial violence perpetrated upon us, and we are forgotten. If people think this is how to honor us, then colonization has really taken hold."

Regardless, the campaign to erase Indian team names and symbols nationwide has been a success. Though Native American activists have made little progress at the highest level of pro sports—officials of the Atlanta Braves, Chicago Blackhawks, Cleveland Indians and Washington Redskins, for example, say they have no intention of changing their teams' names or mascots—their single-minded pursuit of the issue has literally changed the face of sports in the U.S. Since 1969, when Oklahoma disavowed its mascot Little

Red (a student wearing an Indian war bonnet, buckskin costume and moccasins), more than 600 school teams and minor league professional clubs have dropped nicknames deemed offensive by Native American groups.

What's more, the movement continues. On Jan. 9 the Metropolitan Washington Council of Governments, which represents 17 local governments in D.C., southern Maryland and northern Virginia, voted 11-2 to adopt a resolution calling the Redskins name "demeaning and dehumanizing" and asking team owner Dan Snyder to change it by next season. A week earlier former Redskins fullback Dale Atkeson had been told by the California Department of Motor Vehicles to remove his vanity plates reading 1 REDSKN. The word *Redskin* was banned on plates by the DMV in 1999.

"We consider ourselves racially sensitive," says D.C. council member Carol Schwartz, who introduced the resolution against the Redskins, "yet in this one area we are so hypocritical. Since when is a sports team's name more important than the sensitivities of our fellow human beings? For decades we had the Washington Bullets, and [owner] Abe Pollin on his own changed the name [in 1997, because of the high murder rate in D.C.]. Guess what? The world did not stop spinning. Why we would keep this racist term is beyond me."

While those who support names such as Seminoles (Florida State) and Braves can argue that the words celebrate Native American traditions, applying that claim to the Redskins is absurd. Nevertheless, Redskins vice president Karl Swanson says the name "symbolizes courage, dignity and leadership and has always been employed in that manner"—conveniently ignoring the fact that in popular usage dating back four centuries, the word has been a slur based on skin color. Swanson trots out research that traces the term redskin to Native Americans' custom of daubing on red paint before battle. Many experts on Native American history point out that the red paint was used not for war but for burial, and that the word redskin was first used by whites who paid and received bounties for dead Indians. "If you research the origin of *redskin*, no one would want that associated with his team," says pro golfer Notah Begay III, who is half Navajo and half Pueblo. "Trading-post owners used to offer rewards for Indian scalps. Signs would say something like, 'Redskin scalps, worth so much.'"

However, what's most important, Swanson counters, is intent: Because the Redskins and their fans *mean* nothing racist by using the nickname, it isn't racist or offensive. "This has been the name of our organization for 70 years," Swanson says. "We believe it has taken on a meaning independent of the word itself—and it's positive."

Not so, says Harjo: "There's no more derogatory word that's used against us, about us, in the English language. Even if it didn't have such heinous origins, everyone knows that it has never been an honorific. It's a terrible insult."

Harjo is not alone in her thinking. A slew of dictionaries agree that redskin is contemptuous, and so do Native American academics, nearly every Native American organization and three judges on the U.S. Trademark Trial and Appeal Board. In April 1999, responding to a lawsuit brought by Harjo and six other Indian leaders, the board stripped the Washington Redskins of federal protection on their seven trademarks. If the decision stands up under appeal, the team and the NFL could lose an estimated $5 million annually on sales of licensed merchandise.

Even though no team name is under more sustained attack, there's evidence that for the Redskins, a name change would be good for business. In 1996, after much pressure from alumni threatening to withdraw their financial support, Miami (Ohio) University acceded to the Miami tribe's request that it change its team names from Redskins to Redhawks. The following year alumni gave a record $25 million to the school. "Someday it will change," Miami spokesman Richard Little says of the Washington Redskins name. "And you know what? There'll still be a football team there, and there'll still be those ugly fat guys in dresses cheering for it."

Swanson says the vast majority of Redskins fans like the name, and indeed, beyond the protests of politicians, there's no groundswell of outrage against it in D.C. In a city so racially sensitive that an aide to mayor Anthony Williams was forced to resign in 1999 for *correctly* using the nonracial term *niggardly*, there's nothing hotter than the mass pilgrimage of 80,000 fans to Landover, Md., on Sundays in autumn to sing *Hail to the Redskins* at FedEx Field. Williams mentioned changing the name at a press conference once, but "no one really paid attention," says his aide Tony Bullock. "It's not something that anyone is really talking about." Nevertheless, Bullock says, "the mayor believes it is time to change the name."

That the name is offensive to Native Americans is easy for non-Natives to presume. It resonates when an Olympic hero and former Marine Corps captain such as Mills, who speaks out against Indian names and mascots at schools around the country, insists that a team named Redskins in the capital of the nation that committed genocide against Native Americans is the equivalent of a soccer team in Germany being called the Berlin Kikes. Says Mills, "Our truth is, *redskin* is tied to the murder of indigenous people."

Somehow that message is lost on most of Mills's fellow Native Americans. Asked if they were offended by the name Redskins, 75% of Native American respondents in SI's poll said they were not, and even on reservations, where Native American culture and influence are perhaps felt most intensely, 62% said they weren't offended. Overall, 69% of Native American respondents—and 57% of those living on reservations—feel it's O.K. for the Washington Redskins to continue using the name. "I like the name Redskins," says Mark Timentwa, 50, a member of the Colville Confederated Tribes in Washington State who lives on the tribes' reservation. "A few elders find it offensive, but my mother loves the Redskins."

Only 29% of Native Americans, and 40% living on reservations, thought Snyder should change his team's name. Such indifference implies a near total disconnect between Native American activists and the general Native American population on this issue. "To a lot of the younger folks the name Redskins is tied to the football team, and it doesn't represent anything more than the team," says Roland McCook, a member of the tribal council of the Ute tribe in Fort Duchesne, Utah.

The Utes' experience with the University of Utah might serve as a model for successful resolution of conflicts over Indian nicknames. Four years ago the council met with university officials, who made it clear that they would change their teams' name, the Running Utes, if the tribe found it objectionable. (The university had retired its cartoonish Indian mascot years before.) The council was perfectly happy to have the Ute name continue to circulate in the nations' sports pages, but council members said they intended to keep a close eye on its use. "We came away with an understanding that as long as the university used the Ute name in a positive manner that preserved the integrity of the Ute tribe, we would allow the use of the name and the Ute logo [two eagle feathers and a drum]," says McCook. Florida State, likewise, uses the name Seminoles for its teams with the express approval of the Seminole nation.

Like the Ute tribe, most Native Americans have no problem with teams using names like Indians and Fighting Illini—or even imposed names like Sioux. "People get upset about the Fighting

Sioux, but why?" Gross says. "We're not Sioux people, anyway. The French and the Ojibway tribe gave us that name, and they're our hereditary enemies. We're not braves, and we're not really Indians. I know the history. For me those names are not a problem." Many Native Americans are offended, however, by mascots such as Illinois's Chief Illiniwek and others that dress up in feathers and so-called war paint. "Just do away with the imagery—the dancing, the pageantry," says Gross.

Which brings us to the point at which the word problem becomes a number problem. Say you are a team owner. You kiss Chief Wahoo goodbye. Stop the chop. Dump the fake Indian garb, the turkey feathers and the war paint. Get rid of, say, the Redskins name because it's got a sullied history and just sounds wrong. Rename the team the Washington Warriors—without the Indian-head logo—and watch the new team hats and jackets hit the stores. Money is going to pour in, you see, and someone will have to count it.

Questions for Discussion and Writing

1. Price opens with a story or narrative. Is the narrative an effective writing strategy to begin this article? Why or why not?

2. Do you have any personal experience with this issue? Are you aware of a high school or college that changed its name and mascot in order to be more racially sensitive? Write about the public reaction, the process, and your own reaction.

3. A good argument or a thorough analysis of a topic will include multiple perspectives on the issue. How well does Price incorporate opposing viewpoints? Does he interview and quote sources on both sides of the controversy? Is his coverage of the issue balanced or biased? Critique specific parts of the article where he does a good job or parts where he could have done better.

4. Price begins to dissect the word *redskin* to prove that it is not the same as words such as *braves*. Choose a name of a sports team and find the history of the name. Is the history more positive or negative? Based on your research, do you think the name is appropriate for a sports team?

5. Names and mascots create most of the controversy in the media, but Price quotes some Native Americans who are offended by actions such as tribal dancing and the tomahawk chop, as well as fans or school representatives who dress up and ceremonies or pageants that seem to poke fun at Native American customs. Is rhetoric composed only of words? When do actions, sounds, music, and visual elements become rhetoric as well?

Of Polls and Race Prejudice:
Sports Illustrated's Errant
"Indian Wars"

C. RICHARD KING, ELLEN STAUROWSKY, LAWRENCE BACA,
LAUREL R. DAVIS, AND CORNEL PEWEWARDY

The five authors of this piece, which appeared in the Journal of Sport &
Social Issues, *came from five different perspectives to collaborate on
a critique of S. L. Price's article from* Sports Illustrated. *Anthropologist and sociologist C. Richard King has written about a number of
civil rights issues and is a co-author of* Beyond the Cheers: Race as
Spectacle in College Sport. *Ellen Staurowsky is a professor of sport
management, a former college athletic director, and a leading expert
on race issues and gender equity in sports. Attorney Lawrence Baca
worked with the National Native American Bar Association when
this article was published, is a Pawnee Indian, and has served as a
deputy director of the Office of Tribal Justice with the United States
Department of Justice. Sociology professor Laurel R. Davis is a specialist in race, class, and gender issues in sports. She wrote a book
called* The Swimsuit Issue and Sport: Hegemonic Masculinity in
Sports Illustrated. *Cornel Pewewardy is an education professor and
outspoken opponent of Native American mascots in schools. He is
Comanche and Kiowa. As you read their critique of S. L. Price's "The
Indian Wars," consider the backgrounds of each of these authors.
Why might they regularly read and critique* Sports Illustrated? *Does
the fact that some of them are Native American and others are educators impact their initial biases or opinions regarding the* Sports
Illustrated *article?*

◆

The March 4, 2002, issue of *Sports Illustrated* (*SI*) featured a
vividly illustrated, sensationally reported, 7-page article about
the Native American mascots controversy. "The Indian Wars" by
S. L. Price pivoted on views of the use of Indian names and symbols
in sports. From a poll of 351 Native Americans and 743 sports fans
commissioned from the Peter Harris Research Group, supplemented with 10 interviews with Indian and non-Indian individuals,

Price concluded first that the majority of indigenous peoples, like sports fans and citizens generally, supported such mascots, and more, that Native American leaders working against these mascots were out of touch with, even disconnected from, their constituents.

Having studied and worked against Native American mascots for years, we are not surprised by Price's report. We know that some Native Americans not only endorse but also defend the use of Indianness in athletics. We are also familiar with the reactionary backlash that has fostered and fed off efforts to defend the symbols, practices, and privileges associated with Native American mascots. "The Indian Wars" troubles us because of (a) its pronounced bias, seemingly intent to distract from the history and implications of mascots as it derails efforts to challenge them; (b) its use of polling and representations of opinion; (c) its pervasive decontextualization of mascots and the controversy over them; (d) the impression it undoubtedly leaves on its audience that mascots are unproblematic, particularly because indigenous people say so; and (e) the legacies of such inappropriate and inaccurate renderings for public debate and social justice.

In this article, we want to reframe "The Indian Wars." On one hand, we deconstruct the *SI* article, particularly its interpretive frames and signifying practices. On the other hand, we make sense of the sociocultural context shaping the *SI* article, public opinion, and indigenous support. . . .

READING "THE INDIAN WARS"

Arguably, the preferred reading of "The Indian Wars" is that the article offers new insights into the mascot controversy, particularly how Native Americans feel about mascots. In this section, we offer an alternative reading that critically unpacks the structures and meanings of the *SI* article.

The *SI* article begins on the cover. To entice readers, a banner in the upper right-hand corner of the magazine poses the question "Are Indian Team Names Offensive?" with the accompanying teaser "Our poll will surprise you." Inside the magazine, the text of one headline reads, "The campaign against Indian nicknames and mascots presumes that they offend Native Americans—but do they? We took a poll, and you won't believe the results." Later in the *SI* article, a third headline reads, "*SI* polls Native Americans and sport fans in general on the use of Indian nicknames, and got some surprising answers."

This kind of editorial framing of the findings in advance of their introduction can hardly be interpreted as balanced reporting when measured against any journalistic standard (Goldberg, 2001).

The stated purpose of the *SI* article, to consider whether American Indian team names are offensive, is overwhelmed by selected bits of the pollster's data, the imagery, and the frame in which the report is made. The introduction to the article begins with a 2-page foldout of the Florida State mascot "Chief Osceola," a young man whose face is marked with red war paint, his long black hair bound with a matching red bandana, sitting astride a horse named "Renegade," flaming war lance held aloft in a menacing gesture.

At a visual level, readers confront stereotype on stereotype before the reporting begins. Of the six photos that appear in the article, three feature college students dressed up as American Indians (a shot of FSU's "Chief Osceola" that takes up two full pages and two one-quarter page photos); one depicts a player for the Washington football franchise with the "Indian" logo on his helmet; and another features two fans at Turner Field participating in the "tomahawk chop" (which takes up one third of a page). Noticeably, the publishers appear averse to acknowledging Native Americans as real people within the visual context of the article. There are no pictures of Native Americans in nonstereotypical dress and roles, nor are there any pictures of those who work against the mascots. In the visual presentation, why were there no pictures of Native Americans being spat on or harassed for protesting against these stereotypes or being handcuffed and thrown in jail for protesting? Why were there no pictures of the anonymous flyers posted on college campuses where Native Americans have asked for these images to be retired, flyers threatening harm to critics and invoking racial epithets such as "prairie nigger"? Why were there no pictures of the T-shirts emblazoned with dehumanizing words and images such as "Sioux Suck" and worse in North Dakota? This represents a significant departure for *SI* or any other sport publication in which feature articles are uniformly supplemented with pictures of people quoted in them. Not even Billy Mills, the great Lakota runner who won the gold medal in the 10,000 meters in the 1968 Olympic Games, had sufficient athletic stature and pedigree to warrant a present day photo despite providing S. L. Price with the opening narrative for the piece.

Against this backdrop of Native American stereotypes and real Native American invisibility, readers learn that a majority of sport fans apparently do not find Native American mascots and nick-names offensive nor do Native Americans. The filter the reader sifts through on the way to the "hard facts" assumes the dimensions of a racialized gauntlet for those who would dare to point to the missing facts associated with the polling method, the bias of the *SI* article itself, or the more significant "fact" of White supremacy and privilege at the core of these images.

So firm is the magazine's belief in the data gathered that S. L. Price concluded, and the headline editor reinforced the conclusion with red border text set off with arrows, that "there's a total disconnect between Indian activists and the Native American population on this [mascot] issue" (p. 72). The message communicated to readers is that they have essentially been duped by a few vocal Native Americans and their allies who have made an issue out of something that is inconsequential not just to sport fans but to the majority of Native Americans as well. Thus, the readers are the victims of a frame-up that has relied on a race card that does not exist. . . .

ON THE NUMBERS: THE PERILS OF POLLING

A poll of public opinion anchors and animates "The Indian Wars." It legitimates the assertions in the *SI* article and, by extension, makes them less debatable, while fostering a sensational reframing of the mascot issue.

Since the publication of "The Indian Wars," repeated efforts have been made to obtain information directly from *SI* and the Peter Harris Research Group about the methodology used and the identification of subjects interviewed. *SI* has taken the position that the survey itself and details regarding the method used in polling are their exclusive property. Sheryl Spain, the director of public relations for *SI*, has also indicated in response to requests for more details about the study that all the information that readers need to know is contained in the article itself (S. Spain, personal communication, March 11, 2002). This is clearly not the case. In fact, we would assert that *SI* has failed to abide by accepted journalistic standards and practices for the appropriate reporting of survey results. Consequently, we do not know (a) how participants were recruited, (b) how they were contacted, (c) if they were concentrated in one region, (d) if one ethnic group (Cherokee, Dine, or Ojibwe, for instance) is overrepresented, or (e) the exact wording and order of questions. Indeed, because *SI* failed to secure a full, complete, and unambiguous enumeration of the population, its results are problematic at best and invalid and unreliable at worst. Whether *SI* ever discloses how the poll was actually conducted or not, there are several major concerns that can be raised.

Based on the *SI* article, responses were "weighted according to U.S. Census figures for age, race and gender, and for distribution of Native Americans on and off reservations." Having consulted the U.S. 2000 Census of Population and Housing, there is a difference in terminology between that used in the *SI* article and the census itself. The census does not use "gender" as a stratification variable. It uses the term "sex." Furthermore, although *SI* refers to subjects as "Native American," there is no such category in the U.S. Census, which uses American Indian and Alaskan Native. In the census, American Indian and Alaskan Native are listed under "one race" and also under "race alone or in combination with one or more races." Given the terminology used in the article, it is impossible to know exactly what census data were used in shaping the *SI* study itself. . . .

Doing telephone research is not easy and may account for these problems of representation. The *SI* article never discusses what many Americans do not know: Many Native Americans do not have reliable telephone service. How did this shape the study's findings? Did the pollsters take this into account? Whether or not they did, they seem to have conducted a terribly successful study of indigenous public opinion. The notion that unknown pollsters could simply telephone Native American respondents, particularly Native American respondents on the reservation, presents several areas of questions. Researchers who work with Native American subjects often report that Native American subjects are reticent about offering their insights and opinions to strangers. The apparent ability of the Peter Harris Research Group to locate so many Native Americans to talk about this issue over the phone is certainly a feat that other researchers would like to know how it was accomplished. In addition, some Native Americans have questioned how the pollsters determined who they were speaking with at the time of the call. Whereas the report in *SI* indicates that special attention was directed toward geographical locations where more Indians resided to locate an appropriate sample, some Native Americans have pointed out that the racial politics in those regions is such that it would not be unusual for Whites in those areas, on receiving a call of this kind, to identify as Native Americans for the purpose of skewing results (notes taken by Staurowsky, April 7, 2002, in Cleveland, Ohio, during Suzan Shown Harjo's presentation).

The very fact that one of the questions sought opinions about team nicknames derived from other ethnic groups is another area fraught with error. The problematic dynamic of representation within the population versus representation within the mascot collection is never addressed within the context of the *SI* article. At the college level, there is only one Irish mascot. There are 88 mascots with American Indian referents at the college/university level. At the high school level, 1,217 mascots allude to American Indians, only 46 make reference to the Irish (many of these being traced back to the University of Notre Dame). At the same time, the Irish American population is much higher than that of Native Americans by a wide margin. Irish Americans have had access to significant political power within the United States; Native Americans historically have not. Students at the University of Notre Dame, many of whom were of Irish descent, selected the Fighting Irish as the team name and mascot. The same cannot be said for American Indian mascots, the vast majority of which are White inventions chosen by White schools at the time of their adoption. The inclusion of this type of question represents a serious error within the construction of the instrument itself. . . .

Of course, the greatest error of all may be the idea that polling people on these issues is appropriate from the outset. It suggests that popular opinion can settle troubling questions about prejudice, power, and privilege. Hence, if the majority support mascots (or racial segregation or sexual harassment), then such symbols and practices are acceptable. And worse, the *SI* article asserts that if members of marginalized and oppressed groups consent to their marginalization and oppression, then everything is OK. If most Blacks supported racial segregation, would it be a justifiable system? If most women saw nothing wrong with sexual harassment, would we not still want to suggest such actions were reprehensible and problematic? Unfortunately, in the end, "The Indian Wars" encourages Americans to avoid thinking critically about the history and significance of race.

REFERENCES

1. Goldberg, B. (2001). *Bias: A CBS insider exposes how the media distort the news*. Washington, DC: Regnery Publishing.

Questions for Discussion and Writing

1. Analyze the five reasons why the authors say Price's article "troubles" them (listed as a through e). Which reasons seem fair and reasonable? Which ones (if any) seem unfounded? Do you agree with the way the authors characterize Price's article? Refer to "The Indian Wars" as you analyze the authors' reasons for critiquing it.

2. Though the journal article is clearly a rebuttal to or critique of "The Indian Wars," the two articles are essentially about the same topic. Look at the structure of each piece, though, which differs significantly. How do the articles differ because of their format? You might consider issues such as audience, tone, use of language, and organizational structure.

3. One of the points the authors make early in their critique is that the way the *SI* article is introduced (through teasers and subheads, for example) is biased or unbalanced. Was the article meant to be balanced or unbiased? Should it have been? Are the authors correct to criticize the graphic layout of the article as well as the words it contains? Do photos (or lack of), blurbs, and other graphic elements influence the reader and therefore the article? How so?

4. What is your opinion regarding the authors' claims about the survey itself? Is it important to you as a reader to know the origins and details of a survey or do you trust statistics without that kind of background information? What other issues regarding the survey concern you?

5. The authors conclude in this excerpt that "'The Indian Wars' encourages Americans to avoid thinking critically about the history and significance of race." Do you agree or disagree? What parts of "The Indian Wars" encourage you as a reader to think critically? What parts encourage you to avoid such critical thinking?

Latino Players Can Revive Baseball in America
Tim Wendel

Tim Wendel is a versatile writer whose work includes both fiction and journalism. His books range from Castro's Curveball, *the fictional account of a pitcher in Old Havana, Cuba, to* The New Face of Baseball: The One-Hundred-Year Rise and Triumph of Latinos in America's Favorite Sport, *which traces the interest in American baseball through*

Latin American countries and the struggles Latino players have faced while learning America's language and culture. The New Face of Baseball *was named the Top History Book for 2004 by the Latino Literary Awards. Wendel's journalistic articles have appeared in* USA Today, GQ, *and* The New York Times. *He is one of the founders of* USA Today Baseball Weekly. *He has a bachelor's degree in journalism from Syracuse University and a master's in writing from Johns Hopkins University, and has taught fiction and nonfiction writing. As you read this article from* USA Today, *watch for signs that Wendel is writing more than an objective report, and is voicing his opinions.*

◆

In his last turn at bat during a much-anticipated home stand, Rafael Palmeiro of the Texas Rangers drove the ball into the right-field bleachers . . . becoming the 19th player in the game's history to reach 500 home runs.

The first baseman with the sweet, compact swing is symbolic of a major trend in baseball that has implications reaching far beyond home-run records: Players of Latino descent, like Palmeiro and Sammy Sosa, who hit his own No. 500 earlier . . . have come to dominate America's national pastime.

The two sluggers are the first players born outside the USA to join the 500-home-run club. Palmeiro was born in Cuba, and Sosa in the Dominican Republic. But they're not the only Latino stars; pick up any sports section, and you'll find Latino ballplayers making headlines every day. Alfonso Soriano, Jose Vidro and Juan Gonzalez are among the hitting leaders. This generation's pitchers include potential Hall of Famers Pedro Martinez and Mariano Rivera.

Before Jackie Robinson broke the color barrier in 1947, baseball was strictly a white man's game. In the years after Robinson, such black superstars as Hank Aaron, Willie Mays, Bob Gibson and Reggie Jackson took center stage. Now, with Alex Rodriguez the highest-paid player in the game and Vladimir Guerrero likely to be the most coveted free agent . . . baseball isn't just white or black anymore. To crib from commentator and writer Richard Rodriguez, the prominent color has become brown.

The impact of Latinos in baseball will be as important to the sport specifically, and our society in general, as the rise of the African-American athletes in the 1960s and 1970s.

Many consider baseball to be past its prime, better suited for nostalgic old-timers than the X Games crowd. For many kids in this country, baseball moves too slowly, and too little seems to be at stake.

But anyone who has seen baseball as it is played in the Dominican Republic or Cuba knows how exciting the game can be. Outside the borders of the USA, runners relish taking the extra base at every opportunity. Pitchers aren't reluctant to challenge hitters. This quicker, passionate, even more confrontational style of play is what's being brought to the United States.

"Of all the sports, we Latins believe that baseball requires the greatest amount of skill," Hall of Fame player Orlando Cepeda says. "That's why we take such pride in playing it well."

Off the field, Latinos are making inroads into baseball management. . . . Arturo Moreno, a Phoenix businessman, has stepped up to buy the world champion Anaheim Angels from Disney. Omar Minaya, who was born in the Dominican Republic and made history when he was named the first Latino general manager in the major leagues, has kept his Montreal Expos competitive even though the ball club has one of the lowest team payrolls in the game. Not bad for a guy who was passed over by other ball clubs because he didn't have enough "organizational experience."

Just as it took a while for Palmeiro to be recognized, the powers that be in baseball often underestimate the Latino impact. When Major League Baseball announced its All-Century Team in 1999, not a single Latino made the cut. The great Roberto Clemente finished 10th among outfielders, one spot removed from the roster. . . .

Latinos have become the largest minority in America. Yet too often we overlook emerging segments of our population. Sports help us overcome that. The play of Aaron and Mays moved in tandem with civil rights marches and Martin Luther King Jr. in challenging Jim Crow laws and overt racism. Clemente once said that Latinos were a double minority—disregarded because of the color of their skin and their mother tongue. One wonders what Clemente, who died young, would think of this sea change in baseball.

Since our nation's inception, we've prided ourselves on being a melting pot—a place where talent, not connections or family linkage, is the bottom line. While that may be difficult to argue in some fields these days, it still rings true often enough in sports.

In *The Old Man and the Sea*, Ernest Hemingway's fisherman asks which Cuban manager was the best of that time, Dolf Luque or Mike Gonzalez. From such beginnings, the Latino connection with baseball extends like a family tree to Orestes "Minnie" Minoso (the Latino Jackie Robinson), Clemente and Cepeda, all the way to modern-era Sosa and Palmeiro.

What many U.S. sports fans are just beginning to realize is that our national pastime also belongs to the rest of the world. Dreams about baseball extend beyond borders, even past the barriers of language. That can truly be a wonder in a world that's seemingly eager to break along class and racial lines at every turn.

So often baseball offers us the comfort of continuity, a link from one generation to another. What we're only beginning to realize is that the game also can connect Americans to worlds with which we thought we had little in common.

Questions for Discussion and Writing

1. Wendel says that players of Latino descent "have come to dominate America's pastime." Can a minority dominate? Aren't the meanings of those two words—*minority* and *dominate*—in opposition? When are they compatible?

2. Like many others, Wendel compares Latino players to early African-American players such as Jackie Robinson. Is that a fair comparison? How might the Latino experience have been the same as that of African-American athletes and how might it differ? How effective is Wendel's comparison?

3. Wendel paraphrases a popular author named Richard Rodriguez. Conduct some research to find out more about Rodriguez and decide whether Wendel's use of his idea is effective or not.

4. What is Wendel's thesis and where does it come in the article?

5. Wendel criticizes Major League Baseball for not including Latino players on its All-Century Team in 1999. See if you can find other lists of baseball's greatest players. Are there Latinos on the list? How do Latino players seem to be represented in relation to white players, overall? Is Wendel's criticism justified?

Joe Louis' Biggest Knockout
DAVE KINDRED

Though he actually had no control over it, Dave Kindred likes to boast that he was born in Louisville, Kentucky, the hometown of Muhammad Ali. Since then, he has written thousands of articles for

The Washington Post, The Atlanta Journal-Constitution, *and* Sporting News. *In 1991 he was honored for lifetime achievement in sports journalism with the Red Smith Award (Red Smith was one of America's most widely read sportswriters and the first sportswriter to win the Pulitzer Prize for Commentary). Kindred is the author of* Sound and Fury: Two Powerful Lives, One Fateful Friendship, *about the relationship between boxer Muhammad Ali and sportscaster Howard Cosell; he worked with both men in his position as a sportswriter. He also wrote* Glove Stories, *a collection of commentaries and he has co-authored several books on athletes and sporting events. As the turn of the century approached, Kindred's editors at* Sporting News *asked him to reflect on the most significant moments in sports in the twentieth century. The following article is part of that series and the event is second on Kindred's list of the Five Best Sports Events. Incidentally, the first event on the list was Jesse Owens winning four gold medals in the 1936 "Nazi" Olympics in Berlin, Germany. You can find more of Kindred's picks online, including the Five Greatest Athletes and the Five Events That Changed Everything. As you consider the racial implications of this particular sporting event, Joe Louis' defeat of German Max Schmeling, keep in mind the year of the fight.*

◆

When 24-year-old Joe Louis stopped by the White House early in 1938 to meet Franklin D. Roosevelt, the president did what most everyone wanted to do on meeting the heavyweight champion. FDR gripped Louis's arm and said, "Joe, we're depending on those muscles for America."

Louis told the story in his autobiography 40 years later, adding, "Let me tell you, that was a thrill. Now, even more, I knew I had to get Schmeling good."

Max Schmeling, a German, had knocked out Louis in the 12th round of a fight in 1936. The next year, Louis had won the heavyweight championship. Early in '38, the world teetered on the brink of World War II and the Louis-Schmeling rematch had become a metaphor of that coming war.

More than any other sports event, a fight can be laden with meaning beyond itself. That's because boxing is the simplest and rawest of games, hand-to-hand combat by two men with the winner decided by his ability to deliver more punishment than he accepts.

And the drama is all but irresistible because boxing is the beast in the human animal, at once repulsive and compelling.

Never has any fight carried more symbolic weight than Louis-Schmeling on June 22, 1938. That's why it ranks No. 2 on my list of the Five Best Sports Events of the 20th century.

The story really begins in 1935, even before the first Louis-Schmeling fight.

As Adolf Hitler consolidated his dictatorship in Germany and rattled swords at his neighbors, Schmeling once served as a sports diplomat of sorts. Preparing for the 1936 Olympics in Berlin, Americans had criticized Germany's treatment of its Jewish athletes; the U.S. Amateur Athletic Union proposed a boycott of the Olympics. At Hitler's direction, Schmeling delivered a letter reassuring Americans that Germany's Jews would be fairly treated.

Though Hitler admired Schmeling, he worried about the upcoming fight with Louis. Historian Chris Mead, in a study of Louis, wrote: "When he got back to Germany (after meeting American Olympic officials), Schmeling lunched with Adolf Hitler in Munich. . . . The dictator was upset that Schmeling was risking Germany's reputation in a fight against a black man when there was so little chance of victory. With his usual self-confidence, Schmeling assured his Fuehrer that he had a good chance to win, and Hitler presented the boxer with an autographed picture of himself. Schmeling hung the picture of Hitler in his study."

After Schmeling's knockout victory over Louis on June 19, 1936, the New York newspaperman Westbrook Pegler wrote that at no time leading up to the fight had the Nazi government of Hitler attached itself to Schmeling's hopes: "He was absolutely on his own, because there seemed an excellent chance that having already been knocked out by a Jew (Max Baer) he would now be stretched in the resin at the feet of a cotton-field Negro. . . ."

But before the night was over, Schmeling had become a great German patriot, and his unexpected conquest of the colored boy had been taken over as a triumph for Adolf Hitler and his government.

Hitler dispatched a telegram to Schmeling in New York: "Most cordial congratulations on your victory." Propaganda Minister Josef Goebbels also weighed in: "I know you fought for Germany; that it was a German victory. We are proud of you. Heil Hitler! Regards."

On his return to Germany, Schmeling brought his wife to lunch with Hitler in the Reich Chancellery.

Small wonder, then, that two years later, Louis came to the second meeting with Schmeling so intent on victory. The ghost-writer of Louis's autobiography quoted Louis saying, "The whole damned country was depending on me."

The night before the fight, Louis sat with his friend, the New York sportswriter Jimmy Cannon, on the porch of his fight camp cabin in upstate New York.

"You make a pick?" Louis asked.

"Yes," Cannon said.

"Knockout?" Louis asked.

"Six rounds," Cannon said.

"No," Louis said. "One."

He held up one finger. "It go one."

It went less than one. In two minutes and four seconds, Louis knocked out Schmeling.

While Hitler sent a telegram of condolences, most German reports downplayed the defeat as meaningless to the nation's prestige, some claiming Louis had fouled Schmeling with a paralyzing kidney punch. Americans cheered giddily, as in the boxing magazine, *The Ring*: "The World's heavyweight boxing title stayed American and non-Aryan when, in 2 min. 4 sec. on the muggy night of June 22, Joe Louis, Negro champion, knocked out Max Schmeling, the white hope of Germany. . . . The German press fulminated, blaming their hero's defeat on American machinations. But anti-Nazis gloated."

Perhaps the most solidly grounded perspective came from the American sportswriter Heywood Broun in the *New York World-Telegram:* "One hundred years from now some historian may theorize, in a footnote at least, that the decline of Nazi prestige began with a left hook delivered by a former unskilled automotive worker who had never studied the policies of Neville Chamberlain and had no opinion whatever in regard to the situation in Czechoslovakia. . . .

"And possibly there could be a further footnote. It was known that Schmeling regarded himself as a Nazi symbol. It is not known whether Joe Louis consciously regards himself as a representative of his race and as one under dedication to advance its prestige. I can't remember that he has ever said anything about it. But that may have been in his heart when he exploded the Nordic myth with a bombing glove."

Questions for Discussion and Writing

1. The Louis-Schmeling bout has been called a metaphor for World War II. Knowing what you do about what happened in World War II, how accurate is the metaphor? If you need to refresh your knowledge of the major themes of World War II, do some reading first.
2. Compare Schmeling's position in the eyes of his government and country in relation to Louis' position as the hope of America. How might their experiences have been similar or different? What role does race play in each man's position in his country?
3. Read Kindred's descriptive paragraph on boxing as the "simplest and rawest of games." Does he effectively describe the sport of boxing? What words are important in his description? Can you tell from his wording if he is a fan or a critic of boxing?
4. Why is it ironic that Joe Louis would become a symbol of America in 1938?
5. Research this fight in a textbook or a history site on the Web. Also look it up in an encyclopedia (print or online). Compare the rhetorical structure of Kindred's article to the other two pieces. What features do they share? How are they different?

Asian America's Response to Shaquille O'Neal Riddled with Racial-Sexual Anxiety

TAMARA K. NOPPER

Tamara K. Nopper is a graduate of Temple University, where she has taught sociology and American studies. Her research and teaching interests include Asian American communities and politics, Black-Asian relations, immigration, and race theory. Her dissertation research explored how Korean and Korean-American banks and federal government agencies work together to make capital and resources available to Korean immigrant entrepreneurs in the United States. Nopper is also an activist who practices what she calls "public sociology" that addresses her political and intellectual concerns of inequality and resistance. She practices her public sociology through political writing, activism, and organizing public presentations and forums. Nopper's original essay, which follows, did not appear in mainstream publications but she did circulate it to several Web sites. Go online and see how many times you can find the article or references to it. As you read, keep in mind that several of her remarks also ignited angry responses and an online dialogue that sometimes got ugly. Read some of the responses after you read Nopper's essay.

———————— ✦ ————————

By now, Los Angeles Lakers basketball player Shaquille O'Neal's racial comments about Houston Rockets' Chinese-born (and recent immigrant) Yao Ming has become well publicized. On June 28, 2002, O'Neal said, "Tell Yao Ming . . ." and then made what are described in Asian American circles as racial "Chinaman noises." That is, he made sounds that reflect what the non-Asian public would characterize as the sounds that Asian people speak. In short, O'Neal relied on common racial characterizations of Asian Americans, which, in this case, emphasizes what is considered the "foreign" and therefore "unintelligible" aspects of Asian American culture and language.

Recently, O'Neal's comment has been played over and over by different radio stations, sports commentators have chimed in on news radio programs and in the printed press, listservs have bounced around different responses, Asian American publications such as *AsianWeek* and *Asian American Movement E-Zine*, have commented on the situation, and there is currently a petition letter addressed to National Basketball Association (NBA) Commissioner David Stern circulating among Asian American listservs. As of this writing, there were 4,317 signatories to this letter.

This writer was not one of them.

It is not that I am not concerned by this racial characterization of Asian Americans. My own life as an Asian American woman is certainly shaped and structured by this racial characterization. So too, of course, are the lives of many people who are structurally situated similarly to me as Asian Americans. Further, I am not supportive of any ideological sentiment that reflects and reproduces American ideology, which to me, is not about freedom and liberty, but is one of violence and containment through various dimensions of racism, (hetero)sexism, classism, and homophobia.

I say all of this to say that I am not in support of O'Neal's comments about Yao, just as I was not in support of O'Neal calling the Sacramento Kings "queens" because both comments reflect a reliance on an American logic that demonizes that which is non-normative racially and sexually.

So why did I not sign the petition letter? Why am I not joining in the calls for O'Neal to apologize or to be properly punished?

My reasons have to do with my concerns about how Asian America is framing Blackness, Black people, and Black politics in their response to O'Neal's comments. These concerns have to do with the ways in which the criticisms of O'Neal reflect Asian America's racist and sexist anxiety about Black people generally, and in this case, Black men specifically.

Overall, writers have relied on a racist and sexist image of Black men in their analysis of O'Neal's comments. For example, in his widely circulated January [2003] *AsianWeek* column, author Irwin Tang calls O'Neal a "brute." In a January 14 circulated op-ed, *Sacramento Bee* writer Diana Griego Erwin describes O'Neal as "hulking."

The fact that O'Neal has a large build and is tall—standing at seven feet—is not the point. What I find disturbing is that in order to provide a certain image of Yao, who we are to understand is representative of Asian America as a political entity, Asian Americans (and our supporters) must rely on racist and sexist images of Black people, and in this case, Black men specifically.

What is most disturbing is that I do not even think we consider how violent our considerations, perhaps our fixation with Black men's bodies are in our Asian American claims. Yet we rely on the image of Black people as loud, aggressive, and physically and politically threatening in our depictions of Blacks "attacking" Asian Americans. As such, it is necessary for the writers to depict O'Neal as "hulking" and as a "brute" in order to convince the readers that Asian Americans have a just claim. Yet we read or hear little of the fact that O'Neal is actually five inches shorter than Yao. This physiological fact would not serve our racial and sexual imagination, which attempts to depict a struggle between a Chinese David in the face of a Black Goliath, and in the process, create a story of racially weak person versus racially strong, even scary giant.

The subsequent result of this framing is that we turn a blind eye towards the fact that the image of the Black man as hyper-masculine is racist and sexist. Instead, we believe this image is really true and rely on this image in order to situate ourselves as "vulnerable" and "politically weak" Asian Americans. As such, we do not challenge our racist and sexist construction of Black men, nor do we deal with the fact that we, as Asian Americans, have helped to reproduce a structure of violence against Black male bodies. But it is precisely the image of Black hyper-masculinity and beliefs in Black male physical prowess and violence, an image that affects Black straight and queer men alike, that victimizes Black males.

Not only are Asian Americans careless with the use of this racist and sexist imagery of Black men, we also appear to envy it. This is evident in broader discussions of Asian American masculinity generally and in the responses to O'Neal in particular. For example, Tang's *AsianWeek* column ends with the author issuing the following challenge to O'Neal: "Come down to Chinatown, Shaq. You disrespect Asian Pacific America, and we will break you down."

Remember, this is from the same man who labeled O'Neal a "brute." What is interesting is how Tang strategically uses Chinatown as an image of both Asian American "emasculization" and Asian American power. To do so, he must "hyper-masculinize" Chinatown in much the same way he does O'Neal. To me, this shows a sexual-racial anxiety that characterizes most discussions of Asian American masculinity and sexuality more generally. That is, it appears that not only does Tang accept the racist and sexist image of O'Neal as a Black male brute, but he also must make Chinatown (and Asian American men) appear as *potentially* violent and hyper-masculine in order to "break down" O'Neal.

The result is that Tang does not challenge racist and sexist constructions of both Asian American men and Black men. Instead, he relies on both to make his argument. Yet Tang must rely on the racist and sexist construction of Black men to masculinize Chinatown as a site and symbol that can take on the "brute." This is not to suggest that Chinatown is not a site of violence, whether due to it being a place of international division of labor, gentrification, lack of viable housing options, containment by police agencies particularly Immigration and Naturalization Services and Licenses and Inspections, along with all of the terrible aspects of hyper-masculinity that characterize patriarchal family structures and capitalist arrangements. Nor does it suggest that there are not individuals who indeed identify and are committed to a patriarchal, heterosexist, and capitalist identity in Chinatown (or in Asian America, for that matter). What I question is how Tang must masculinize Chinatown in order to see it as a symbol that can appropriately "take on" a "brute" like O'Neal with the anticipated result of "breaking" him down.

This racist image of Black male sexuality also informs the idea that Asian Americans are not viewed as threatening enough, an idea that Tang discusses, as do others. For example, consider a statement made in a letter to the editor posted on the *Asian American Movement E-Zine*: "I am going from one Asian site to another in hopes of arousing anger and a sense of disgust to provoke Asians and sound minded non-Asians to wake up and realize that unless we are actively vocal and tenacious about our plight in America, Asians will always receive the second-class treatment and viewed as weak wimps and nerds by rest of America."

What I wonder is, Asian Americans are not threatening enough . . . compared to whom? It appears that the answer is Black people. Asian Americans seem to think that we need to be more threatening, just like Blacks. As such, we do not question the function of racist and sexist image of Blacks as threatening for the expansion of state violence through policing, prisons, and state-sanctioned death. Instead, we appear to desire the very aspect of Blackness that we also appear to hate. That is, we want to be more vocal, more aggressive and more powerful just like Blacks, because supposedly, Black people have been able to do so successfully. Indeed, the desire by many Asian Americans for Yao to do well in the NBA comes from both a racial and sexual desire for Asian American men to break into what is considered a "Black man's game," and in the process, prove that they are "real men," i.e., hyper-masculine.

Unfortunately, this image of Black people is not only racist and sexist, it also reproduces a certain image of reverse racism against non-Blacks by Black people. This idea of Black racism is evident in the responses to O'Neal. For example, the aforementioned writer of the letter that appeared in the *Asian American Movement E-Zine* says, "I think for too long there has been a double standard in American media when it comes to blacks and the racist comments they make. If an Asian or white or any other group would have made similarly racially insensitive comments about blacks, the black community (i.e., Jesse Jackson, Al Sharpton and the NAACP, by the way it should be NAABP because really they only represent the blacks and not all people of color like their acronyms suggest 'National Association of Advancement for Colored People') would be in an uproar. Why isn't Jesse Jackson or the 'honorable' Al Sharpton up in arms when blacks make racist comments? Just pure hypocrisy, that's why!"

Not only does this writer need a history lesson to understand the establishment and trajectory of the NAACP and the term "colored." Not only does he make an implicit attack on Black political leadership, which is often viewed as too showy, disingenuous, selfish, and subsequently too successful by non-Blacks. What we also have is an image of Blacks as the "true" or "new" racists. This is exemplified by the likening of O'Neal to the recently retired Senator Trent Lott (who praised Dixiecrat Strom Thurmond's anti-desegregation platform) that has been made in different commentaries, notably those by Tang and Erwin.

Yet I do not think that Black people have become less the subjects of racist-sexist comments or depictions, or that Black political leaders have been met overwhelmingly favorably. Nor do I think that Black people's position as the most detested, despised, and contained racial group since the foundation of the US has changed, even as the positions and placement of other ethnic and racial groups, including Asian Americans, have. Nor do I, unfortunately, think Asian America as a political project, really cares that this is the case, and if anything, must resist this analysis to make its political claims.

Subsequently, the image of Black racism against non-Blacks seems to shape Asian America's racial claims, as it does the rest of America's. The country has become even more neo-conservative as it moves towards a so-called color-blind perspective in the post-1965 era that has anchored contemporary racist projects by whites (and some Asian Americans and Latino/as), such as the current dismantling of affirmative action.

Yet this neo-conservativism is not just against the consideration of race and racism, per se. This neo-conservativism is also inherently anti-Black. The impetus for doing away with race and for ending talks about racial power, discrimination, and oppression was, and is in response to the aggrandized fears of Black mobility, access and power. This fear of Black power, or more aptly put, of Blacks actually experiencing some aspect of non-slavery, has always been met with retaliatory violence, whether it was in the forms of lynching, the shutting down of Reconstruction and the movement of Union troops out of the south, the burning and murdering of Black towns and economies such as Rosewood and Tulsa, legal mandates such as the Dred Scott decision, hyper-segregation, or the creation and expansion of the current police state and the prison industrial complex.

One major component of this anti-Black neo-conservativism is the belief that racism against Blacks is a thing of the past or has been remedied. Therefore, we assume that Blacks should be grateful for the institutional gains they now have. An implicit aspect of this perspective is the idea that Blacks now have political power and therefore have the same power as whites to be racist. As such, Blacks can now be just as racist against Asian Americans as whites can be.

This understanding of racial power is clearly evident in the claims made against O'Neal. What has been overwhelmingly demonstrated with these situations is that if anything, Asian Americans need the racist and sexist image of Black people, and in this case, Black males, to make their claims. That is, we need a group to both chastise and hold up as models of how one makes political claims. Black people are that group. The result is, we have hatred towards Blacks for being too loud, too pushy, too vocal, too visible, and for overall, taking up too much space politically. We talk about how Blacks don't share, or we say statements such as, "people need to realize that a lot of groups are racially oppressed" or, "Blacks aren't the only ones who experience racism," or, the popular "we need to go beyond black and white." We even hijack Ralph Ellison's consideration of Blackness as invisible as he wrote in 1952's *Invisible Man* to make our claims against Blacks, who we purport to be successfully visible (never considering whether they are actually viewed as human). Consider how many times Asian Americans have been able to successfully get resources, whether it be college programs, funding for non-profits, or sometimes just sympathy for our causes by using these claims. In short, consider how often Asian Americans have attempted to make claims in opposition to Blacks and subsequently how we have been fairly successful at doing so. It appears that Asian America cannot leverage our claims without relying on the image of Blacks as over-powerful and selfish.

In the process, we lay out the following agenda for Asian American politics: we must be more aggressive, more physical, more "scary," and more "threatening." The fact that we rely on the racist caricatures of Blacks fails to concern Asian America. The fact that these racist caricatures help organize and structure the lives of Black bodies—even rich people like O'Neal, who, as the editor of the *Asian American Movement E-Zine* puts it, "is not just another African American on the street"—seems to be of little concern to us. The fact that Black men are the victims of this racist and sexist caricature as clearly shown by the containment they experience through state violence such as police violence, imprisonment, and death seems to be of little concern. The fact that Asian Americans have yet to figure out how to make our claims against white supremacy, capitalism and (hetero)sexism (if we have these claims at all) without attempting to silence, displace, and in some ways, hijack Black political claims seems to be of little concern. The fact that despite supposedly not being heard effectively, we have somehow been able to live lives structurally different from Blacks in terms of state violence, racial and sexual characterization, etc. appears to be of little concern.

Nor does the fact that Asian Americans work with white institutions and white people to police Black people (and many times can be successful at doing so) seem to be a concern of ours. Yet this is precisely what Asian Americans are attempting to do in this case. Calling on NBA Commissioner David Stern, a white man who also has institutional power, to chastise and punish O'Neal is a form of policing Black men just as Asian grocers calling on police to protect their stores in Black neighborhoods is.

And who says women can't police Black men? Think about California Democrat Assemblywoman Judy Chu's letter to Stern, in which she demanded the commissioner "prevent and publicly punish" racist behavior from players. The desire to have O'Neal "publicly" punished by a white man is disgusting, as is Chu's suggestion to Stern that O'Neal be forced to perform community service in LA's Chinese American community.

In closing, it is not that I am not concerned or bothered by O'Neal's statements. Nor do I want Asian Americans to not fight back against capitalism, white supremacy, (hetero)sexism, and homophobia. I am just not interested in promoting a response and a political agenda that reproduces racist and sexist constructions and treatment of Black people generally, and in this case, Black men specifically. I am seeking for an Asian American response to O'Neal that can put forth a claim and an analysis that does not reproduce, and call for violence towards Black people. Perhaps, though, this request, rather this plea, may be unanswerable.

Questions for Discussion and Writing

1. Nopper obviously feels uncomfortable restating the actual words Shaquille O'Neal said that insulted the Asian-American community. Yet the words themselves are widely available all over the Internet. If you find them, read

them and note your first reaction. What purpose did Nopper have for not including the actual words in her essay?

2. In reference to those who signed a petition to the NBA to punish O'Neal for his words, Nopper writes one dramatic stand-alone sentence: "This writer was not one of them." Why do you think Nopper chose this rhetorical strategy? What impact does this sentence have on you as a reader and on how you read the remainder of the essay?

3. Over the course of several paragraphs Nopper explains her theory that society perceives racism against blacks is over and that now society is afraid blacks have too much power and can actually be racist against other races. She also notes that she thinks Asian Americans need to perpetuate this perception of black power in order to legitimize their own claims of racism. In doing so, she uses some complex language. Summarize her views in your own words. Be careful not to interject your own opinions into the summary. Compare summaries with your classmates to see if anyone understood Nopper's points differently.

4. Yao Ming has been viewed by many as Asian Americans' hope for breaking into basketball. Is he really representative of most Asian Americans? How is he? How is he not? How is he described and perceived by the media?

5. Examine Nopper's introduction and conclusion. Do they provide effective "bookends" to her argument? Why or why not?

Debate on Women at Augusta Catches Woods Off Balance
JERE LONGMAN WITH CLIFTON BROWN

As a reporter for The New York Times, *Jere Longman has written primarily about sports. He spent three years covering the NFL's Philadelphia Eagles football team for* The Philadelphia Inquirer. *He has also written several books, including* If Football's a Religion, Why Don't We Have a Prayer: Philadelphia, Its Faithful, and the Eternal Quest for Sports Salvation; The Girls of Summer: The U.S. Women's Soccer Team and How It Changed the World; *and* Among the Heroes: United Flight 93 and the Passengers and Crew Who Fought Back. *He has covered several controversies in sports, including the alleged use of drugs in cycling, athletes who have been arrested for criminal behavior, and the effectiveness of headgear in preventing concussions among soccer players. In this article from* The New York Times,

Longman reports on the awkward position of Tiger Woods, who is of African-American and Thai descent, when asked about his position on discrimination against women at Augusta National Golf Club.

———————— ✦ ————————

Tiger Woods, who is rarely caught off guard on a fairway or a putting green, was surprised that he had become such a lightning rod in the divisive issue over whether women should be admitted as members of Augusta National Golf Club, home of the Masters tournament.

"I didn't see it coming to this degree," he said in an interview on Friday in Lake Buena Vista, Fla., where he is playing in the Walt Disney World Resort Golf Classic this weekend. "Yes, I've always wanted to impact lives in a positive way. But I like to pick my own causes, and not be forced into having to do something."

Augusta National is a private club in Georgia, but because it plays host to the nation's pre-eminent golf tournament and draws network coverage and sponsorship from corporations whose own cultures espouse equal treatment for all, the exclusion of women as club members has become an incendiary issue.

In his most extensive comments on the Augusta's membership, Mr. Woods rejected the suggestion that he steers clear of political controversy for fear it will harm his corporate interests or affect his income from endorsements. "There's no validity to that at all," he said. "I'll say what I believe, but I'll choose when."

Then Mr. Woods took his cap off and rubbed his forehead in frustration.

"I'm also trying to win tournaments here," he said. "Do people understand that?"

At the British Open in July, when Mr. Woods was first asked about the matter, his response was terse. "It would be nice to see everyone have an equal chance to participate, but there is nothing you can do about it," he said.

When Mr. Woods, the world's top-ranked golfer, was asked again last week for his thoughts on the dispute, his response was slightly more expansive. "Do I want to see a female member?" he said. "Yes. But it's our right to have any club set up the way we want to."

Mr. Woods then called on the dispute's two major voices on the issue—William Johnson, the chairman of Augusta National, and Martha Burk, the chairwoman of the National Council of Women's

Organizations—to meet and work out a compromise. "If they both sat down and talked about it, it would be resolved a lot better than what is going on right now," Mr. Woods said Wednesday.

To many, Mr. Woods's remarks were enormously disappointing. They view Mr. Woods, whose father is African-American and whose mother is Thai, as essentially condoning discrimination and, in the process, turning his back on more than a half-century tradition of high-profile black athletes who used their celebrity status to advocate for civil rights.

But others, including several retired black and female athletes who spoke up forcefully against discrimination, viewed Mr. Woods's latest comments quite differently. They said they perceived an evolution in his social consciousness, however subtle. Given his standing as perhaps the world's best-known athlete, they said, Mr. Woods's gentle push for mediation represented a shrewd strategy.

In Friday's interview, Mr. Woods seemed astonished that his views resonate so much and that he has been pressured so hard to speak out on Augusta National and other social issues.

"I have my foundation," he said, referring to the Tiger Woods Foundation, which encourages minority youngsters to play golf and teaches them the game. "We're trying to do a lot of different things. But what I've found is that a lot of people want me to be the head of their cause. It's hard. I certainly understand what they're trying to accomplish at Augusta. I also understood the Confederate flag issue a while ago. But I'm trying to keep my focus on my foundation, and what we're trying to do. I don't think it should be the responsibility of celebrities, or sports figures, to have to be the champion of all causes."

Like some other star athletes, Mr. Woods contended that he was criticized sometimes for speaking out and at other times for not doing so.

"I have the feeling that sometimes I can't say anything, because I'm going to get criticized," he said. "And what's unfair about that is, people always ask my opinion. They ask for my opinion, and then sometimes when I give it to them, they don't respect what I have to say. If that's the case, then don't ask."

Mr. Woods smiled when he was asked if he thought it unfair that he constantly heard the question of whether women should be admitted to Augusta National, especially since legendary white golfers like Arnold Palmer and Jack Nicklaus—who are members of Augusta National—are seldom asked about it.

"Yeah, I know what you're talking about," he said. "I know exactly what you're talking about. It's certainly interesting. I'm not a member. Those guys are."

THE PRESSURE TO SPEAK OUT

Like it or not, Mr. Woods has been drawn into the debate over Augusta National's all-male membership. Many people insist that star black athletes have an obligation to speak out on social issues. Because of his multiethnic background, they say, Mr. Woods should be helping to break gender and racial barriers in his sport, which was long a preserve of affluent white males.

The Rev. Joseph Lowery, a founder of the Southern Christian Leadership Conference, credited Mr. Woods for "trying to do the right thing," but was sharply critical of what he had to say.

"He said they're both right, didn't he?" Mr. Lowery said. "He sounds like a politician. It's a good thing he doesn't play golf that way. That's so nonaggressive, so milquetoast, so lukewarm."

Mr. Lowery added: "I guess it's his way of being politically correct and safe. But you can't be all things to all people. Sometimes you have to take a principled stand. I understand that as the point man for the game of golf, and who's done more for the sport than anyone else, he doesn't want to get embroiled in controversy. But some things you can't avoid getting embroiled in."

Mary Jo Kane, a sports sociologist at the University of Minnesota, said that Mr. Woods's comments should be considered in the context of the history of racial and religious discrimination in golf clubs. "The minute Tiger Woods says it's perfectly fine for Augusta to do what it wants," Ms. Kane said, "the immediate response is, 'Is that what you would have thought a decade ago when Augusta would not have allowed you to be a member?' "

While she said she thought it was important for Mr. Woods to take a stand, Ms. Kane added: "It's curious to me why other male athletes are not asked to take a similar position. Why have they been protected?"

But there were varying opinions on Mr. Woods's responsibilities and varying assessments of his position. Several retired athletes who were celebrated and sometimes scorned for publicly advocating for civil rights said Mr. Woods deserves credit for endorsing the idea of opening Augusta National to women.

"Very diplomatic," Tommie Smith, the champion sprinter who raised a gloved fist at the 1968 Olympics in Mexico City, in protest of the treatment of black Americans, said of Mr. Woods's latest comments. "I think he's coming out in his social development."

Billie Jean King, who helped revolutionize women's tennis, applauded Mr. Woods's latest comments. "I thought they were right on," Ms. King said. "He said they should get together, person to person, and have a dialogue."

Of Mr. Woods's apparent reluctance to be dragged into the middle of the dispute over Augusta National, Ms. King said, "You have to be truthful to yourself and comfortable with it, no matter what others think."

She added, "You have to be respectful and have dignity and say it in a nice way at first, and then escalate it if people are not cooperative."

'ENTIRELY IN A NO-WIN SITUATION'

David Duval, the 2001 British Open champion and one of Mr. Woods's closest friends on the professional golf tour, said he thought that Mr. Woods was in an extremely uncomfortable position.

"There's a firestorm around him," Mr. Duval said. "We've talked about it. Regardless of the position he takes, he's wrong. He's not ever going to be right, unless he agrees with the party that is really upset. He's entirely in a no-win situation that way."

Duval said that Mr. Woods has become a pivotal figure in the dispute over Augusta National—because he is the world's top player, and also because of his race.

"I think most of it's because he's not white," Mr. Duval said. "He's looked to pick up where Jim Brown, Michael Jordan and some of these guys have left off. That's a tough spot to be in."

Mr. Duval, like some of Mr. Woods's other friends on the pro tour, wishes that people would leave him alone.

"He's 26 years old," Mr. Duval said. "Let him play golf. I imagine you'll see him take positions here and there, but I don't think his focus right now should be social change and social influence. He's just starting his career."

Until the current dispute over Augusta National's all-male membership, golf's most-publicized membership dispute occurred in 1990, before the PGA Championship at Shoal Creek Country Club in Birmingham, Ala. Before the tournament, Hall Thompson, chairman of Shoal Creek, was asked about the club's membership and responded, "We don't discriminate in every other area except the blacks."

That statement focused national attention on club membership policies, and it resulted in Shoal Creek hurriedly adding a black member before the tournament. The PGA Tour, the PGA of America, the United States Golf Association and the Ladies Professional Golf Association have all instituted policies requiring private clubs that play host to tournaments to have integrated memberships. Augusta National added its first black member in the aftermath of Shoal Creek.

Now, to pressure Augusta National to admit women as members, Ms. Burk, the chairwoman of the National Council of Women's Organizations, has been publicizing letters she has sent to corporate chief executives who are members of the club. Several of the chief executives have publicly released letters they have written in response that expressed support for admitting women at Augusta National.

Some people think that pressure on these chief executives, who belong to Augusta National and have professed a commitment to equal opportunity in their jobs, will have more influence in changing Augusta National than will any words spoken by Mr. Woods or other golfers.

THE CORPORATE INFLUENCE

Golfers, like most contemporary athletes, not only make salaries that dwarf those of previous generations of professional athletes, but they also earn far more by endorsing products like sneakers, video games, fast food and clothing.

For top athletes like Mr. Woods and Mr. Jordan—paradigms of the athlete-businessman—lucrative associations with companies like Nike, American Express, McDonald's and Buick provide disincentives to speak out on social or political issues, said Chris Bevilacqua, a former director of global negotiations for Nike.

"Alongside their great talent, intellect and intelligence, they're just smart businessmen," Mr. Bevilacqua said. "They're not going to shoot themselves in their heads if they go out and alienate a part of their businesses."

Corporations seeking to improve their images through their associations with athletes generally do not want controversy; they want consensus builders, not crusaders.

"You go after a celebrity to create a synonym between the company and the athlete to move products and services," said Nova Lanktree, executive vice president of Lanktree Sports, which matches companies with athletes.

Bob Kain, the president of the International Management Group, which represents Mr. Woods, said that financial considerations often come into play. "Companies don't want spokespersons who alienate half the population," he said. "They like spokespersons who are well liked, and it makes top athletes who make a lot of money in endorsements think long and hard before they speak out."

"We wouldn't recommend that Tiger not speak out about things that are meaningful to him," Mr. Kain added, "but he doesn't have to speak out on every issue. It's not his role."

Mr. Kain also said that star athletes, especially relatively young athletes, are not particularly well versed about social and political issues and often have vaguely formed opinions. "They're very tunnel-visioned and they don't feel they have much expertise," he said.

Regarding Mr. Woods's careful yet slowly evolving views about Augusta National, Mr. Kain said: "He keeps giving it more thought, so he's giving more bits and pieces about how he's feeling. He's not surprised the question hasn't gone away, so he's giving a little more about how he feels."

David Falk, the agent who represents Mr. Jordan, said it was never the basketball star's nature to be a social commentator. Mr. Jordan was criticized for failing to challenge publicly Nike's labor practices in its Asian factories.

"If Michael went in and said, 'We have to reverse this policy 180 degrees,' Phil Knight would listen," Mr. Falk said, referring to Nike's chairman. "But ultimately Michael doesn't run the company. People assume athletes have more power than they have."

But it is also not clear that a public figure of Mr. Woods's stature would really risk much by more pointedly challenging Augusta National's all-male membership and advocating equal opportunity for women.

For example, while Nike has not commented specifically about Augusta National, it did issue a statement saying that it believes in inclusion in sports. "We don't believe that anybody should be excluded from anywhere," Christopher Mike, director of marketing for Nike Golf, said. "But we can't control what happens at Augusta National."

Questions for Discussion and Writing

1. Longman says that Tiger Woods was put on the spot several times regarding his opinion on whether or not women should be allowed to play in golf's premier tournament, the Masters. He has said, "I like to pick my own causes, and not be forced into having to do something." Woods seems frustrated that he's expected to comment on social issues when he's "also trying to win tournaments." Does he have a valid complaint? Should athletes be expected to address social issues or should they be free to concentrate on their sports?

2. Are racial and gender discrimination the same thing? What makes them similar? What makes them different? Does Longman indicate a difference between the two?

3. Longman quotes several former and current athletes, as well as civil rights leaders and sociologists. Summarize the various opinions in your own words. Then analyze the differences between athletes' opinions and those of leaders and sociologists. What might account for the differences?

4. The Rev. Joseph Lowery is quoted as saying that Woods has "done more for the sport than anyone else." What has Tiger Woods done for the sport of golf? Is there appropriate evidence to support any claims regarding Woods' contributions? Does Longman's tone insinuate that he agrees with this theory?

5. Longman points out that prior to the Augusta controversy the last dispute in golf was at Shoal Creek Country Club in Alabama in 1990. Read that paragraph again. What is your initial reaction to that situation? How does this example enhance Longman's research?

Making Connections: Writing

1. Define the word *activist*. Look up some prominent activists in history. S. L. Price mentions activists who oppose Indian mascots. Tamara Nopper is an activist in the Asian-American community. Tiger Woods is expected to be an activist, whether he wants to be or not. Why is it important to understand what an activist is in order to fully analyze controversial issues?

2. Tiger Woods has been criticized by members of his own race. Such race-on-race criticism is also the basis for Tamara Nopper's essay. Respond to her claims. She references other articles on the Shaquille O'Neal controversy, including one from *AsianWeek* that created quite a stir. Go online or use one of your library's information databases to find responses from Irwin Tang, the author of the *AsianWeek* article, and others. Compare those responses to your own.

3. Go to a game or event in a sport that is dominated by a particular race. Suggestions might include a martial arts tournament or a golf match. Keep a

journal of your observations. Do most of the players belong to one race? What about the fans? After the event, research the sport and write about the racial makeup and history of the sport.

4. Answer a question posed in many of these reading selections: What constitutes racist language? Is Irwin Tang's threat to "take" O'Neal "down" equally as racist as O'Neal's comments or is one "worse" than the other according to Tamara Nopper? Was it right for America to depend on Joe Louis to represent the country that wouldn't let him use the same facilities as whites? Who decides? You respond.

5. Examine statistics in these reading selections. Are they all logical? Believable? Backed up by evidence? Why might you question some of the statistics? What is the purpose of the statistics? Compare statistics that appear to be rooted in fact and those that appear to be "sensationalized."

6. Choose an issue from this chapter and find a statistic to support your opinion. Use it in a sentence so that it sounds credible and fact-based. Rewrite the sentence, this time making the statistic seem sensationalized or manipulated.

7. Analyze the reading selections from newspapers or magazines: S. L. Price's article from *Sports Illustrated*, Tim Wendel's article for *USA Today*, and Jere Longman's article for *The New York Times*. Are the articles objective in the journalistic sense? Can you detect signs of bias? How do the writers keep their reports objective? Do they offer balanced evidence from both sides of the argument?

8. S. L. Price calls the mascot issue "sport's thorniest word problem." Would you agree? What about racist names for African Americans, Asian Americans, and Latinos? You might also answer the question now, read some of the selections in Chapter 6 (on sports and rhetoric), and then write about this question again.

9. The authors of the article "Of Polls and Race Prejudice" say up front that they "critically unpack" the article, "The Indian Wars." Write a rhetorical analysis— an essay that "critically unpacks" a text—on another reading selection from this chapter.

10. Conduct a survey among your peers. Each of the issues in this chapter deserves attention. But how large a place do Native American concerns or Asian-American concerns or Latino concerns occupy in race relations in the United States? Construct survey questions to see how aware your peers are of racial issues other than those between blacks and whites. Include at least one open-ended question to allow explanation.

Books Worth Reading

Beyond Glory: Joe Louis vs. Max Schmeling, and a World on the Brink by David Margolick. Comprehensive report of the boxing match that pitted a black American against a German on the brink of World War II and Nazism.

Black Planet: Facing Race During an NBA Season by David Shields. Author followed the Seattle Supersonics to explore white spectators' relationship to black athletes.

Counting Coup: The True Story of Basketball and Honor on the Little Big Horn by Larry Colton. Tells the story of a high school girls' basketball team in Crow Agency, Montana, and its struggle with racism.

Days of Grace: A Memoir by Arthur Ashe. Autobiography by one of tennis' only black players and an advocate for racial and social justice.

Forty Million Dollar Slaves: The Rise, Fall, and Redemption of the Black Athlete by William C. Rhoden. Author argues that the sports industry exploits the talents of black athletes.

The New Face of Baseball: The One-Hundred-Year Rise and Triumph of Latinos in America's Favorite Sport by Tim Wendel. Based on interviews and research, examines the history of Latino baseball players in America.

Only the Ball Was White: A History of Legendary Black Players and All-Black Professional Teams by Robert W. Peterson. Comprehensive look at baseball's Negro League.

Unforgivable Blackness: The Rise and Fall of Jack Johnson by Geoffrey C. Ward. Biography of the first black boxing heavyweight champion in history who fought and beat Jim Jeffries, "The Great White Hope."

Wokini: A Lakota Journey to Happiness and Self-Understanding by Billy Mills with Nicholas Sparks. Updated edition of inspirational words from the Native American Olympic medalist turned motivational speaker and Indian activist.

You Gotta Have WA: When Two Cultures Collide on a Baseball Diamond by Robert Whiting. An inside look at Japanese baseball.

Films Worth Watching

American Pastime (2007). Explores a dark time in America's history—the internment of Japanese Americans during World War II—and the Japanese-American families' struggle to deal with their internment through baseball.

Chiefs (2002). PBS documentary about high school basketball and life on Indian reservations.

The Jesse Owens Story (1984). Worth checking out at a library, the story of the black athlete who won four gold medals in the 1936 "Hitler's Olympics."

Viva Baseball! (2005). Documentary explores the racial struggles and discrimination of Latin Americans playing Major League Baseball; narrated by Marc Anthony.

The Year of the Yao (2004). Documentary about Yao Ming's journey from China to America's NBA.

Sites Worth Surfing

http://www.nascsports.org
Home of the Native American Sports Council.

http://www.latinosportslegends.com/
Stories and statistics about Latino athletes.

http://www.asianathlete.com/
News about Asian and Asian-American athletes.

http://www.blackathlete.net/
Site of the Black Athlete Sports Network.

http://www.chineseathlete.net/
Site of the Chinese Athlete Sports Network.

Barriers or Breakthroughs: What Role Does Gender Play in Sports?

As the old cliché goes, "You've come a long way, baby." The phrase seems to apply to women in sports. But does gender still pose a barrier for many athletes? In their dramatic photographic book *Superwomen: 100 Women, 100 Sports*, Jodi Buren and the Women's Sports Foundation's Donna Lopiano quote a number of female athletes on their sports' progress. It's shocking to see just how recently a number of strides have been made. According to race car driver Janet Guthrie, "Until 1971 women were not allowed in the pits, the garage area, or the press box at the Indianapolis 500 for any reason whatsoever. It was a major ban. A woman could own the race car, but she couldn't get close to it." It wasn't until 1983 that marathon runner Kathrine Switzer was finally able to have women's marathon declared a sport in the Olympic Games. The Women's Professional Football League wasn't formed until 1999. Says player Andra Douglas of her first championship: "It was a fantastic feeling of success after hard work, but it was an opportunity that should have been afforded me twenty years ago." Certainly, there have been breakthroughs. But how many barriers still exist? And while women get the brunt of the attention when it comes to gender issues in sport, what breakthroughs and barriers can men claim? Chapter 5 examines these questions.

The chapter opens with an historical analysis of the All-American Girls Professional Baseball League. Most people associate that organization with the movie *A League of Their Own*. While the film is worth watching and does attempt historical accuracy, Patricia

Vignola's study in the baseball journal *Nine* points out deeper issues. Sure, the All-American Girls Professional Baseball League was a positive step for women. But, as Vignola points out, the players wore skirts for uniforms, attended mandatory charm school, and were often covered in the media's society pages rather than in the sports section. Did the League help to maintain the stereotype of female athletes as fragile and pretty? Why, decades later, is professional women's baseball defunct while women's softball is gaining popularity?

Likewise, the second reading in this chapter, "Sex Sells, and Many Athletes Are Cashing In," looks back into history. But this article also looks into a controversial topic's current and future impact on society. Female athletes, like their male counterparts, depend on endorsements and advertising for much of their income. But for women, whose salaries are typically much lower than those of male athletes, there's a growing trend of earning extra money by posing in men's magazines or in suggestive ads. Does posing half-clothed (or less) perpetuate the exploitation of women's bodies? This article delves into the recent history of this controversy and offers perspectives from both sides of the argument.

The remaining selections, in varied ways, examine gender issues involving both men and women in sports. Mariah Burton Nelson argues that, while it has become more acceptable for women to compete as ferociously as men, our culture still has problems completely accepting competitive females. In an excerpt from her book *Embracing Victory: Life Lessons on Competition and Compassion*, she uses the example of figure skater Nancy Kerrigan, who was criticized for her competitive nature in favor of more graceful and feminine behavior.

The advocacy organization Children Now became so concerned about sports' impact on young boys that they commissioned a study by sports and gender scholar Michael Messner. Excerpts of this study, "Boys to Men," point out many barriers males experience in sports. How do messages of violence and aggression in sports affect boys who don't see themselves as "tough"? Do stereotypical women in television commercials influence the way boys perceive women's roles in society? Another organization, the Women's Sports Foundation, advocates for women in sports but is no less concerned about the impact of perceptions on boys and men. In their position statement on Title IX, the controversial law aimed at creating gender equality in sports in schools, the Foundation asserts that it is "not in favor of reducing athletic opportunities for men as the preferred method of achieving Title IX compliance." Instead, the Foundation offers several suggestions for improving women's sports without harming men's.

As you read the selections in this chapter, you will notice that all the writers make arguments of some type. However, there are many ways to make and support an argument. Vignola, for example, makes her argument regarding the influence of the All-American Girls Professional Baseball League by supporting it with facts and historical evidence. Huang, in his article on sex appeal, writes more objectively because the piece appeared in a mainstream newspaper. Yet can you identify possible bias? Is bias always a negative quality in persuasive writing? As advocacy organizations, Children Now and the Women's Sports Foundation are free to be more clearly biased. See if you can identify language that clearly defines these organizations as advocates. Finally, Mariah Burton Nelson, a former athlete and sports activist, argues much from personal experience. Does her personal experience enhance her argument? Does personal experience always enhance an argument? As you read, consider what makes a good argument and all the ways a writer can make an effective argument.

This chapter is intended to prompt you to think about gender and sports, particularly about women and sports. Most people are familiar with female athletes who made early breakthroughs: Billie Jean King, who beat a man in tennis; golfer and grand slam winner Annika Sorenstam; Olympians Jackie Joyner-Kersee and Bonnie Blair; and IndyCar racer Danica Patrick. But even these legendary athletes had to break down barriers first, and not all women find the success of soccer's Mia Hamm or basketball's Lisa Leslie. And what about men? How are boys and men in American culture supposed to react to the drastic changes in women's sports? Are men who compete in traditionally female sports viewed as wimps? How are sports media helping or hampering gender equality? There are breakthroughs when it comes to gender issues in sports, but there are still barriers. Which one is winning?

The Patriotic Pinch Hitter: The AAGBL and How the American Woman Earned a Permanent Spot on the Roster

PATRICIA VIGNOLA

As a graduate student at Rutgers University, Patricia Vignola secured an internship at the Baseball Hall of Fame in Cooperstown, New York. Her interest in baseball continued with an academic article about the Negro League and this one, about the All-American Girls Professional Baseball League, published in Nine: A Journal of Baseball History. Nine *publishes scholarly articles on historical aspects of baseball and the cultural connections to baseball around the world. The journal also hosts an annual conference on baseball scholarship, aptly called Spring Training. The All-American Girls Professional Baseball League was founded by Philip Wrigley, the chewing gum mogul and one-time owner of the Chicago Cubs. The League actually began in 1943 as the All-American Girls Softball League. In her article, Vignola examines the origins of women's baseball as a patriotic gesture to fill in for men's baseball during World War II. She claims that the League had a lasting impact on women's sports in American society.*

———————————— ✦ ————————————

During World War II, that lovely, patriotic pinch hitter "Rosie the Riveter" stepped up to bat, entering the workforce so her boyfriend, "Charlie," could take it for the team by going to war. Once she saw her MVP rounding third, Rosie happily slid into her warm, safe home, gratified by a job well done. However, contrary to popular belief, Rosie was no mere pinch hitter. Throughout the 1940s the American woman was capable of being more than a temporary hire. She was a professional musician, a war correspondent, and a member of the United States Congress as well as a professional baseball player. The All-American Girls' Baseball League (AAGBL) began as wartime entertainment; however, it would last nine years after World War II with its effects still reverberating today. . . .

By autumn 1942 many minor baseball leagues had closed down due to the lack of wartime manpower. By 1943 only eleven leagues were operating, a thirty-one-team drop-off from two seasons earlier. It appeared that by 1944, Major League [B]aseball might have to close its own ballpark gates.[3] Diamond stars, such as Joe DiMaggio, were putting on military uniforms. Even if the government did not shut down professional baseball, team owners became concerned that the player quality would suffer and fans would lose interest.[4]

In late 1942 Philip K. Wrigley, owner of the Chicago Cubs, tapped Ken Sells, the assistant to the general manager of the club, to head up a task force to brainstorm on the issue. After exploring several options the committee recommended a professional softball league with female players. Softball was as popular as baseball at the time.[5] However, it cannot be ignored that softball was a game dominated by women and that women were one of the few sectors of the American population, aside from children, the disabled, and the elderly, who were guaranteed exemption from the draft. Sells's commission led to the founding of the AAGBL in 1943; however, the league began its auspicious history as the All-American Girls' Softball League (AAGSL).[6] And a girls' league it would be, as all of the players ranged in age from their teens to their twenties.[7] However, a few were married and held professional careers as well as being mothers. It should be noted that these players took no offense at the moniker "girl." Today, in a post-NOW (National Organization for Women) era, these women still refer to themselves and their former teammates as "the girls."

A professional organized athletic league had never been successfully attempted with women to this point, so Wrigley called on the support and expertise of fellow Major League Baseball executives. Ken Sells was named president of the league.[8] Wrigley also called on Cubs attorney Paul V. Harper and Brooklyn Dodgers general manager Branch Rickey to become the league's first trustees. When the league was officially announced, Wrigley claimed that it was time for "softball to take its proper place among American girls and women as one of the country's major sports." However, to make the AAGSL stand out among other recreational softball leagues, the girls would play a hybrid game of softball combined with the more aggressive aspects of baseball. Immediately, the male-dominated world of sports commentary speculated on a feminine bastardization of the national pastime, predicting a league with such teams as the "Glamour Gals" and the "Rockettes". This sports commentary facilitated a common American view of sports at the time as "inherently masculine and of women athletes as, therefore, charming but temporary impostors, freakish anomalies, or threatening transgressors of sexual and gender boundaries."[9] At the time, for a woman to forge any "independent life outside marriage carried enormous risks of . . . social ostracism."[10]

PATRIOTIC

The AAGSL would be presented as available outdoor entertainment for millions engaged in war work.[11] The femininity of these women would become a "patriotic" enterprise, low-cost entertainment to boost public morale. As a patriotic gesture, the players would line up on the field in a "V" formation before each game.[12] Wrigley wanted his players to exert a Betty Grable quality, reminding America what it was fighting for. They would play exhibition games on training bases, and servicemen and servicewomen would be admitted free to the ballpark.

Unlike their comrades in arms in Major League [B]aseball, each signed AAGSL player was required to go to charm school. Wrigley demanded that his girls be different from the "other" female athletes. He wanted to prove that women could play as hard as men could as well as retain their femininity. Besides, a pretty girl in a skirt could fill the seats—at least in the beginning. Ironically, at the same time, Rickey was promoting a "clean cut," "collegiate" image with his Brooklyn Dodgers. America was threatened by class and race conflict in the mid-twentieth century. The Anglo mainstream felt comforted by the idea of being able to identify their nonthreatening "All American" girls and boys.

The charm school was run by cosmetics entrepreneur Helena Rubinstein and based on "gracious living programs" at Smith, Wellesley, and Vassar.[13] Each player learned makeup application, posture, and carriage. Advice included tips such as running the fingers through a bar of soap before a game so a player would not get dirt underneath her fingernails. Each player also received a guidebook with mandatory rules of comportment. The league felt the need to institute these rules of "behavior" for the girls' "own good" as well as for "that of the future success of baseball." Most interesting were the etiquette rules regarding sportsmanship, dealing with the public and, in particular, [male] baseball fans. As the guide stated: "You [should] know she is a lady as soon as she opens her mouth."[14] The players were always "ladies first" and ballplayers second. In wartime America the AAGSL would have met a premature end commercially if stereotyped as a transgressing lesbian league.

Wrigley's marketing machine required the players to live up to glamour pinups for the league to find commercial success; however, these rules also substituted as motherly advice for these players in mid-twentieth-century America. Far from home and their mothers, playing this traditionally male sport, players still could not escape the expectations of American womanhood. Many ex-players look back on the rules of comportment with ambivalence. Gloria Cordes (Elliot), who played from 1950 to 1954, "really didn't have a problem with it," although she did not go to the Rubinstein school, which was disbanded after the first couple of seasons. Cordes pointed out that the "League *stressed* femininity. It wasn't as much about beauty as it was about being *not* masculine."[15] Again the threat of sexual transgression reared its head. In 1990 a survey was taken of surviving players regarding the rules of comportment. Seventy percent of the ex-players felt that these restrictions were necessary to have a good image for the public. Propagating the feminine stereotype was an occupational hazard. However, the survey did not inquire whether players felt that they had to sacrifice aspects of their personal identities for the opportunity to play the game professionally.

The players' and the league's images were protected by chaperones, the front line of defense. Each team had a chaperone, who upheld the players to the *high* moral standards of the time. Beyond protecting the public image, chaperones provided needed services for the players that a male manager was unable to and assured parents that their daughters were well taken care of.[16] One aspect of a chaperone's job was to make sure that the players were always accompanied. Long-distance parents were comforted by the fact that their daughters were not expected to fend for themselves in big cities such as Chicago. The players lived under rules similar to what they might have experienced at home, with curfews and guardian approval of all entertainment.[17] Of course, some found ways around chaperones at night. However, for the most part, the chaperone played "den mother" to the players. In the later years of the league, the chaperone was a former player.[18]

UNIFORMS

Otis Shepard, art director for the Wrigley Company, designed the players' uniforms. With the assistance of Ann Harnett, one of the first players signed to the league, Shepard designed the uniforms in a tunic style to ensure practicality as well as style. The uniforms were modeled after tennis and field hockey outfits of the day.[19] Wrigley wanted to disassociate his players as much as possible from the common "Bloomer Girl" look of shorts or pants. One Kalamazoo Lassies first baseman, describing the experience of playing in a skirt, said that "the uniform looked great on the girls and they didn't interfere with the quality of play." Former player Shirley Jameson would concur, "except for sliding."[20] When sliding into bases the girls would receive large, bloody bruises on their thighs, which they referred to as "strawberries." When asked if the short tunic skirt made her any less likely to slide into a base, former player Dolores Moore replied, "Heck no. I just slid head first."[21] . . .

In 1943, 400 prospective players arrived at Wrigley Field for 60 slots at that first midwestern tryout. Each player worked out for four hours each morning, had a break for lunch, and then had a long afternoon workout, culminating with time in charm school. Each team carried a sixteen-woman roster and played up to 125 games, almost all at night, over the course of a seven-month season. Impressively, that first season players made upward of $85 a week, an unprecedented working wage for a female and an *unheard-of* wage for a female athlete.[23] . . .

EXPANSION

These girls were definitely as competitive as their male counterparts, going as far as to spike and throw at one another in retribution. Ex-player Dottie Kamenshek remembered sliding into a second baseman with her cleats first, because the second baseman cleated Kamenshek's teammate.[29] The players, as well as the managers (and on occasion, chaperones), would be sanctioned for a team's rough play and "conduct unbecoming a lady," in the form of fines. The most drastic punishment was banishment from the league. There was no union organized to protect a player in this case, and *most* importantly, nowhere else to play professional women's baseball.

Although the players were not unionized, they were not completely devoid of power. In 1947 the Peoria Redwings voted to fire
their manager Johnny Gottselig and replace him with Leo Schrall,
a move that received the blessing of the league's administration.[30]
Although these women faced daily discrimination on the basis of
their gender, their agency would not be taken from them. The
League recognized the Redwings' political power to choose a new
leader, augmenting scholar Joan Wallach Scott's theory that gender is a societal construction that can be overcome.[31] Just because
these players were women did not mean that they were powerless
in a culture that fostered a gender caste system.

Although she was no longer attending charm school, an AAGBL
player had a busier schedule, wore a shorter skirt, played a purer
form of baseball, and got paid better than her AAGSL sisters. Gloria
Cordes began with a starting salary of $50 a week, after making
$30 a week as a clerk in Manhattan. By the end of the league's
tenure in 1954, she was making upward of $100 a week.[32]

For most of the league's history, the AAGBL drew a good attendance. In the first year, attendance grew 50 percent between
the first and second half of the season.[33] In 1945 the Fort Wayne
Daisies were outdrawing the local male teams by approximately
800 spectators a game. The AAGBL was even able to charge
more admission, 75 cents to the going average of 50 cents a
ticket.[34] By 1946 the Racine (Wisconsin) Belles reached the
750,000 mark.[35] During spring training in Havana, Cuba, the
AAGBL drew more than 30,000 people for four exhibition games.
They outdrew the Brooklyn Dodgers, who were there for their
own spring training. The AAGBL success gave birth to the Latin
American Feminine Baseball League, which would produce a
number of players for the AAGBL.[36] At its height the AAGBL
consisted of ten teams and entertained nearly a million fans in
mid-sized midwestern cities.[37] . . .

AMERICAN BEAUTY

A devastating blow to the AAGBL was the missed opportunity for
media expansion. Baseball was first introduced to television in the
late 1940s; however, television would not become a significant
mode of media until after the league dissolved. Could the AAGBL
have made use of the new media? Men's baseball had made the

transition successfully, and some AAGBL teams, such as the Belles, had been on the radio already. However, the era of autonomous team ownership (1951–54) left the AAGBL in disarray. Players would never get a chance to see if they could make it in the new medium. As they bought out Meyerhoff, owners stripped the league office of most of its administrative powers. Each owner was solely concerned with his own team, so no one watched out for the league as a whole.[50] There was no united league front to capitalize on the economic advantages of the expanding media. This missed opportunity was characteristic of the mounting problems of the AAGBL. The lack of political infrastructure brought the league to an end, even though it was still drawing over 1,000 spectators a night in Minor League parks in its final season.[51] . . .

To trace the history of the AAGBL, you would think that any remnants of the league fell off the face of the earth in September 1954. Most players stopped talking about their baseball experience. These women were re-entering a society that had never truly seen viable, successful female athletes. Few people understood their accomplishments. Nonetheless, many went on to become doctors, lawyers, and teachers, professions that they could not have afforded before their baseball careers.[56]

If and where does the AAGBL fit into the feminist narrative? Although it lasted only twelve years, its results can still be measured today. Once afforded the opportunity, these women made a mockery of the postwar American feminine stereotype. They looked like Rita Hayworth and played like Ted Williams. Players proved, at least by Joan Wallach Scott's model discussed earlier, that gender is a societal convention manipulated by whomever is in political power at the moment. Although they were told by society that they were of the more demure sex, in many cases they proved that they were as strong as their Major League brethren—physically as well as emotionally.

In a time when the postwar American woman was most restricted by society, these women had agency. The women were able to transcend class, though regrettably not race. Unlike Rosie the Riveter, these professional women were not temporary. They played the game for nine years after the war ended; after the league folded, many went on to postsecondary education as well as other professions. Not only did these women provide a model of a successful team sport, but they provided a model of how women collectively can make a political and social impact.

NOTES

3. Joan Winter, *The History of the All American Girls Professional Baseball League* (n.p.: AAGPBL, n.d.), p.1. Winter was a pitcher with the Racine Belles from 1943 to 1950.
4. Susan E. Johnson, *When Women Played Hardball* (Washington: Seal, 1994), p. xix.
5. Winter, *History*, p. 1.
6. David Young, "Seasons in the Sun," *Women's Sports* 4 (October 1982): p. 50.
7. Tim Wiles, National Baseball Hall of Fame historian, telephone interview by author, February 1, 2002.
8. Winter, *History*, p. 1.
9. Susan K. Cahn, "Sports Talk: Oral History and Its Uses, Problems, and Possibilities for Sports History," *Journal of American History* (September 1994): p. 599.
10. Elaine Tyler May, *Homeward Bound: American Families in the Cold War Era* (New York: Basic Books, 1988), p. 36.
11. Winter, *History*, p. 15.
12. Gai Ingham Berlage, *Women in Baseball: The Forgotten History* (Westport CT: Praeger, 1994), p. 135.
13. Berlage, *Women in Baseball*, p. 139.
14. *A Guide for All American Girls—How to Look Better, Feel Better, Be More Popular* (n.p.: All-American Girls' Baseball League, n.d.), pp. 1–10. Each player was required to have a beauty kit, which included cleansing cream, lipstick, rouge, cream deodorant, mild astringent, face powder, hand lotion and hair remover. The guide shared grooming methods, food habits, and exercises as well as a suggested travel wardrobe, because choosing an outfit could be "one of woman's great problems."
15. Gloria Cordes Elliot, AAGBL pitcher (1950–54), interview by author, February 10, 2002, Staten Island NY. Cordes remembers ways in which some of the players would push the envelope regarding the rules of comportment. A player was required to keep her hair long, which became uncomfortable under her cap in the summer heat. Cordes would keep her hair naturally curly, making it harder to detect if she chose to cut her hair in the midsummer heat.
16. Berlage, *Women in Baseball*, p. 140.
17. Johnson, *When Women Played Hardball*, p. 66.
18. Gloria Cordes Elliot, interview by author. Cordes, who was chaperoned by several of these former players, felt that you truly "could talk to [your chaperone] about problems that you couldn't bring up to your manager."
19. Winter, *History*, pp. 2–7.
20. Young, "Seasons," p. 52.

21. Tim Wiles, "Let's Play, Too," *League Championship Series* (New York: Major League Baseball, 2000), p. 59.

23. Young, "Seasons," pp. 51, 52.

29. Young, "Seasons," p. 51; Winter, *History*, p. 7.

30. Johnson, *When Women Played Hardball*, pp. 77, 105–6, 187.

31. Joan Wallach Scott, *Gender and the Politics of History* (New York: Columbia University Press, 1999), pp. 16–27.

32. Young, "Seasons," p. 51; Gloria Cordes Elliot, interview by author.

33. Young, "Seasons," p. 52.

34. Berlage, *Women in Baseball*, p. 146.

35. Sports clipping (name of publication unknown), Kenosha WI, 1946.

36. Berlage, *Women in Baseball*, p. 147.

37. Winter, *History*, p. xv.

50. Johnson, *When Women Played Hardball*, p. xxiii.

51. Gloria Cordes E[l]liot, interview by author.

56. Barbara Gregorich, *Women at Play: The Story of Women in Baseball* (New York: Harcourt Brace, 1993), p. 88.

Questions for Discussion and Writing

1. Why does Vignola begin her examination by discussing Rosie the Riveter instead of a female baseball player? Do you know who Rosie the Riveter is? What does she represent?

2. Some people predicted that women's baseball teams would have names like "Glamour Gals" and "Rockettes." In reality, there really were Daisies, Chicks, Belles, and Peaches, but also Comets, Blue Sox, and Redwings. Why would team names have been so important during the early years of the League? What about now, looking back historically?

3. Vignola says Wrigley wanted his baseball players to be different from "other" female athletes. Research female athletes in the 1940s and write about the characteristics they possessed that Wrigley might have wanted to avoid. Does Vignola effectively address these characteristics in her article?

4. Wrigley sold the League in 1944 and it officially became known as the All-American Girls Professional Baseball League. As the League evolved, the women began to gain more power, even forming a union. Did their power and more exciting style of play make them more masculine or simply more accepted by society? Try to research expert views before you voice your own opinion and compare the two. Also consider Vignola's view.

5. How does Vignola support her claim about the League's impact far into the future, even today? What evidence does she offer and how effective is it? How does she further connect the League with other areas of women's lives such as work and family?

Sex Sells, and Many Athletes Are Cashing In

THOMAS HUANG

Thomas Huang has served at The Dallas Morning News *in several capacities, including staff reporter, features editor, and lead editor for narrative writing. Huang has also been involved with training new and current journalists: for example, he teaches other journalists how to write mission statements. "By that, I mean crafting a couple of paragraphs about your life's purpose," he says. Huang came from a family of scientists and engineers, so his first inclination was not to become a writer. But he says, "I was driven by a personal mission to step outside of my own experience, gain some wisdom about the world and write about it." Huang's article on female athletes' use of their sex appeal appeared in* The Dallas Morning News *in 2004 during the Athens Olympics.*

◆

Athens, Greece—She graces the cover of the men's magazine, pressed close to four other women. Barely concealed in their white bikinis, they look like models from a Victoria's Secret ad.

But look more closely at this month's *FHM* magazine and you'll see that it's Olympic high jumper Amy Acuff, along with volleyball player Logan Tom, long jumper Jenny Adams and swimmers Amanda Beard and Haley Cope.

"We work hard for our bodies," said Ms. Acuff, 29, of Austin.

All are competing at the Athens Games, except Ms. Adams, who failed to qualify.

"Ten or 20 years ago, it wasn't in vogue to be competitive, aggressive or sweaty," Ms. Acuff said. "Now you see the athletic body has become the standard."

The athletic body, in various states of undress, is getting a lot of exposure these days, as several female Olympic athletes have decidedly gone sexy. And while it's true that athletes in the ancient Games competed in the nude, the modern-day athletes have the benefit of mass-circulation magazines and the Internet.

Ms. Acuff and Ms. Cope are in this month's *Playboy*. Basketball phenom Lauren Jackson disrobed for an Australian magazine. A group of U.S. swimmers and water polo players appeared in *Stuff* magazine. Softball player Jennie Finch gets as much attention for her attractiveness as she does for her pitching. And doesn't the TV camera always seem to linger just a second or two longer than necessary on the bikini-clad beach volleyball players?

Advocates for women's sports don't blame the athletes for taking advantage of the Olympic spotlight—and potentially earning more money and corporate sponsorships. But they argue that this "sexualization" of female Olympic athletes diminishes their accomplishments—and ends up hurting other women.

Historically, female athletes have often been photographed in feminine poses—in such outfits as prom dresses and cheerleading uniforms. "But more and more, there's an alarming parallel between how women athletes are portrayed and soft pornography," said Mary Jo Kane, director of the University of Minnesota's Tucker Center for Research on Girls and Women in Sport.

The Olympic athletes "get so little exposure and have such a short period when they're in the news," said Dr. Kane, professor of kinesiology. "It costs a lot of money to be an elite athlete. I understand why they do what they do. But it's not about advancing the cause of women's sports."

Michael Dolan, *FHM* magazine's deputy editor, disagrees: "So much of what you see is their athletic ability. Hopefully, if the piece succeeds, it shows them a bit more in three dimensions. . . . These women are beautiful, strong athletes, good people."

CULTURAL 'INDICTMENT'

Dr. Kane and other experts argue that several factors are behind this trend:

- The success of tennis player Anna Kournikova and pro volleyball player Gabrielle Reece showed that athletes could parlay their good looks into lucrative careers. The proliferation of their images on the Internet only increased their profile.
- Some younger female athletes are less inhibited about posing nude, because they're not as aware of the struggle that female athletes have gone through to gain an equal footing with men.
- The sports industry is a huge entertainment machine, and, just as with the film and music industries, the media are constantly on the lookout for sexy celebrities.

- Even as the popularity of certain women's sports soars, some assert that there's a societal backlash against women participating in more aggressive sports, like basketball, softball and track and field.

"It's an indictment of the sports media culture," said Donna Lopiano, chief executive of the Women's Sports Foundation in Long Island, N.Y. "It's a predominantly male culture. They're deciding what sells, and they're not willing to sell legitimate female athletic achievement. . . . It's a way that culture has tried to diminish a woman by relegating her to sex object or decorative object.

"This is an entertainment medium," she said, "and even if you think the Olympics is the epitome of amateur sport and all that is good and right, the media is going to cover it as it's used to covering it—as an entertainment and celebrity deal."

To be sure, men are getting into the act, as well. Australian swimmer Michael Klim appeared in the same magazine spread with Lauren Jackson. His countryman Ian Thorpe launched his new underwear collection with sexy images. Swimmer Michael Phelps wore a tight Speedo on the cover of *Time*'s Olympic preview.

But "for every image of a male athlete that supposedly sexualizes him, there are thousands and thousands of pictures of male athletes who are simply great athletes," Dr. Kane said. "That's not the case for women," she said. "If it was true that whenever I turned on ESPN, I saw women athletes as athletes, I'd be less troubled by *Playboy*."

And it's not like male athletes are baring all. "Unless you're seeing men's genitals, they're not nude. . . . Tiger Woods doesn't pose in the nude," she said.

HISTORICAL PERSPECTIVE

"There's a long tradition of the objectification of female Olympic athletes, and it's intensifying at this time," said Margaret Carlisle Duncan, a sociologist at the University of Wisconsin at Milwaukee. "People are getting sponsorship endorsements and are doing this for commercial reasons. . . . It's like going for all you can get, because you might as well capitalize on the moment."

The post-Title IX generation doesn't "have the history of how women have struggled to make their presence known in sports," she said. They "don't have the sense that they need to protect the gains that women have made."

Dr. Duncan studied media coverage of female Olympic athletes in the 1970s and '80s. She found that the media often focused on the physical appearance of these athletes, including Florence Griffith-Joyner, Janet Evans and Katarina Witt. Ms. Witt posed for *Playboy*, as did Ms. Reece, the volleyball player.

Then came a high-profile moment in 1999. To celebrate a game-winning penalty kick at the Women's World Cup, soccer player Brandi Chastain took off her jersey to reveal a black sports bra. That same year, she posed nude in *Gear* magazine. Not long afterward, Ms. Acuff and 11 other female track and field athletes posed, mostly nude, for a calendar to raise money for charity. The Canadian women's cross-country ski team and the Australian women's soccer team did the same thing.

Shortly before the Sydney Games in 2000, Olympic swimming legend Jenny Thompson stirred up controversy when she posed for *Sports Illustrated* without a top on, covering her breasts with her fists.

"The quiet message is that men's sports are better, stronger and more powerful, and women will never measure up," said Karen Weiller, associate professor of kinesiology at the University of North Texas.

Some female athletes draw the line at posing for sexy magazine covers. Jennie Finch, who was voted ESPN.com's "hottest female athlete," reportedly turned down offers from *Playboy* and *Maxim*. "I'd rather not pass judgment on any other athletes," she told reporters in Athens. "Muscles on women are beautiful. It's great. But my personal opinion—decision—would be not to do that. I love being a role model for young girls."

HELPING ATHLETES

Others argue that such calendars and magazine photo spreads don't belittle the accomplishments of women athletes—they help them.

"Some of these folks are brilliant athletes, and they make so little money," said Mr. Dolan of *FHM*. "Any opportunity to raise money to help them train and not starve doing what they love—it's hard to hold that against them."

Ms. Beard, who won the gold in the 200-meter breaststroke Thursday, said she has fun posing for magazines. "It's a thing to do outside of swimming, and I enjoy it. And as long as I enjoy it, I'll keep doing it."

Evan Morgenstein, Ms. Beard's agent, has watched her grow up from a 14-year-old with a teddy bear to a 22-year-old Olympian who also models. She has appeared in *Men's Fitness* and *Shape* magazine, and she has deals with Speedo, ThermaSilk, Gateway, Red Bull and Oroweat.

"It's the benefit of having success and expectations and beauty," Mr. Morgenstein said. The sponsors "have the expectation that the athlete doesn't crawl into a hole. They want the public to get to know her. I told Amanda this is an opportunity to get exposure and help your sponsors. [It could] lead to new deals. That's why you do this: money, opportunity and visibility."

That's a major reason why Ms. Acuff posed in the magazines. "It's beneficial to me financially to have exposure, to be on the cover of *FHM*," she said. "I see the body as a miraculous machine, and I don't see sexuality when I see a woman's body. I see strength, athleticism and beauty.

"If someone is so narrow-minded, I feel sorry for them," she said. "People are so reductionist in their thinking, they miss the bigger picture. . . . People have different standards of what's acceptable. I'm sure we'd be stoned to death in the Middle East just for wearing our track uniforms.

"I don't see it as shameful," she said. "We're promoting pride in our bodies."

Dr. Kane agrees that athletes should be proud of their bodies. "But if they think posing in *Playboy* is showing off their bodies as competent athletes, they are either naive or fools," she said.

"I mean, what muscle group does the bare breast belong to?" she asked. "Let's at least be honest about what the purpose is: to have men buy those images of her and have her become part of locker room titillation."

Questions for Discussion and Writing

1. Huang points out that athletes in ancient Olympic Games often competed in the nude. But he also states that today's athletes have "the benefit of mass-circulation magazines and the Internet." What point is he trying to make? What impact has technology had on this issue?

2. Does Huang offer a balanced view of the controversy? How does he incorporate quotations from advocates of women's sports, for example? Why is it important to include the opposing viewpoint from an editor at *FHM* magazine? Evaluate Huang's use of argument and counterargument.

3. What impact did soccer player Brandi Chastain's actions have on this controversy? Are the other situations Huang describes different? What distinguishes between the actions of the athletes involved?

4. How could posing nude or provocatively *help* athletes in terms of their careers? Does Huang address these ideas?

5. Do an Internet search for Amy Acuff or some of the other names mentioned in this article. How many of the sites discuss the athletes' sports? How many are celebrity or entertainment sites? Look to see if the athletes have their own sites and how they represent themselves. Do the same with some prominent male athletes, such as David Beckham and LeBron James. Why isn't there much coverage of male athletes using the same marketing tactics?

Embracing Victory: Life Lessons on Competition and Compassion
MARIAH BURTON NELSON

Mariah Burton Nelson played basketball at Stanford University, where she graduated in 1978. She was the leading scorer all four years. She played professionally in France and in the United States' first women's professional league (before the WNBA), the Women's Basketball League or WBL. Since then, Nelson has written several books and hundreds of articles for publications such as The New York Times, Newsweek, Shape, Working Woman, Ms., Glamour, Cosmopolitan, Redbook, USA Today, Self, *and* Women's Sports & Fitness. *Her books include* We Are All Athletes *and* The Stronger Women Get, the More Men Love Football: Sexism and the American Culture of Sports. *She wrote the first nationally syndicated women's sports column for Knight-Ridder/Tribune newspapers and has appeared on the* Today *show,* Good Morning America, Larry King Live, *and* Crossfire. *As executive director of the American Association for Physical Activity and Recreation, Nelson is an advocate for lifelong participation in sports and recreation. In this excerpt from her book* Embracing Victory: Life Lessons on Competition and Compassion, *Nelson argues that female athletes can and should be as competitive as male athletes but that society frowns on such attitudes in women. She uses as an example the case of*

Olympic figure skater Nancy Kerrigan, who won silver instead of gold in part because she had been attacked by a friend of rival Tonya Harding.

———————— ✦ ————————

When she was young, Nancy Kerrigan wanted to play ice hockey with her older brothers. Her mother told her, "You're a girl. Do girl things."

Figure skating is a girl thing. Athletes in sequins and "sheer illusion sleeves" glide and dance, their tiny skirts flapping in the breeze. They achieve, but without touching or pushing anyone else. They win, but without visible signs of sweat. They compete, but not directly. Their success is measured not by confrontation with an opponent or even by a clock or a scoreboard. Rather, they are judged as beauty contestants are judged, by a panel of people who interpret the success of the routines. Prettiness is mandatory. Petite and groomed and gracious, figure skaters—like cheerleaders, gymnasts, and aerobic dancers—camouflage their competitiveness with niceness and prettiness until it no longer seems male or aggressive or unseemly.

The most popular sport for high school and college women to play is basketball. More than a million fans shelled out an average of $15 per ticket in 1997, the inaugural summer of the Women's National Basketball Association. But the most televised women's sport is figure skating. In 1995, revenue from skating shows and competitions topped six hundred million dollars. In the seven months between October 1996 and March 1997, ABC, CBS, NBC, Fox, ESPN, TBS, and USA dedicated 162.5 hours of programming to figure skating, half of it in prime time. Kerrigan earns up to three hundred thousand dollars for a single performance. National champion Michelle Kwan pocketed a million dollars in 1996.

Nearly 75 percent of the viewers of televised skating are women. The average age is between twenty-five and forty-five years old, with a household income of more than fifty thousand dollars. What are these women watching? What are they seeing? What's the appeal?

Like golf, tennis, and gymnastics, figure skating is an individual sport favored by white people from the upper classes. The skaters wear cosmetics, frozen smiles, and revealing dresses. Behind the scenes they lift weights and sweat like any serious athlete, but figure skating seems more dance than sport, more grace than guts, more art than athleticism. Figure skating allows women to compete like Champions while dressed like Cheerleaders.

In women's figure skating, smiling is part of "artistic expression." In the final round, if the competitors are of equal merit, artistry weighs more heavily than technique. Midori Ito, the best jumper in the history of women's skating, explained a weak showing at the world championships this way: "I wasn't 100 percent satisfied. . . . I probably wasn't smiling enough today in my performance. That could have been one of the problems with the competition."

At the 1988 Olympics, Debi Thomas wore a black unitard similar to an outfit her friend Brian Boitano used to wear. The Lycra accentuated her muscular thighs and looked more appropriate on her, somehow, than any four-inch skirt ever did. But she received poor marks for artistic impression, and soon afterward the International Skating Union rewrote the women's rules to outlaw unitards. Like pants, unitards are not girl things.

The media portray female figure skaters as "little girl dancers" or "fairy tale princesses" (NBC commentator John Tesh); as "elegant" (Dick Button); as "little angels" (Peggy Fleming); as "ice beauties" and "ladies who lutz" (*People* magazine). Commentators frame skaters as small, young, and decorative creatures, not superwomen but fairytale figments of someone's imagination.

After Kerrigan was assaulted by a member of Tonya Harding's entourage, she was featured on a *Sports Illustrated* cover crying, "Why me?" When she recovered to win a silver medal at the Olympics that year, she became "America's sweetheart," and rich to boot. But the princess turned pumpkin shortly after midnight, as soon as the ball was over and she stopped smiling and started speaking. Growing impatient during the Olympic medal ceremony while everyone waited for Oksana Baiul, Kerrigan grumbled, "Oh, give me a break, she's just going to cry out there again. What's the difference?" Later, asked whether she should have won, she complained, "I was so perfect. . . . I was flawless. . . ." Kerrigan's popularity took another nosedive when, surrounded by Mickey Mouse characters during a tour of Disney World, she observed, "This is so corny. . . ."

What were Kerrigan's crimes? That she felt too old to cavort with cartoon characters. Isn't she? That she expressed anger and disappointment—even bitterness and bad sportsmanship—about losing the gold. But wasn't she supposed to want to win? What happens to baseball players who, disappointed about losses, hit each other or spit on umpires? What happens to basketball players and football players and hockey players who fight? Men can't tumble from a princess palace because we don't expect them to be princesses in the first place, only athletes.

Americans fell out of love with Kerrigan not because they couldn't adore an athlete who lacked grace in defeat but because they couldn't adore a female athlete who lacked grace in defeat. They couldn't abide a Miss America who, instead of prettily waving her white gloves from atop the float, honestly commented on the absurdity of the situation. As soon as Kerrigan proved herself to be less than a charming prince the applause stopped. Three years later she claimed implausibly in *Sports Illustrated Women/ Sport*, "I never cared that much about winning."

Questions for Discussion and Writing

1. Nelson begins this piece with a story about Nancy Kerrigan wanting to play hockey but skating instead to satisfy her parents. How does this introduction appeal to you? What makes the story an effective (or ineffective) rhetorical strategy?

2. Read Nelson's second paragraph about figure skating and gymnastics. Is she being critical or condescending toward traditionally female sports? What do her word choice and tone tell you about her opinions? Examine the rest of the excerpt for critical, sarcastic, or opinionated word choice as well.

3. If beauty and femininity are prerequisites for success in sports such as figure skating and gymnastics, then how does society view males in these sports? How *should* we view male athletes in these sports? Does Nelson indicate her opinion?

4. Nelson offers statistics from the mid-1990s, when the WNBA was founded. If basketball is more popular than figure skating, then why do figure skaters earn so much more money? Do some research and see what today's female basketball players and figure skaters earn, how much television coverage they get, and how many endorsements they receive. What has changed since the 1990s? How so?

5. According to Nelson, what did society's reaction to Kerrigan's competitive behavior do to Kerrigan? What are the long-term consequences, not just for Nancy Kerrigan, but for all competitive female athletes? Is this idea Nelson's thesis? If so, how so?

Boys to Men: Sports Media—
Messages About Masculinity
A national poll of children, focus groups, and content analysis of sports programs and commercials
CHILDREN NOW

Children Now is a national advocacy organization. The organization's primary concern is promoting children's needs and prompting changes in public policy. To do so, the organization conducts research on issues related to children, seeks ways to promote a positive media environment for children such as appropriate television shows and video games, advocates for access to affordable health care for all children, and works to improve access to quality childcare, preschool, and after-school programs. Children Now also runs a Talking with Kids program that helps parents talk to children about issues like sex, drugs, and alcohol. The group's research is used and published by politicians and policy makers, business leaders, academics, and parents. Children Now commissioned this study, "Boys to Men," through Michael Messner, a nationally known sociologist and an expert on gender issues and sports. Messner's books include Power at Play: Sports and the Problem of Masculinity; Sex, Violence & Power in Sports: Rethinking Masculinity; *and* Taking the Field: Women, Men and Sports. *His work has been published in numerous journals and he is a past president of the North American Society for the Sociology of Sport. As you read, ask yourself why Children Now might have deemed this issue—sports media's impact on young boys—important enough to commission such a detailed study.*

———————— ✦ ————————

Sports programming plays a significant role in the media messages that American boys receive today. While a full range of American boys watch sports, the effects of their media consumption may differ depending on who they are and what messages are being sent. . . . Do girls receive the same messages that boys do? What roles do men and women play in the games, on the sidelines or during the commercial breaks? Who are the coaches, the commentators, and the voices of authority on these sports shows? How are violence and aggression presented in sports programming? Above all, how does sports programming affect a boy's sense of self and his potential?

By looking at the quality of a representative selection of sports programs and their accompanying commercials, Children Now begins to explore the many messages that sports programming—athletes, games, broadcast networks, commentators, promoters, commercials—presents to its audience.

ANALYZING SPORTS PROGRAMMING

Boys are five times more likely than girls to watch sports programs on a regular basis. On average, one out of three boys across all races watch every day. With its fundamentally male "cast"—athletes and anchors, coaches and commentators—sports programming sends uniquely powerful messages about masculine behavior.

- *Aggression and violence among men is depicted as exciting and rewarding behavior.* One of sports coverage's dominant messages is that the most aggressive athletes are rewarded. Viewers are continually immersed in images that highlight and commentary that praises athletes who most successfully employ physical, aggressive play, as well as toughness.
- *Athletes who are "playing with pain" or "giving up their body for the team" are often portrayed as heroes.* Commentators laud athletes who engage in dangerous plays or compete while injured; conversely, they sometimes criticize athletes who remove themselves from games due to injuries, often raising questions about their manhood. For example, a SportsCenter commentator asked, "Could the Dominator be soft?" when an NHL goalie decided to sit out a game due to a groin injury.
- *Commentators consistently use martial metaphors and language of war and weaponry to describe sports action.* On an average of nearly five times per hour of sports commentary, announcers describe action using terms such as "battle," "kill," "ammunition," "weapons," "professional sniper," "taking aim," "fighting," "shot in his arsenal," "reloading," "detonate," "squeezes the trigger," "exploded," "attack mode," "firing blanks," "blast," "explosion," "blitz," "point of attack," "lance through the heart," "gunning it," "battle lines are drawn," and "shotgun."

- *More than half of the children in our poll (57%) said they see violence in sports programs often.* When asked how often they see violence on sports programs, 15% said "a lot of the time" and 42% said "some of the time." As one 12 year-old boy remarked, "Yes, like in the sports games, the violence is, like, normal. They grab somebody and then just throw them or push them and they fall."

ANALYZING COMMERCIALS IN SPORTS PROGRAMMING

Whether it is TV commercial time, celebrity endorsement or tournament sponsorship, advertising plays an integral role in professional sports and a significant part of the messages that all young people receive from watching sports programming. Almost one quarter of the sample consisted of commercials (722 in total), selling products that ranged from automobiles and alcohol to fast food and video games. What do these engaging images and catchy phrases tell kids about sports, media, and themselves? What overall messages are boys getting from the sports shows that they watch the most, including the commercials?

Products

- *Automobiles, shows on the same network, and snacks/fast food are the primary products advertised on the sports programs that boys watch.* Automobile-related ads represented the largest proportion of recorded advertising across all programs (20.5% overall) and were the highest percentage of commercials for each sports program except Extreme Sports and the NFL. Following closely were ads for other shows on the same network (14.1% overall) and snack/fast food commercials (11% overall). Notably, alcohol advertisements were a significant proportion of commercials for all sports programs, except Extreme Sports and Wrestling.

Commercial Sponsorships and Tie-ins

In sports programming that boys consume, the relative invisibility of women magnifies the importance of the female images that do appear. Although women are more visible in the commercials than in the programs themselves, the frequency and quality of representation raises concerns.

- *Women often appear in stereotypical and/or background roles.* The images of women as sexual objects, prizes, and supportive props for men's success in sports programming are reinforced by the commercials that play during the games. On average, a sports programming viewer watching shows and commercials will see these images twice an hour.

  In commercials that feature both women and men, women are often cast as beautiful and sexual rewards for men who purchase the right product. A typical storyline involves the transformation of a formerly nerdy or insecure man who is now adored and desired by beautiful women. For example, a Keystone Light Beer commercial shown on ESPN Sports-Center features a nerdy White guy who drinks bitter beer and repulses women. After the character drinks Keystone Light, he is surrounded by two beautiful young women and proclaims, "I hope my wife's not watching!"

  Accordingly, some women are also cast as "controlling," "emotional" wives and girlfriends who must be rejected in favor of beautiful, sexy women. In a Sony PlayStation spot shown on Extreme Sports and during NBA games, a male is shown with a female watching a romantic film. The male is then ridiculed and taunted by cartoon characters for being "whipped," watching a "chick flick," and doomed to domestic chores. At the end of the commercial, the female is harassed by a cartoon clown and locked out of the room, while the male is playing a video game and accompanied by a big-breasted cartoon woman.

Self Images

- *Many sports programming commercials that boys watch play on male insecurities about being "man" enough.* A common formula in commercials is to play on the insecurities of the audience, convincing them that purchasing a particular product will help them overcome their fears, embarrassments, and shortcomings. In sports programming, many of the commercials play on male fears of being a geek or a nerd who is not cool, aggressive, or attractive to women. Commercials for products such as Rogaine (hair loss) feature formerly insecure, unattractive men who acquire confidence and success after using the product.

• *Traditionally masculine images of speed, danger, and aggression are often used in the sports programming commercials that boys watch.* Echoing the images that pervade sports programming, commercials often employ storylines that emphasize speed, danger, or aggressive behavior to attract viewers to their products. For example, 27% of the commercials on Extreme Sports place actors in such situations.

CONCLUSION

Ninety percent of our nation's boys regularly or often watch televised sports programs, with their accompanying commercial advertisements. What messages do boys and young men receive from these programs and ads? What values and ideas about gender, race, aggression, and violence are being promoted? How do these messages and images define what it takes to be a "real" man?

According to the sports programming that boys consume most, a real man is strong, tough, aggressive, and above all, a winner in what is still a man's world. To be a winner, he must be willing to compromise his own long-term health by showing guts in the face of danger, by fighting other men when necessary, and by "playing hurt" when he's injured. He must avoid being soft; he must be the aggressor, both on the "battle fields" of sports and in his consumption choices. Whether he is playing sports or making choices about which products to purchase, his aggressiveness will win him the ultimate prize: the adoring attention of beautiful women and the admiration of other men.

These messages are promoted, in varying degrees, in the NFL games, NBA games, MLB games, Extreme Sports, SportsCenter shows and in their accompanying commercials. In the dramatic spectacle of Professional Wrestling, these messages are most clear, presented to audiences as an almost seamless package. While there are differences across the various types of sports programs and commercials, the messages and images reinforce dominant themes outlined in this report—themes which can be summarized as a "televised sports masculinity formula." Recognizing the extraordinary number of boys who consume televised sports and its exceptional power to influence, more diverse media messages defining masculinity could powerfully influence the positive development of **boys to men.**

Commissioned by Children Now, this study was conducted by Michael A. Messner, PhD; Darnell Hunt, PhD; and Michele Dunbar, MA, from the Department of Sociology at the University of Southern California. The sample set of programming aired May 23-29, 1999. This study also incorporates findings from research conducted by Lake Snell Perry & Associates.

Questions for Discussion and Writing

1. The study analyzes the impact of sports media on boys through various perspectives, including commercials, athletes, and games themselves. As you read the study, try to decide which entity probably has the biggest impact on boys and why. Is it the advertising boys see in commercials? The athletes they view as role models? What evidence does the study provide to support the influence of each of these entities? Do you find yourself changing your mind as you read as a result of the evidence?

2. Watch the commercials during the sports segment of the news on two or three different channels. If you can, also watch a show like *SportsCenter* on ESPN. How are men and women portrayed? Keep a log of your observations and compare them to the results of this study.

3. Find a product that is endorsed by both male and female athletes—sports drinks, for example, or perhaps a clothing and equipment line such as Nike. Examine the print ads for the product online or in magazines. Are female athletes represented in the same way as male athletes? Are they dressed more provocatively or the same? Do they appear as athletic? How might these ads impact young boys?

4. Though our first thoughts regarding advertising are of women being exploited, what about men? Think about commercials that make men feel inferior in some way, especially if they are portrayed as not manly enough. What qualities does it require to be manly and how are these qualities conveyed to young boys? How effectively does the study examine this issue?

5. Analyze the organizational structure of the study. How well did the writers organize the vast amount of research and statistics into a readable document? Point out areas that are clear and understandable as well as those you think need clarity.

Dropping Men's Sports—Expanding Opportunities for Girls and Women in Sport Without Eliminating Men's Sports: The Foundation Position

WOMEN'S SPORTS FOUNDATION

The Women's Sports Foundation exists to "advance the lives of girls and women through sport and physical activity." Founded in 1974 by tennis legend Billie Jean King, the Foundation offers educational programs, services, and national initiatives to help girls and women advance in sports. Past board members and volunteers include several Olympic medalists, such as softball player Lisa Fernandez, gymnast Dominique Dawes, and figure skater Peggy Fleming, plus entertainers such as Holly Hunter, Sheryl Crow, and Geena Davis. The Women's Sports Foundation has become a source of research and opinion for many sports organizations, politicians, and school leaders. Part of the Foundation's mission is to make its position clear on controversial issues. When the Title IX law was passed in 1972, it was credited with improving girls' sports in schools and colleges. But many also criticized the law for harming or eliminating boys' sports. The assumption was that to add opportunities for girls, schools had to take away opportunities for boys. In this position statement, the Foundation asserts that it does not agree with taking opportunities away from male athletes and that there are other ways to create equality. Half of the statement is a position argument and half seems like a proposal. Do the two parts work together effectively?

◆

The Women's Sports Foundation is often asked whether it has a position on the elimination of sports opportunities for men as a method of complying with Title IX of the Education Amendments of 1972, the federal law that prohibits sex discrimination in educational programs or activities at schools and colleges that receive federal funds. This question usually stems from situations in which schools cite insufficient finances to add more sports opportunities for women, cut a men's non-revenue sport and use these funds to start a new women's team. When alumni and students complain about the decision, the institution blames the law (Title IX requires no such reduction in opportunities for men) and female athletes. The Foundation is not in favor of reducing athletic opportunities for men as the preferred method of achieving Title IX compliance.

The real problem can be simply described. Your first two children are boys. You give them everything. Their rooms are palaces of athletics privilege—full of every sport gift imaginable—gloves, balls, bats, hockey sticks, football helmets, etc. They go to two or three sport camps every summer. They play Little League Baseball, soccer and Pop Warner football. One becomes an outstanding football player and the other excels in tennis. Then, you have another child, a girl, and your income doesn't change. She comes to you one day and says, "Mom, Dad—I want to play sports." What are your options?

Option A: Tell your last born son (i.e., drop the men's tennis team) he can't play sports any more so you still have only two children to provide for.

Option B: Tell your daughter she can't have the same privileges as her brothers. If she want[s] a glove she has to go to work and save up to buy it. Tell her she can't go to a summer sports camp unless she earns her own money and pays for it herself. Suggest that she sell cookies or get together with her girlfriends to have a bake sale (this is the way it was before Title IX) to scrape up enough money for equipment to play.

Option C: You gather the family around the kitchen table and explain to your children that your daughter is just as important as your sons and you don't have the dollars to provide the same privileges for your daughter as you did for your sons . . . but that you are going to try your best to give all of your children every opportunity to participate in sports. You tell your sons that it is important to share their equipment and all you have provided for them. You probably come up with a system where each child gets to choose one summer sports camp instead of each attending several. The family gives up spring vacation in Disney World and tightens its belt. Everyone sacrifices and each child makes do with a smaller piece of the pie because now there are three (the Title IX situation).

The solution is Option C. Institutions that are dropping men's teams are choosing Option A not because of Title IX, but because they are being terrible parents (educational leaders). The answer to Title IX is very simple: If revenues don't increase, then everyone must make do with a smaller piece of the budget pie. The NCAA and its athletic conferences are simply refusing to legislate lower costs and a lower standard of living for men's sports in order to free up money for new women's teams.

Men's revenue sports are issuing threats regarding their own demise if their budgets are reduced in any way. First, tightening a sport's budget will not cause this sport business to fail. Commercial entities initiate such cost cuts every day to eliminate fat, increase profit margins and satisfy stock holders.

Second, and more important, there can never be an economic justification for discrimination. No one should ever be permitted to say that I can't comply with the law because I can't afford it. It is the same as saying, "I should be allowed to practice racism (or sexism) if I can't afford to initiate a change in the way I live or do business."

Using an employment discrimination example, the analogy would be that reducing the salaries of all employees is the preferred method of generating funds in an effort to increase salaries for the group that has historically experienced discrimination. This never happens. Rather, the salaries of the disadvantaged gender or individuals are always raised to the level of the advantaged group. As in the area of salary discrimination, the goal should be to bring the treatment of the group experiencing discrimination up to the level of the group that has received fair treatment, not to bring male athletes in minor sports down to the level of female athletes who simply were not provided with opportunities to play.

Even worse, when an institution eliminates a men's team in the name of Title IX, such action usually results in the development of destructive acrimony, pitting the men's non-revenue sports against women's sports. Alumni of the dropped men's sport get upset. An unnecessary domino effect results in the development of attitudes antithetical to solving discrimination in the long run. Gains for the underrepresented group come grudgingly and at a high cost to the previously advantaged group.

The last alternative should be cutting opportunities for students to participate in an educational activity. Other solutions, in order of preference, that should be considered are:

1. *Raising new revenues.* Gender equity can be used as an opportunity to raise new funds in much the same way as the need for a new building is used to initiate a capital campaign. However, it is essential that there be a positive spin on alumni solicitations for this purpose like adding one or two dollars to the current price of all sport tickets "so our daughters will have an equal chance to play" and other similarly creative revenue solutions. "Providing an equal opportunity for women to participate in varsity athletics" is also an excellent theme for an annual giving campaign targeted to female alumnae and supporters.

   The demographic shift in higher education toward increasing percentages of women in undergraduate and graduate schools must also be noted. These are future generations of alumnae. Any position which antagonizes a group of future donors to the institution is short-sighted.

   Presidential or school principal leadership is essential. The institution has the choice of "taking the high ground" and calling upon alumni and supporters of men's sports to "dig deeper" so our daughters are given the same chances to play as our sons, or pitting the have-nots against the have-nots by cutting men's sports teams. At many institutions, the resentment against Title IX has prevented athletic directors from "seeing the forest for the trees." The result has been the adoption of less than exemplary solutions to a very difficult problem.

2. *Reducing excess expenditures on the most expensive men's sports and using the savings to expand opportunities and treatment for the underrepresented gender.* There are many expenditures in the budgets of well-funded sports which can be eliminated without having a negative impact on either competitiveness vis-a-vis other institutions or the quality of the athletics experience. Such reductions include: provision of hotel rooms the night before home contests, ordering new uniforms less frequently, reducing the distance traveled for non-conference competition by selecting others as competitive opponents in closer geographic proximity, etc.

3. *Athletic Conference Cost-Saving.* The conference can adopt across-the-board mandated cost reductions that will assist all

schools in saving funds while ensuring that the competitive playing field remains level (i.e., travel squad limits, adding the same sports for the underrepresented gender at the same time in order to ensure competition within a reasonable geographic area, etc.).

4. *Internal Across-the-Board Budget Reductions.* All sports can be asked to cut their budgets by a fixed percentage, thereby allowing each sport to choose the way it might least be affected, to free up funds for expanded opportunities for women. This method is preferred in that it does not have a disproportionate impact on low-budget sports.

5. *Moving to a Lower Competitive Division.* At the college level, Division I programs can move to Division IAA or Division II competition, thereby reducing scholarship and other expenses.

6. *Using Tuition Waiver Savings to Fund Gender Equity.* States can initiate legislation which provides for waiver of higher education tuition for athletic scholarships to members of the underrepresented gender, similar to the law adopted by the State of Washington. This legislation mandates the use of these scholarship savings to expand opportunities for the underrepresented gender. Such initiatives recognize that correcting gender inequities is an institutional obligation, not just an athletic department issue. There are other precedents for states to enact laws which confer financial relief in an effort to remedy widespread discrimination. The states of Washington, Florida and Minnesota have all enacted state laws to provide funding to achieve gender equity in athletics.

Unfortunately, at most institutions, it is easier for a college president to cut wrestling or men's gymnastics than to deal with the politics of reducing the football or men's basketball budgets. Simply put, educational leaders need to demonstrate better leadership and do the right thing.

Questions for Discussion and Writing

1. The authors use an analogy of a family to illustrate their point that taking away from one to give to another is wrong. Does the analogy work as effective writing? Why or why not?

2. The Foundation argues that controlling budget and finances can help create equality in sports. What evidence do you see on your own campus that budgets might need to be equalized? Take a tour of the athletic facilities on your

campus or one nearby. Does everyone have ample workout equipment? Are the practice fields and courts well maintained? What do the locker rooms look like? Are any of the facilities "fancier" or obviously more expensive than others? Write down your observations. Then analyze your findings. Do the facilities have anything to do with gender? Does your school spend more on men's sports or women's, or is there a balance?

3. The position states that "there can never be an economic justification for discrimination" and compares such an argument to acceptable racism. Do you agree with this statement? Are there cases when economics could justify some sort of discrimination? Does your opinion impact whether or not you are convinced by this argument?

4. Examine the Foundation's suggestions for other ways to balance costs. Which ones seem logical and feasible? Which ones seem too difficult to implement? Why? In what ways is this argument both a position and a proposal?

5. Write a letter to a leader on your campus: the athletic director, a group of coaches, or perhaps even the president. Argue (respectfully) some strategies that might help your school balance costs in men's and women's sports. Use evidence from this position if you like and find more evidence for your argument online or in print publications.

Making Connections: Writing

1. Compare the rules of the All-American Girls Professional Baseball League, such as attending charm school, obeying chaperones, and wearing uniforms, to Mariah Burton Nelson's remarks on the rules of figure skating. How are they the same? How are they different? Based on this comparison, how much have women's sports changed?

2. Controversial issues often prompt public outcries or calls for change. Of the issues discussed in this chapter, research which ones have prompted the most response from the public. Compare the responses and analyze the public's role in creating change.

3. Female baseball players and figure skaters have rules to follow but so do men and boys, according to Michael Messner's research for Children Now. Interview a male and a female athlete about the rules of his or her sport. Which of the rules are enforced for safety or because they are traditional rules of the game and which of the rules are there because of society's perceptions of femininity and masculinity?

4. One of the concerns that Thomas Huang brings up in his article on female athletes using their sex appeal is that these athletes risk destroying years of work by their predecessors to tear down stereotypes about women. Consider

what supporters of Title IX might think about this issue. Write a letter to the Women's Sports Foundation stating your position on the controversy. Back up your claims with support.

5. Patricia Vignola traces the impact of the All-American Girls Professional Baseball League and Thomas Huang discusses female athletes who have competed alongside men in the Olympics. Research an event or person of historical significance in sports and gender, whether it's a co-ed competition or a particular man or woman who broke gender boundaries. Write a profile analyzing the impact of that person or event on contemporary gender issues in sports.

6. The authors of the selections in this chapter write in very different styles. Take an issue discussed in one selection and re-write it in the style or rhetorical mode of a different selection. For example, you might write about the impact of sports advertising on young boys as an historical analysis much like Patricia Vignola writes about the All-American Girls Professional Baseball League. You might write a position statement on athletes using their sex appeal in the same form that the Women's Sports Foundation takes a position on Title IX. Or you might write about competition from the perspective of boys as discussed in the Children Now piece rather than from the perspective of women as Mariah Burton Nelson does with Nancy Kerrigan.

7. Write an exploratory essay on either femininity or masculinity. What is the historical definition of each? How have definitions changed? Find some examples of the ideal of each. You might even incorporate photos into your essay to support your ideas.

8. The report for Children Now discusses how boys view females in sports. Mariah Burton Nelson shows how society reacted to Nancy Kerrigan when she showed the competitive spirit normally associated with a man. Write an essay based on a personal experience you have had competing with the opposite gender. Don't limit your experience to a sporting event but write about a time you competed on anything: a musical contest, an academic competition, or perhaps a debate.

9. Respond to the side with which you disagree on an issue in this chapter. If you disagree that women are treated unfairly in sports, for example, respond to Thomas Huang's article on sex appeal or the Women's Sports Foundation's position on Title IX. If you do feel that women are treated unfairly in sports, respond to Children Now's selection on the media's impact on boys.

10. Analyze the construction of two or more arguments in this chapter. For example, what are the differences between the Women's Sports Foundation's position on Title IX and the newspaper article on athletes using sex appeal? Write about the evidence each piece uses, the organization of each piece, and how well each writer addresses the audience.

Books Worth Reading

A Place on the Team: The Triumph and Tragedy of Title IX by Welch Suggs. Journalist examines the successes, failures, opportunities, and pressures of the Title IX law.

A Whole New Ball Game: The Story of the All-American Girls Professional Baseball League by Sue Macy. Provides an historical and social background of the League.

Girls of Summer: The U.S. Women's Soccer Team and How They Changed the World by Jere Longman. Compares the 1999 World Cup victory with the USA men's hockey team triumph in the 1980 Olympics.

Inside Edge: A Revealing Journey Into the Secret World of Figure Skating by Christine Brennan. Sports reporter examines the competitive world of figure skating.

In These Girls Hope Is a Muscle: A True Story of Hoop Dreams and One Very Special Team by Madeleine Blais. Pulitzer-Prize winning journalist tells the story of a high school girls' basketball championship season; female companion to *Friday Night Lights*.

Little Girls in Pretty Boxes: The Making and Breaking of Elite Gymnasts and Figure Skaters by Joan Ryan. Journalist examines the struggles—including sometimes fatal eating disorders—of elite Olympic athletes.

Marathon Woman: Running the Race to Revolutionize Women's Sports by Kathrine Switzer. Runner recounts her struggle to establish women's marathon as an Olympic sport, even after being attacked by a director of the Boston Marathon in 1967 in an effort to get her ejected from the all-male race.

Nike Is a Goddess: The History of Women in Sports edited by Lissa Smith. A collection of 12 original narratives, each on the top female athletes in a particular sport.

Taking the Field: Women, Men and Sports by Michael Messner. Argues that despite changes, sports still differentiate between men and women.

Women at Play: The Story of Women in Baseball by Barbara Gregorich. A photographic and historical examination of women who have played baseball.

Films Worth Watching

A League of Their Own (1992). Fictional, but includes a lot of accurate history of the All-American Girls Professional Baseball League.

Dare to Compete: The Struggle of Women in Sports (1999). An HBO documentary that explores issues in women's sports such as racism, sexism, and homophobia.

Heart Like a Wheel (1983). Based on the life of Shirley "Cha Cha" Muldowney, the first woman licensed to drive a Top Fuel dragster; find it if you can. Nominated for an Oscar.

Sites Worth Surfing

http://www.womenssportsfoundation.org
Site of the Women's Sports Foundation advocacy organization.

http://www.aagpbl.org/
Home page of the All-American Girls Professional Baseball League.

http://www.iwflsports.com/
Official site of the Independent Women's Football League. Also see

http://www.womensfootballassociation.com/
The National Women's Football Association.

Trash-Talk or Free Speech:
What Do Words Mean
in Sports?

As we conclude *Sports Talk* with this chapter, we end much where we began—with a discussion of sports' impact on writing, reading, and language. We don't often associate words with sports—words are typically thought to be intellectual, while sports might seem more tangible and physical. But the two are more related than we might think. Consider this: An athlete can hardly voice an opinion without prompting responses from writers, broadcasters, fans, and critics. Sports often "speak" for our culture and what we represent—or want to represent. The language associated with our sports can help define us, both to each other as well as to others around the world. Many of our words and phrases originated from sports. Likewise, many sports words and phrases originated from other facets of American culture such as business. And our language, like our athletes and sports, often creates controversy. Like sports, rhetoric is pervasive in American society. Combine the two—sports and rhetoric—and you find a powerful force in America. Chapter 6 examines such issues.

Some of the reading selections in this chapter revolve around the negative uses of language in sports. An article from *The Chronicle of Higher Education*, for example, examines how "free speech" at colleges and universities sometimes turns into the use of vulgar and offensive language. When do students' rights take a back seat to the rights of spectators and athletes on opposing teams? And should students watch their language when impressionable children are at sporting events? In another article, David Haugh of the *Chicago Tribune* examines what he calls "competitive rhetoric," better known as trash-talking, or the practice of taunting an athlete or a team.

195

Trash-talking can range from the innocent Little League chimes "Hey batter, batter!" to personal and offensive remarks about an athlete's family or personal hardships. Former teacher Nancy Huppertz, in "The Importance of Language," focuses on language bias related to women and argues that writers and broadcasters—and society, overall—must do more to avoid making women feel inferior in athletics. While not overtly offensive, terms like the "Lady" Bearcats in reference to a women's team belittle women as second-class in sports.

Not all of the reading selections examine language from a negative standpoint, though. Steve Rushin, known for his more lighthearted, sometimes humorous pieces in *Sports Illustrated*, offers an introductory roundup of words and phrases associated with sports. Some originated in sports but are seeping into other areas of culture, such as calling the practice of "holding five-year-olds back from kindergarten an extra year . . . redshirting." Other phrases are taken from their origins and applied to sports, as in the football player who "can play the piano" because he can fend off blockers with his hands while running with his legs. On a more serious note, professor Ann E. Cudd makes the link between sports metaphors and business in the United States in her journal article, "Sporting Metaphors: Competition and the Ethos of Capitalism." She makes the point that competition is the common thread in both sports and capitalism, as evidenced by phrases such as "no pain, no gain" for athletes and managers who must make difficult decisions, and "marathon" for a long day at work.

The reading selections cover not only a variety of issues in this chapter, but a variety of writing models. Hoover's piece on fan speech in colleges, for example, seems to be primarily a report. It's not without bias or opinion but it seeks primarily to engage readers in the topic. Haugh's piece on trash-talk, however, though it also appeared in a newspaper, seems to offer more argument or opinion. He often quotes sources to support his claim that athletes would be better off if they ignored trash-talking. Huppertz clearly makes an argument for inclusive language in her piece, beginning with a powerful opening that "the power to persuade begins with language." She also ends the essay with instructions on how to enforce her proposed argument. Cudd, while she does make an argument, uses more scholarly evidence than anecdote. And Rushin takes the opposite approach, writing in a conversational and even humorous tone.

Notice how the selections are also aimed at various audiences. Some are meant for a general readership through newspapers. Even those, however, are probably aimed at sports fans because of the topics. Hoover's piece from the *Chronicle* is aimed at a specific audience. Cudd's analysis is aimed at a scholarly audience. Can you identify the audience for Huppertz's piece?

Finally, the reading selections in this chapter relate to many of the issues earlier in this reader. For example, each culture has its own system of slang and popular words and phrases. Consider how trash-talk might be different in the United States (Chapter 1) than it is in other countries (Chapter 2). Would a sports fan from a socialist economy understand Cudd's thesis in her journal article on the metaphor for capitalism? It would be interesting to examine the impact of sports language on economies other than capitalism. Sometimes language can provoke violence, the issue in Chapter 3. How many times have riots broken out, both in college and in professional sports, because of something a fan or athlete said? How often do athletes on the floor or field come to fists because of something one of them said to the other? Speech or language can also impact racial (Chapter 4) and gender (Chapter 5) issues. Sportswriters and broadcasters must be careful not to use language with racial or gender-biased undertones that might insult or offend someone.

This chapter serves to help you connect the relationship between words and sports. The two are not exclusive. Have you ever thought about how many of the words and phrases you use originated in sports? Have you ever examined your own speech at games when you were passionate about your team? Is language a positive or negative force in sports? What do you think?

Crying Foul Over Fans' Boorish Behavior
ERIC HOOVER

Eric Hoover is a reporter for The Chronicle of Higher Education, *a weekly print newspaper and daily online source of news and information for college and university faculty and administrators.* The Chronicle *is known for its in-depth news reports and lively discussion forums in academia. Hoover has reported on varied issues in higher education, but a few stand out as related to rhetoric or language. For example, he reported from the campus of Virginia Tech in 2007 when 32 people were killed by a gunman and interviewed dozens of students who "couldn't stop talking about the horrible things he [the gunman] had said on his video tapes." He has also written about the controversy of free speech vs. student rights in campus codes of conduct and about the sometimes controversial language used when media rank colleges and universities. This article was published in* The Chronicle *in 2004 and examines whether students should be allowed to use profanity or insulting language at sporting events.*

—————————— ✦ ——————————

The final buzzer sounded at the National Collegiate Athletic Association men's basketball championship this week, ending a season in which student spectators cheered, jeered, and hurled four-letter words.

In sports arenas throughout the nation, boos have become passé, and fans are getting personal.

During a basketball game at the University of Kentucky last month, for instance, students both chanted "Matt is gay" at Matt Walsh, a forward on the visiting University of Florida team, and then hoisted signs that insulted his girlfriend, a *Playboy* magazine Playmate.

In January students at Iowa State University yelled "rapist!" at Pierre Pierce, a guard for the University of Iowa who pleaded guilty to a[n] assault-causing-injury charge in 2002.

Last December students at Florida taunted D.J. Strawberry, a guard for the University of Maryland at College Park, by referring to the drug problems of his father, Darryl Strawberry, a former professional baseball player.

Incivility at sporting events is as old as blood-boiling collegiate rivalries, and perhaps, just as inevitable. Still, some administrators, tired of plugging their ears, are trying to promote more tasteful cheering—a delicate task in an era when students believe they have a right to say what they please while supporting the home team.

Although some institutions, including St. Joseph's University, boot students out of arenas for bad language, many colleges tolerate isolated showers of expletives in deference to fans' free-speech rights. But some legal experts say both public and private colleges can prohibit indecent language at athletics events without stomping on the First Amendment.

Last month an assistant attorney general of Maryland advised the state's flagship institution that it could constitutionally restrict vulgar chants and signs at games with a "carefully drafted policy."

Even if the law supports them, college officials who have confronted the issue say efforts to clean up speech must include—if not begin with—students themselves. Lectures or warnings from administrators alone might not inspire anyone to put soap in his own mouth.

"It has to sink in with students at some kind of a voluntary level that they are fouling their own nest," says Gary M. Pavela, director of judicial programs at Maryland. "If your dominant image of a particular university is that of a howling, obscene mob, then you are not going to be favorably disposed."

VULGAR DISPLAYS

Maryland's administrators had red faces after a nationally televised home basketball game against Duke University on January 21 [2004]. Dozens of students at the game sported T-shirts that applied the F-word to the visiting team. They also chanted an expletive at J.J. Redick, a Duke guard who scored a game-high 26 points.

National sports commentators lampooned the Terrapins' fans. Maryland alumni, some of whom had taken their children to the game, complained about the coarse language, a recurring problem at basketball games. (Students have long chanted, "Hey, you suck!" at visiting players before tipoff.)

After the Duke game, Maryland's president, C.D. Mote Jr., asked the state attorney general's office if the university had any latitude to adopt a speech policy prohibiting offensive language at athletics events.

In a March 17 letter to Mr. Mote obtained by *The Chronicle*, John K. Anderson, the state's chief counsel for educational affairs, advised the university that such a policy was feasible. "While First Amendment law is complex, it does not seem reasonable for the university to be utterly without any means to address a phenomenon that has proved to be upsetting to large numbers of fans," Mr. Anderson wrote. "The applicable case law does not, in my view, leave the university powerless."

In his analysis, Mr. Anderson noted that the speech policy could not include criminal punishments, citing *Cohen v. California*, a 1971 case in which the U.S. Supreme Court held that states could not remove a particular word, however offensive, from the public's vocabulary: "One man's vulgarity," Justice John Marshall Harlan wrote in the majority opinion, "is another's lyric."

The speech in question at Maryland is constitutionally protected because it is neither defamatory nor obscene under the Supreme Court's definition. Nonetheless, Mr. Anderson wrote that the court's reasoning, in *Cohen* and in other cases, suggested that states could regulate "lewd or profane words" in specific locations, particularly those where "captive auditors," including children, are present.

At Maryland's arena, he wrote, "offensive language comes without warning . . . people attending the game cannot avoid it by averting their eyes. They are captives whose only recourse is to leave the stadium or stop attending games."

The university would have to word such a policy carefully, ensuring it was neither too broad nor too vague. Maryland would also have to publicize the restrictions, train its arena personnel to enforce it, and perhaps provide a means of contesting sanctions, which could include ejection from the arena and campus-judiciary punishments for students.

Such "practical problems" might persuade the university to regulate speech only if all other means were ineffective, Mr. Anderson concluded.

Officials at the university say they will consider a speech policy, among other strategies, over the summer.

Maryland's Mr. Pavela concedes that enforcing a speech restriction may be impractical: Sending a battalion of security officers after swearing students could spawn "First Amendment martyrs" who might cause a greater stir than foul-mouthed fans.

But he says the university can refer to the nuances of the law to inform discussions of sportsmanship among students, who tend to believe the First Amendment protects them against any restraint of expression.

"If we frame it at the outset as a punishment issue, then we will probably lose—then it's not about the sportsmanship standards involved," Mr. Pavela says. "We've got to get students to think. . . . we're not just dealing with the First Amendment rights of speakers, but also with the rights of people in the audience."

'DOING THEIR PART'

Some athletics conferences have confronted the issue with policy changes. Last summer the Big Ten passed new crowd-control measures, stating that it would hold colleges "responsible" for student sections that singled out athletes for verbal abuse. But those measures do not include procedures for disciplining or ejecting students during games.

One complication for colleges is that students know that administrators welcome most of the noise they make. Coaches encourage students to make their home courts "hostile" environments, places their opponents fear. Some arenas were designed to intimidate: At Maryland's new Comcast Center, the stands behind the visitor's basket during the second half rise at a steep angle, thrusting a "wall of fans" into the action.

So how do administrators ask students to go crazy, but not too crazy?

"It's very difficult in a college setting because you're trying to market to different groups," says Bob D'Amelio, an assistant athletics director at Western Michigan University. "You want students there, you want families there, you want them to coexist peacefully."

Athletics officials say students tend to listen to appeals from coaches and players. After Western Michigan students rained the F-word on a referee during an ice-hockey game a few years ago, the university's hockey coach took the ice before the following game and urged students to refrain from swearing.

Mr. D'Amelio says that fans' behavior improved, though some problems endure. When a player on the visiting team goes to the penalty box, some students continue to yell, "See ya, bitch!"

Security officers occasionally remove fans for shouting the F-word. (Mr. D'Amelio could only remember one such instance this season.) Students who get booted must report to the campus judiciary office, where they receive "verbal reprimands," Mr. D'Amelio says.

Some colleges recommend that coaches talk to students at the beginning of the season, before problems arise. Broadcasting reminders about sportsmanship from coaches or players just before big games may help, too. Western Michigan's code of conduct for sporting events, which includes warnings about using abusive language, is read over the public-address system before each game and posted in the arena.

Daniel L. Wann, a professor of social psychology at Murray State University and the editor of *Sports Fans: The Psychology and Social Impact of Spectators* (Routledge, 2001), says students are more likely to engage in verbal abuse when facing a bitter rival whom "they perceive as a threat."

Persuading fans to root a certain way is not easy, though, given that many of them believe they can influence the outcome of a game.

"When fans yell at officials, there's no belief in their mind that it will help the team—it's just aggression," Mr. Wann says. "But when they yell at opposing players, they feel like they're helping the team win, doing their part."

Students are matter of fact about why they give visiting teams hell.

"We get into their heads," says Donald Wine, a senior at Duke and a member of the university's infamous "Cameron Crazies," who see themselves less as spectators than as participants in basketball games.

Mr. Wine gets so worked up in the stands that he spends hours afterwards just sitting around, chugging orange juice and vitamins. He is certain, though, that he and his fellow Crazies helped limit Julius Hodge, North Carolina State University's star forward, to just seven points on January 15 by chanting "anything and everything" at him all night.

Duke students pride themselves on creative cheers and publicly eschew the use of expletives. Their philosophy stems from a 1984 letter Terry Sanford, then the president of Duke, sent to students, criticizing them for their "crudeness, profanity, and cheapness" during games. The missive, which Mr. Sanford titled "An Avuncular Letter," urged students to clean up their language and to "taunt with style."

But Duke fans have their four-letter lapses, as some Crazies admit. When playing host to its hated rival, the University of North Carolina at Chapel Hill, Mr. Wine says, the "line" distinguishing appropriate from inappropriate fan behavior shifts, allowing for more vicious and personal jibes.

Among student fans, politeness is a relative term. Before the game against Maryland this season, some Duke students debated whether they should taunt Mr. Strawberry about his father's drug abuse (one idea was to fill sandwich bags with sugar and shake the "cocaine" at him). The Crazies decided against the tactic, though decency was not necessarily the deciding factor.

"Strawberry was not a big threat," explains Matt Kawecki, a senior at Duke. "It wouldn't have been worth any sort of fallout."

The Crazies usually enjoy a good relationship with Duke's athletics department and Mike Krzyzewski, the men's basketball coach, who also tells fans when their chants cross the line.

Other colleges cite communication between students and administrators as a key to improving fan behavior.

After students at Stanford University hoisted fake joints to taunt a visiting player with a drug history in the late 1990s, administrators told them the stunt was too personal. Now the athletics department regularly discusses its expectations with leaders of the student fan group.

At the University of Missouri, a notorious student group known as the Antlers lost its priority seating at basketball games because the athletics department became frustrated with the students' "questionable" chants and signage, says Chad Moller, the university's director of sports information.

Now Missouri reserves prime seats for two university-approved groups, the Student Athletic Board and the Zoo Crew, which both emphasize sportsmanship. Each group has a faculty sponsor, "which lends them a little more credibility," Mr. Moller says.

A CULTURE CHANGE?

Following the game against Duke in College Park, Coach Gary Williams talked to students about the importance of appropriate behavior. Fans did not reprise their profane January performance for the rest of the season.

Administrators at the university are working with student leaders to develop a game plan for better sportsmanship.

In February Ben Maggin, a senior at Maryland who was frustrated by the four-letter jeers, created "the Sixth Man," a student group that plans to organize more-creative—and decent—cheers in the next season. Within weeks of its founding, more than a hundred students had signed up to help.

Mr. Maggin, who has attended Terrapins games since he was a child, attributes students' bad behavior to "a combination of frustration and not having anything else to say."

He encountered some resistance from students who worried that he was trying to stifle their passion, but Mr. Maggin says the group will not dictate how fans behave—just provide a presence that might help prevent "a lapse back into profanity."

And there are indications that wit may replace invective in the stands. Recently some Maryland students appeared at games holding signs that read "Expletive" and "I dislike the other team."

Questions for Discussion and Writing

1. Hoover points out that college administrators are trying to get students to tame their behavior "in an era when students believe they have a right to say what they please while supporting the home team." The key word in this sentence is *believe*. What rights do students have? Is this a free speech issue or an issue of college rules?

2. Write about a personal experience you have had with profanity and insults at a sporting event. You might write from the perspective of an athlete, a spectator, or even the person using the language. How did the experience impact you?

3. Hoover describes the lengthy process a college would have to go through in order to restrict speech. Knowing how difficult legal jargon can be to understand, read Hoover's explanations. Does he effectively explain information without using "legalese"? Give specific examples from the text.

4. Why do students yell at games? Hoover quotes a social psychology professor who claims that students yell at officials just to release aggression, but they yell at opposing players because they think they're helping the team. What is your opinion? What are other possible reasons?

5. Other than pointing out a few expletives by students, Hoover waits until more than halfway through the article to quote a student. Is that strategy fair to students? Why or why not? How does the publication's audience impact Hoover's organization?

Trash-Talk? Hear No Evil: Barbs May Cross Line, But Athletes Hurt Only Themselves by Taking Bait

DAVID HAUGH

As a football player at Ball State University in Indiana, David Haugh was part of the school's 1989 Mid-American Conference champion team. He went on to earn a master's degree from Northwestern University and spent a decade covering Notre Dame football for the

South Bend (Ind.) Tribune. *In 2000 Ball State's journalism program honored Haugh with a Young Alumnus Award. Haugh began his career at the* Chicago Tribune *as a beat writer covering the Chicago Bears football team. Some of his essays appear in the newspaper's book* Super Bears: The Remarkable Story of the 2006 Chicago Bears. *This article appeared in the* Chicago Tribune *in 2006.*

———————————— ✦ ————————————

Earplugs.
    World Cup peace might have been preserved if the French soccer team simply had supplied captain Zinedine Zidane with something to block out the noise. That way Zidane never would have heard Italian instigator Marco Materazzi insult his mother or sister in the Cup final, according to a man few would disagree is an expert in trash-talking.

"A $3 set of earplugs and Zidane could have ignored it, kicked the winning goal and given Materazzi something to think about for four years, but instead he lost it like Ron Artest," said Robin Ficker, a notorious NBA fan who knows all about using words to try to push athletes over the edge.

Ficker, a lawyer from Bethesda, Md., once showed up at an NBA game holding a sign that read "Ason" when Jason Kidd was in town to play the Washington Wizards. Kidd asked why.

"Because you've got no 'J,'" Ficker retorted, referring to his jump shot.

Ficker got under Larry Bird's skin by calling him Larry Nerd, waved money in Michael Jordan's face in the midst of gambling rumors and used to heckle NBA players so incessantly from the first row of U.S. Airways Arena that more than a few threw drinks in his face.

"I'd tell them it was the only thing they hit all night, and they'd call me many F-words besides Ficker," said Ficker, 63. "But I never made any racial or sexual remarks or ever about their children or mom. (He did once invoke the names of Scottie Pippen's ex-girlfriends.) It was all in fun.

"If Zidane would have just answered with humor to [Materazzi], then he might have stuck around to kick the winning goal."

Instead, if you missed the soccer version of the Zapruder film last week, Zidane responded to the insult with a head butt on Materazzi and received a red card that cost France its best player for the remaining 10 minutes of overtime and the crucial penalty shootout that ultimately decided the World Cup.

Besides giving Jay Leno more fodder for France jokes, Zidane's visceral reaction raised questions about where the line exists for athletes who use trash-talking either to motivate themselves or to antagonize their opponents. The outcry also stirred debate over what type of personal insult in the heat of action might justify retaliation as shocking as a head butt.

"I don't care what that guy called his mother or sister, he's the captain of that team at the most important time of the game, so he was stupid to respond," said Steve McMichael, an outspoken former Bears defensive tackle who heard his share of insults. "It can get nasty, but if you're getting trash-talked, it just motivates you to play even harder."

IT'S NOTHING NEW

Documented trash-talk dates back to the beginnings of baseball in the late 19th Century, when Hall of Fame manager John McGraw would annoy opponents with constant barbs from the dugout. Ty Cobb once was said to have barked at an opponent, "Don't come back until you have a note signed by your mama!"

In the NBA, as the league evolved in the 1960s, centers Bill Russell and Wilt Chamberlain started going at each other in the paint—and between the ears.

"In the 1965 playoffs," Russell wrote in his autobiography, "I said [to Chamberlain]: 'I never thought I would see the day when you would push me.'

"To which he replied: 'Cut that out, baby. You ain't psyching me.'"

By the contemporary era, trash-talking had spread from the playgrounds to professional sports because it generally stayed more humorous than hurtful. Mostly, it represented ways competitive athletes tried to gain the mental edge on opponents.

Muhammad Ali, whose mouth was as mighty as his right hook, set the modern standard before his 1974 fight with George Foreman when he proclaimed, "Float like a butterfly, sting like a bee, nobody beats the greatest, Muhammad Ali."

Larry Bird forever established his laser-tongue legacy before the three-point-shooting contest at the 1986 All-Star Game when he asked his competitors, "So who's playing for second place?"

Charles Barkley, with one of the most active mouths ever to play on an NBA floor, liked to attempt to rattle devoutly religious A.C. Green when they played by asking, "A.C., if God is so good, how come he didn't give you a jump shot?"

Barkley also rendered Ficker speechless one night—the oral equivalent of holding Jordan to single digits. After Ficker had loudly mocked Barkley's political aspirations by asking him his views on NAFTA and health care, the player turned and said: "I do have a view on the death penalty. They should use it on you."

Bulls coach Scott Skiles, while playing for Michigan State, once chided rival Antoine Joubert after wearing out the chubby guard on the floor, "Yo, 'Toine, we're comin' to Ann Arbor in a couple of weeks. Lose 10."

In a game against Georgetown, a defiant Skiles hit a couple of shots in a row, then asked intimidating Hoyas coach John Thompson, "If you're such a good defensive coach, why don't you get somebody out here to stop me?"

Without humor as its core, trash-talking can devolve into the type of language or harassment that no workplace would tolerate. And sporting arenas are where athletes work.

"If no one on the court would consider it funny, then it probably has crossed the line and is too personal," said Dallas Mavericks owner Mark Cuban, the most vocal owner in sports. "It doesn't have to be politically correct, but it has to have some level of wit combined with something factual. Otherwise it doesn't work and might be taken the wrong way."

Even before the World Cup incident allowed international sports fans to eavesdrop on the heated exchange, trash-talking had become as much a reality of big-time sports culture as agents and baggy shorts.

Adidas even sponsored a camp in China for the country's elite basketball players that included Kareem Abdul-Jabbar teaching the dos and don'ts of trash-talking, American-style. Likewise, University of Pittsburgh linguistics professor Alan Juffs broached the topic when giving a seminar to Chinese and German players on the finer points of competitive rhetoric.

"The focus was court language, but we also had to make sure they knew the right time to use 'Get that [shot] out of my kitchen' so they didn't get themselves in trouble," Juffs said.

Shoe companies have exalted the art of trash-talking in commercials that, in essence, encourage young athletes to find their inner Barkley. It makes for a more colorful experience on fields, courts and diamonds, though it's not always more courteous.

The Pro Bowlers Association, for example, has improved its TV ratings and overall appeal since five years ago when new leadership began encouraging players to goad each other with taunts such as, "You're going down!"

"Most trash-talking does cross the line of sportsmanship, but we have just become so inoculated by it that it has become the norm," said Kay McDaniel, a sports psychologist who helps arm student-athletes for oral warfare at Lee University in Cleveland, Tenn. "Each athlete should have a personal and professional ethical boundary that restrains him or her from going too far."

Zachary Minor, a consultant for all four major sports leagues on life-skills issues over the last 18 years, tells the professional athletes he counsels that their bravado has gone too far when they start referring to their opponents as people rather than players. When the NHL faced a crisis in the late 1990s after a handful of incidents in which trash-talking escalated into racial slurs, the league hired Minor before the 2000 season to discuss with players where that line exists.

The experience helps Minor understand, but not excuse, what drove Zidane to lose control of his emotions and commit one of soccer's all-time blunders. Watching the head butt "horrified" Minor.

"Whatever the words were, absolutely [Zidane] should have walked away," Minor said.

KEEP YOUR HEAD

McMichael remembers walking away many times in 15 NFL seasons if the banter crossed the line, as it often does on a football field. The worst example in McMichael's memory came his rookie year with New England, when he heard racist comments directed at a teammate.

"The worst I ever did was bark like a dog, but some guys got personal," McMichael said.

Former Bears linebacker Bryan Cox, now an assistant coach with the New York Jets, regularly included wives, mothers and girlfriends in his rants the way Materazzi allegedly did with Zidane. So did notorious ex-Minnesota Vikings pass rusher

John Randle, who terrorized the Bears for years with a mouth as explosive as his first step.

But one game, lined up over former Bears guard Todd Burger, Randle misfired. He thought Burger's wife's name was Jennifer and started saying things about "Jennifer," trying to rattle Burger. Turned out that Burger's wife was named Denise, and Jennifer was the name of left tackle Andy Heck's wife, rendering Randle speechless when a Vikings teammate finally told him why Burger did not react.

In college football, the talk can be just as bold. When Wisconsin coach Brett Bielema played linebacker for Iowa in 1991, for example, he told Iowa State coach Jim Walden how much he enjoyed kicking the Cyclones' tails for four straight years. Then-Hawkeyes coach Hayden Fry didn't start Bielema the next game, holding him accountable for words that can be as powerful in sports as any deeds.

"I realized," Bielema said of that incident, "how 10 seconds of stupidity can affect you for a long time."

It is a lesson Zinedine Zidane is just beginning to learn.

Questions for Discussion and Writing

1. Haugh says that athletes use trash-talk either to "motivate themselves" or to "antagonize their opponents." Why would trash-talk be an effective strategy in either case? How could it be effective in opposite situations?

2. Where is the line between innocent trash-talking and hurtful or dangerous remarks? Who determines the line?

3. Haugh uses the phrase "competitive rhetoric" to describe trash-talking. When can trash-talking almost become a sport in itself? Can trash-talk ever overtake the sport?

4. Some sports encourage athletes to trash-talk. The Pro Bowlers Association, Haugh says, encourages bowlers to taunt each other in order to improve television ratings. Haugh says, "It makes for a more colorful experience on fields, courts and diamonds, though it's not always more courteous." Do you agree? Does trash-talking make sports so much more entertaining that it should become part of the sport? Write about your position.

5. Though it was published in a newspaper, Haugh's article clearly presents an argument. It does not appear objective; the author does give his opinion. Identify the elements of an argument—claim or position, evidence or support, counterargument—in Haugh's article. Is his argument effective? Why or why not?

The Importance of Language
NANCY HUPPERTZ

A former teacher, Nancy Huppertz now provides sexual harassment and gender equity training for schools, agencies, and workplaces. She says in her philosophy of training, "Information about laws and internal policies and procedures related to sexual harassment are an essential part of training, but to my mind, only the beginning of real understanding." Her workshops are intended to help people stop thinking in terms of stereotypes such as "boys will be boys" and, in the case of sports language, phrases such as "man-to-man defense" and gender-based league names like the NBA and WNBA. Huppertz has chaired many organizations, including the National Coalition for Sex Equity in Education. She is a supporter of women's athletics and held season tickets to watch the short-lived Portland Fire WNBA team. In this article, which she wrote for the Women's Sports Foundation, Huppertz criticizes gender-biased language in sports.

———————————— ✦ ————————————

The power to persuade begins with language. Advertisers who want us to buy their product know it, politicians who want our vote know it, and government leaders who want to advance their agendas and minimize their weaknesses know it. Spinning, parsing and propagandizing are language skills. So are inspiring, encouraging and comforting. Linguists have said that language creates and conveys the culture. Youngsters learn about the world by not only what they see, but also what they hear.

People who talk about sports—particularly sports reporters and commentators in the media—have an important opportunity to expand upon the considerable progress that has already been made in women's sports participation. By use of language that is inclusive of women, they can subtly but powerfully shift the perception that women's sports are add-ons, auxiliaries or less important than men's sports toward the notion that they are important in their own right.

In English it has been common practice to use masculine words to include females. "Mankind" means everybody—sometimes. "Man" and "men" mean everybody—sometimes. "He," "his" and "him" also mean "her"—sometimes. When used this way the masculine words are referred to as generic. In fact, linguists know that people take the language very literally. When they hear "he," "him," "his," "man" or "mankind," the mental image is masculine. It is only through context that the words might be construed as inclusive of females, but even then, it is not always clear. For example, a sentence such as, "Studies show that in the south men are more likely to get gray hair at a younger age than in the north." In that sentence it is not at all clear whether "men" includes women. Were women included in the study? Do they also get gray at an earlier age? The meaning is not clear.

In the context of sports, we still hear the language used in a number of ways that convey the secondary status of women—most often in basketball. How often have we heard, "In basketball tonight Duke beat North Carolina, Purdue upset Notre Dame, etc. . . . and now, turning to the women, the Lady Bulldogs defeated the Lady Bruins." Teams referred to by just the school or mascot or city name are male, while the "women" or "lady" tags are used for the women's teams. Equitable, inclusive language requires that if the feminine tags are used for the women's teams, masculine tags should be used for the men's teams. This is called parallel language or parallel construction.

The same thing happens in talking about leagues or tournaments. We have the NBA and the WNBA, the PGA and the LPGA. We all know that the NBA is not going to change its name to MNBA, and the PGA is not going to change to the GPGA (gentlemen being the parallel term for ladies), but if people started calling them that, a subtle shift toward equal importance just might begin to occur. When sportscasters talk about the NCAA, the Big Dance, the U.S. Open, the NIT, invariably they are talking about the men. If they talk about the women at all, it is always with the tags women or ladies. To be equitable they should use parallel language meaning using male tags for men's events and female tags for women's events.

The important thing to know about imbalance in the use of language, often called language bias, is that readily available alternatives exist, such as parallel use of tags. Also, sportscasters calling women's basketball games still use the term "man-to-man." It would be just as easy to say "woman-to-woman" or "one-to-one." A reporter at the Salt Lake City Olympic Winter Games, in talking about a women's bobsled team, referred to the individual in the forward position as the "front man." She was not a man; she was a woman. Defenders of traditional usage might argue that the reporter was talking about a position, not a person. So, what is the function of the person in that position? Driver? Then call her or him "driver."

Using inclusive language is not a brand new concept. For years many universities and organizations and journals have required that theses, documents and articles be written in inclusive language. More than 20 years ago the U.S. Department of Labor adopted alternative language for all occupation titles ending in "—man," sample alternatives being fire fighter, flight attendant and police officer. It may seem awkward at first to change language habits, but the language changes all the time. The change to inclusive language is in the interest of creating a more equitable society, so a little initial awkwardness is a small price to pay.

Opportunities for women and girls to play sports have increased dramatically since the passage 30 years ago of Title IX. But women athletes are still paid less, women's sports receive far, far less coverage in the media, attendance at women's sports events is, with notable exceptions at some university basketball games, far less than at men's events, and athletic-related violations of Title IX abound—most unreported. Using inclusive language will not alone eliminate the inequities in sports, but it will reflect progress, convey the notion of equality, help the self-concept of young female athletes and increase respect for women's sports.

Suggested guidelines for equitable use of language related to sports:

1. Avoid using male terms as generic. They are not. Use alternatives. Examples:

   Wrong: Man-to-man defense
   Better: One-on-one, One-to-one, Player-to-player

   Wrong: She's guarding her man.
   Better: She's guarding her woman or player.

2. Use masculine tags for teams and tournaments in the same way that feminine tags are used.
   Examples:

   Bearcats and Lady Bearcats
   Bearcat men and Bearcat women

   The Final Four and the Women's Final Four
   The Men's Final Four and the Women's Final Four

3. Avoid using so-called generic pronouns. Use female terms when talking about females and male terms when talking about males. Use inclusive construction when talking about both.

Examples:

Every player has his ankles taped.
All the players have their ankles taped.

Every athlete at the university is required to keep his grades up.
Every athlete at the university is required to keep her or his grades up.

4. Use parallel terms for male and female leagues in the same sport.
Examples:

NBA and WNBA MNBA and WNBA
PGA and LPGA GPGA and LPGA

All the commonly accepted benefits of sports are as true for girls and women as they are for boys and men. People who care about equal opportunity in sports should do all they can to continue to make sports and athletics a hospitable endeavor for females. Coverage, commentary and conversation about sports have a long way to go to become both equal and equitable. The fair use of language is a big step toward those goals.

Questions for Discussion and Writing

1. Huppertz begins with a powerful opener: "The power to persuade begins with language." Many writers choose to begin with an anecdote or example and work their way up to their thesis. Why do you think Huppertz begins by making her strongest point right away?
2. Is all language persuasive in nature? Why or why not? Explain your reasoning.
3. Huppertz notes that other areas of society, such as the government, have already changed language usage to avoid "language bias." Do her examples make a change in sports language seem more feasible? Why or why not?
4. Watch a sports report on the evening news or a cable channel like ESPN. Keep a journal of the biased language you hear in regard to women's sports or female athletes. Would you characterize any of the language as inappropriate or offensive? Explain.
5. At the end of the article Huppertz shows how broadcasters can change gender-biased language. Do a similar exercise: Find examples of sexist or biased language in print publications or on broadcasts and re-write the language to avoid sexism or bias.

Sport Makes the Words Go Round
STEVE RUSHIN

At age 25, Steve Rushin became the youngest senior writer on the Sports Illustrated *staff, gaining such status after three years with the magazine. A graduate of Marquette University, Rushin grew up in Chicago and Minnesota, where he once had a job selling hot dogs and soft drinks at Minnesota Twins and Vikings baseball and football games. He landed the job at* Sports Illustrated *just two weeks after graduating from college. He has since been nominated for several writing awards and is well-known for his sense of humor, sarcasm, and his skill at feature writing. His article on Roone Arledge, the creator of* Wide World of Sports *and* Monday Night Football, *appeared in* Sports Illustrated's *40th anniversary issue as the longest story to appear in a single issue (at 24 pages). One of his books,* Road Swing: One Fan's Journey into the Soul of American Sports, *is a travelogue chronicling his hilarious, year-long road trip on the eve of his 30th birthday to some of America's most sacred sports shrines, including the Iowa cornfield where* Field of Dreams *was filmed. About his writing style, Rushin has been quoted as saying, "I try to follow the rule that the easier something is to read, the harder it was to write, and the harder it is to read the easier it probably was to write." Rushin left* Sports Illustrated *in 2007 to spend more time with his wife, former University of Connecticut and WNBA star and ESPN analyst Rebecca Lobo, and their daughters, and to write more books.*

◆

"In the NFL," says a league veteran, "every team has a get-back coach, a guy whose job is to hold up his arms and yell, 'Get back!' when [bench players] get too close to the field."

Get-back coach is a felicitous linguistic invention, like Gretzky's office (for the area behind a goal in hockey) or exercise bulimic (for anyone trying to sweat off the calories they've just eaten). And sports are constantly minting these coinages. If language is a breathing organism, our games hyperventilate.

When the next edition of *The Dickson Baseball Dictionary* is published in 2008, it will contain 10,000 words and phrases, twice as many as in the first edition, published in 1989. "First you have run batted in, then RBI, then ribby, then rib eye and now steak," notes author and word nerd Paul Dickson, whose new book is *Slang: The Topical Dictionary of Americanisms*.

To explain why Luis Castillo didn't bunt during a crucial at bat in the Twins-A's playoff series, Minnesota manager Ron Gardenhire said, "They were banzaiin' all over the place." Translation: Oakland infielders were charging the plate. Baseball—like surfing—has taken the World War II cry of the kamikaze pilot and applied it to another suicidal act.

It works in reverse too. Phrases from sports are constantly crossing over to the real world. And so the current vogue for holding five-year-olds back from kindergarten an extra year is called redshirting.

Has there ever been a more apt appellation than the one given to English soccer groupies: goaldiggers? Rodeo groupies have long been called buckle bunnies, a phrase that entered—and was thus interred?—in *The New Oxford American Dictionary*, along with Texas Hold 'Em, the poker game that is a hothouse for slang. In Texas hold 'em, a pocket hand of ace and king is called an Anna Kournikova, and not just because of the way it appears (A, K) when fanned out in front of you. It's also a hand that looks great but often doesn't hold up against lesser opening cards.

There are more names for mullets than the Inuit have for snow, among them hockey hair and NASCAR sunscreen—incidentally, a NASCAR winner's postrace practice of putting on a dozen different baseball caps, each bearing the logo of a sponsor, is called a hat dance—but the best neologism defines something that was crying out for a name. Take those A-list stars (such as Joe Montana and Tiger Woods) who do lucrative commercials in Asia that they'd never do in the West. The website that exists to out them takes its name from a necessary new verb: Japander.

Two hundred years ago British cockfighting and boxing writer Pierce Egan invented all manner of terms still in use today, including cock of the walk and battle royale. In soccer the free kick that bends around or over a defensive wall and dips past a goalkeeper is called, in Portuguese, a folha seca, which means "dry leaf." You need only look out a window to see a swirling leaf afloat on the wind to know why. Like lullaby or Brigitte Bardot, folha seca is the rare word or phrase that is every bit as beautiful as the thing it describes.

It also happens to be a specialty of Roberto Carlos, a Real Madrid galáctico, which is European soccerese for the rank above superstar, an all-galaxy player. The word started in Spain but quickly went viral, spreading to the rest of the globe, if not yet the rest of the Milky Way.

Much great slang remains obscure occupational jargon. According to pro football writer Vic Carucci, NFL scouts say that a linebacker who uses his hands well to shed blockers while moving laterally can play the piano. Other slang is commissioned. A few years ago *The Washington Post* asked readers to name the act of sneaking peeks at a football game on TV during a party. The winner was ESPN-age, as in espionage.

And yet, despite our best efforts, much of the sports world remains linguistically unmapped. Let's remedy that. I'll spot you two new ones to get started. Persona non grotto: Any athlete (such as Cade McNown) banned from the Playboy Mansion. Imbecell: that fan on the phone behind home plate, waving to his buddies at home.

Some slang will live forever. Rookie was first recorded by Rudyard Kipling. (It was a 19th-century British barracks corruption of recruit.) And some new phrases grow so tiresome so quickly that we can't bear to hear them even one more time. (Let's take Throw him under the bus and throw it under the bus.)

Of course, most current coinage is rendered hopelessly passé simply by its appearance in *SPORTS ILLUSTRATED* or any other mass medium—a phenomenon that has a neologism of its own. "It's called the Couric Rule," says Dickson, sighing. "Once a popular talk-show host uses a word like bling-bling or def, it's gone."

Questions for Discussion and Writing

1. Rushin begins with an interesting point that sports practically breed language. He says, "If language is a breathing organism, our games hyperventilate." Why is it, do you think, that sport creates so many phrases and words?

2. Brainstorm a list of all the sports metaphors, words, and phrases you can think of. Are most of the sports-oriented phrases humorous or are there some that are offensive? Who decides what is funny and what is not?

3. Steve Rushin has a knack for writing in a conversational tone. What areas of his article make you feel like he is talking directly to you? Is his tone effective in this article? Why or why not? Use specific examples from Rushin's writing to support your answer.

4. What kind of research did Rushin have to do in order to write this article? Where is his research evident? How would you begin researching language associated with sports? What might make some good sources?

5. Read the example that explains how the term *ESPN-age* was coined. What drives this fascination Americans have with creating new words and phrases? How many of the other examples Rushin uses were you familiar with? How many did you have to look up? What do these words and phrases say about American culture?

Sporting Metaphors: Competition and the Ethos of Capitalism
ANN E. CUDD

Ann E. Cudd is a philosophy professor and director of Women's Studies at the University of Kansas. She has a number of academic interests, including feminism, capitalism, liberalism, globalization, and the philosophy of social science. When she's not teaching or writing, Cudd is an avid runner and enjoys reading essays on running. She has written dozens of articles and has written books including Analyzing Oppression and Feminist Theory: Philosophical Reflections on the Resistance to Feminism. *This article appeared in the* Journal of the Philosophy of Sport, *which focuses on contemporary philosophy in sports. In the article, Cudd merges her interests in capitalism and sport. Along the way, she makes some humorous and interesting observations about the common languages of sports and business.*

——————— ◆ ———————

That is the law which again and again throws bourgeois production out of its old course and which compels capital to intensify the productive forces of labor, because it has intensified them, it, the law which gives capital no rest and continually whispers in its ear: "Go on! Go on!"

Karl Marx *Wage Labor and Capital*

"You give 100% in the first half of the game, and if that isn't enough in the second half you give what's left."

Yogi Berra

The English language is replete with metaphors that use sport to describe daily life as a kind of game. Many of our sports metaphors date back to an earlier time when the most popular games were games of chance, poker and horse racing. In the latter part of the 19th century the team sports of baseball and football (to be followed by basketball and hockey and later still by lacrosse and soccer) began their ascendancy to the top of the American imagination. At the same time, capitalism was becoming the dominant economic system in America. As capitalism became more industrial, team sports gained in popularity (10). These sports are face to face and hard hitting, emphasizing quick, strategic decision making; athletic moves; and team play. Throughout the phases of 19th- and 20th-century capitalism, from personal to managerial to fiduciary (3), capitalism has come to value similar skills in its executives, managers, and investors.

This connection between sports and capitalism is reflected in and emphasized by our metaphorical language connecting sports and work. No metaphor is more powerful than competition and the idea of the competitive market as a winner-takes-all, no-holds-barred dogfight. This article examines metaphors that illuminate the competitive aspects of capitalism and its focus on winning but also metaphors that emphasize cooperation and ways that capitalism improves the lives not only of the winners but also of all who choose to play the game by its rules. Although sports metaphors invoked to describe capitalist competition may appear to cast an unflattering light on both capitalism and sport, on a deeper analysis those metaphors appeal to many of us because they reveal a closer resemblance to the Latin root of the word "competition" and its cooperative, pareto-improving implications. Just as healthy competition in sports requires cooperation, healthy capitalism is also, ultimately, a cooperative endeavor. . . .

SPORTING METAPHORS

Most theories of sport define it as activity that meets at least the following three criteria: Persons voluntarily engage in the activity, the activity is rule governed, and the activity poses a competitive challenge to the persons engaged in it. Perhaps the most influential definition of games, which was proposed by Bernard Suits, poses the following definition (16). A game involves (a) the prelusory goal, a state of affairs specifiable independently of the rules of the game, that the players are trying to attain; (b) the (lusory) means for attaining the goal permitted by the constitutive rules; and (c) the lusory attitude on the part of the players that they accept the constitutive rules. The crucial insight in this definition of "game" is that a game involves voluntarily using only the means allowed by the rules to reach the goal, and these means are characteristically not the most efficient means for doing so. A sport for Suits is a game that also requires physical activity. Thus, some theories emphasize that sport must be physically challenging (1) in order to rule out such games as poker or chess, but I would rather cast a wider net for my purposes here. In this article I am not trying to set out a novel definition or understanding of sport, but rather I am trying to examine capitalism and its ethos through sports metaphors that are commonly used to discuss the business of capitalism.

By capitalism I mean an economic system whose core, defining feature is that it allows private ownership of the means of production, that is, of capital inputs to production. In such a system, under very minimal assumptions of differences in preferences and/or initial distribution of capital inputs, markets will develop, including markets for labor. The definition of capitalism entails that these markets are to be free of undue government intervention so that we may enjoy freedom of movement and enjoy the products of work and trade.

The most important aspects of the concept of sport for its analogy to capitalism revolve around the rule-governed nature and competitively challenging nature of the activity. Sport is governed by two kinds of rules: constitutive rules that define what moves are permitted and how the game is scored and rules of decency and fair play. Metaphorical relations that come out of the constitutive rule-governed nature of sport include "foul," "fair," "in the ballpark," "extra innings," "from the word go," "tackle," "score," "no holds barred," "down for the count," and "level playing field" (13). The injunction to "play by the rules" is a standby of business ethics. The primary metaphor from the rules of decency and fair play that surround sport is that of the "good sport."

Sports pose a competitive challenge to their players in several ways. They often pose physical challenges of skill, athleticism, stamina, or endurance. Sports always pose mental challenges by requiring quick and effective decisions, the ability to assess opponents (and teammates) and react to their strategic decisions, and emotional strength in the form of confidence, determination, flexibility, and persistence. Each of these aspects of challenge in sports engenders metaphorical relations that form a part of our conceptual scheme of capitalism.

Metaphorical relations that begin in the physical challenges of sport may seem to poorly fit the challenges of economic life in capitalism. But many such relations are metaphorical for the determination and persistence that are rewarded by success in business. "No pain, no gain" might be used by managers to justify a decision to streamline a company, despite the complaints by workers and public officials that the company might endure (not to mention the physical suffering of the workers themselves, who can only cynically be described as gaining from their layoff). A long session at work is a "marathon," and someone who works hard will "go the extra mile." One who is deft is "on the ball." A person with determination might "make a comeback" after suffering a "setback."

Decision making in games such as poker, chess, and gambling holds many similarities with the decisions made by capitalists and is a rich source of metaphors. Game theory, an important theoretical model of capitalist interaction, exploits this analogy explicitly. Many metaphors that are useful in understanding capitalism, then, have to do with taking risks. Entrepreneurs are said to "take a shot" at developing new products, even when the "stakes are high" and more timid persons would not "bet on it." The stock market's most secure capital are its "blue chip stocks." When there is little information on which to make a prediction, however, "all bets are off." Managers must be good at making decisions and taking responsibility for the results. They might "toss an idea around" with their associates, but ultimately they must "call the signals" and "make a move" or just "go for it." If they find that they are outdone by a competing firm because they are "out of their league," then the "buck stops" with the manager.

What about the voluntariness criterion of sport—are there important metaphorical relations engendered by this aspect of the concept that form a part of our concept of capitalism? Some metaphors that might fit this bill would be "free agent," "for the love of the game," "call the signals," "freestyle," or perhaps "go for it." But metaphors that reveal coercion or force are just as common here. Consider "backed into a corner," "pinned," "cut one's losses," "tackled," "in over one's head," or "fall guy." On Jan Boxill's view of sport, sport must be voluntarily engaged in if it is to have positive moral value for us. The same can be said of capitalism. Yet capitalism has been criticized as coercive. Indeed, Boxill contrasts sport with work in capitalism to illuminate how sport, unlike work, is free, unalienated activity. The metaphorical ambivalence, I will argue, is reflected in our ambivalent feelings about capitalism and its social costs and benefits.

Sport and capitalism are analogous in some ways and disanalogous in others. I have characterized sport already as activity that is voluntary, rule-governed, and competitively challenging. Capitalist interaction is likewise rule-governed and voluntary, if it is legal. The economic models of capitalist interactions are termed "competition," as in "perfect competition" or "monopolistic competition." . . . In broad terms, sport and capitalism both describe systems that structure large portions of most of our daily lives. There are important voluntary and nonvoluntary aspects to each of them. Sport can be avoided but at the cost of not being able to speak the lingua franca of contemporary popular discourse. Capitalism can be avoided at a cost, as well, although the cost may be one's ability to survive. Whole subcultures live among us that avoid sports or capitalism, such as academics and the Amish, but neither is completely free of what they shun; they live on the periphery, not over the edge. For members of this culture, opting in to either sport or capitalism is far easier than opting out. . . .

SPORTING METAPHORS OF COOPERATION AND COMPETITION

Level Playing Field

An important sports metaphor that extends and refines the metaphorical concept of competitiveness in capitalism is the level playing field. This metaphor conjures up the image of a flat field in which no team is forced to play uphill and where round balls roll evenly, without surprising bounces. In sport, having a literal or metaphorical level playing field is important so that an effective challenge can be mounted by roughly equal players who are making their best efforts to win within the rules of the game. This, after all, is the point of sport—to test one's own and one's opponents' skills by attempting to meet each other's challenge within the rules. This is the meaning of Simon's claim that sport is a mutual quest for excellence or Hyland's understanding of sport as mutual striving (5: p. 64). A level playing field is necessary not only for a good match but also for a fair one. If the playing field is not level, then the challenge is greater on one side and lesser on the other. It may lead to a blowout, which is a situation in which the competitive challenge no longer exists, and is unlikely to be either "mutual" or a successful "quest for excellence." The metaphor of the level playing field thus connotes both fairness and the requirements for a good, successful, satisfying competition.

A level playing field is important in capitalism also to ensure competition as a way to maintain the balance between firms, consumers, and workers that I discussed previously as an important component in a successful capitalist economy. Because competition is the central metaphor of capitalism, the metaphorical relation of the level playing field as preserving and enhancing competition is mirrored in our capitalist discourse. For example, in debates over laws governing antitrust or trade subsidies parties often argue that such laws will make or disrupt a level playing field.

Unlike the metaphor of competition, the metaphor of the level playing field itself carries little ambivalence for us. Fairness is an unmitigated good; a level playing field is a requirement of justice. However, like competition, the metaphor of the level playing field is clouded by ambiguity in its meaning. Achieving or recognizing a level playing field is politically loaded, reflecting the political ambiguity of what it means to enhance or inhibit competition, let alone ensure justice. A good example of this is debates over international trade policies (i.e., "fair trade") where some parties will argue that subsidies or quotas are needed to level the playing field for American firms since they face higher taxes or environmental standards, while others will point to American firms' labor costs as the obstacle to a level playing field. On the other side are countries whose firms produce at lower costs because their workers do not have the luxury to forego work and income in order to demand better environmental standards or higher wages. They complain that there is not a level playing field when U.S. policies effectively prohibit consumers from buying goods made by poorer workers, thus further impoverishing them. What counts as fair thus depends on how one describes the conditions on which the competition is based.

Playing by the Rules

An important metaphor for understanding fair competition in capitalism is the concept of rules and what it is to "play by the rules." Rules imply guides for behavior that are commonly known, or at least assumed by most of those playing the sport to be commonly known, and enforced to a greater or lesser degree so that if one is in clear violation of the rules one can expect negative consequences. In sport we can distinguish two kinds of rules: constitutive rules and rules of decency and fair play. The constitutive rules of a game are explicit and formal and describe the aim, the allowable moves, and the penalties for violating them. Rules of decency and fair play describe what moves, strategies, and behaviors are informally allowed. Since sport is a practical activity, even the constitutive rules have to be interpreted and tend to change organically over time to fit external and internal circumstances. For instance, when Lew Alcindor (later Kareem Abdul Jabbar) played college basketball he dominated the game so much that a new rule was introduced to rule out scoring by forcing the ball through the hoop with one's hands within the rim of the basket—what we now call dunking. But when many more players could perform this athletic feat it was reintroduced as an element that enhanced the athleticism and excitement of the game.

In capitalism, we can distinguish similar kinds of action-guiding principles, namely, laws, that are the constitutive rules of capitalism, ethics, and the rules of decency and fair play. Laws define property and property rights and thus are definitive of the economic system itself. If persons can be property, then we have slavery. Likewise the law of property can make a system feudal or capitalist or socialist by assigning certain sets of rights and obligations to persons based on their historical relations to material and other wealth-conferring or -creating objects. Property rights define theft, which is a particularly salient way of failing to play by the rules. In our contemporary culture we talk about people who play by the rules and manage to make a living or fail to because of some kind of hard luck. Those who steal or cheat are said to be not playing by the rules and, therefore, in need of legal or social sanction. Law also defines fair and unfair competitive practices and prevents monopoly power, collusion, or insider trading from thwarting competition. Although there are many ethical prescriptions for individuals in all societies, the ones that could be said to be the ethical prescriptions specific to capitalism are the ones that concern the behavior of firms, businesspersons, and managers more than workers, who are constrained mainly by the laws regarding theft of one kind or another. Businesses are expected to show a certain amount of generosity or philanthropy in order to be said to be playing by the rules.

Constitutive rules that define property rights have also changed in response to new external conditions. For example, antitrust legislation arose to respond to techniques of production that vastly increased returns to scale and the ability of large firms to engage in far more rapid communication and investment than smaller firms. These conditions led to massive firms that could corner the market, creating the inefficient and otherwise socially undesirable conditions of monopolistic competition. In an attempt to level the playing field for smaller firms and workers, antitrust legislation redefined what it meant to play by the rules. A similar situation is at hand with the advent of digital music and the ability to share files. Although property rights in recorded music used to consist of owning a plastic disc, which allowed only one person at a time to play that disc, now it is commonplace to make multiple copies of the same music file so that many can use it at once. This situation, in which music recordings are no longer "rival" in economists' terms, may create the socially undesirable situation of fewer musicians being willing to create music since there is less financial incentive to do so. Furthermore, it just strikes many of us as unfair to the musicians. Our constitutive rules of property are only beginning to catch up, but we have the sense that if the new technology is to benefit everyone, a system of rules will need to be established.

In either the legal or ethical sense, then, "playing by the rules" in capitalism concerns the maintenance of the competitive environment as a mutually beneficial, or a cooperatively competitive, one. Thus, the metaphorical use of the positively normative phrase playing by the rules supports competition in capitalism in a way that, on inspection, reveals the important cooperative element of competition.

Teamwork

The metaphor of the team and teamwork is explicitly cooperative. Typically it conveys the notion of cooperation in capitalism when used to describe workers or managers in a firm. Yet the sense of cooperation is ambivalent in this metaphor, as well. A sports team is not a purely cooperative situation but rather more of a cooperative competition. Each team member has an interest in working well with the team to defeat an opponent, but each also wants to play individually well enough to maintain her position in the starting lineup. While the benchwarmers would like the team to win, and so will work to improve the play of the other team members in practice, each would also like to outshine the others in order to earn a starting position. As the metaphor is imported into capitalist discourse, it can also carry with it the implicit understanding that while teams work together, teammates are not only altruistically motivated to maximize the performance of the team, but are also interested in their individual standing on the team. One is often encouraged to be a team player when one is being asked to sacrifice individual interests for the good of the team.

In economic theory, firms, which might be considered the quintessential economic teams, are sometimes modeled as having a single set of desires or preferences, as represented by a single utility function, in which the utility of the firm is positively proportional to financial wealth (i.e., money). But just as team members in sport have their own desires to succeed as individuals, individual employees' utilities are opposed to each other in that each one wishes to gain individual wealth (and perhaps also status), even if it costs the firm as a whole some financial wealth. Economic theorists have more recently noted this competitive situation within, as well as between, capitalistic firms (6).

Slam Dunk; Step Up (to the Plate)

This brings us to my final two sporting metaphors, each of which emphasizes the individual achievements and roles of team players. A slam dunk in basketball is an especially violent dunk. The basketball player performs a slam dunk in order to intimidate the other team, a team-oriented motivation, and impress them and the fans with the individual dunker's athleticism and raw power, an individualistic motivation. A slam dunk is also nearly a sure thing—one almost cannot miss the shot when the ball is stuffed into the basket. The metaphorical use of this term particularly conveys either or both aspects of the concept. A product that is a "can't miss" success is a slam dunk. A person who makes a particularly good business presentation is said to have made a slam dunk, meaning that it was a display of individual virtuosity in business acumen and that it will certainly succeed.

Taking credit for one's individual actions and performance implies that one also takes responsibility for one's actions. The metaphor of "stepping up" or to "step up to the plate" reveals this dual aspect of individual responsibility. "Stepping up to the plate" literally describes a baseball player as he comes up to bat and steps into the batter's box at home plate. At this point he is the one offensive player on whom the immediate future of the game rests. There is no other player at that moment who can affect the game like the batter will, particularly if he should hit a home run. Metaphorically, an individual who steps up to the plate (or simply steps up) is taking the responsibility for attempting to either secure her organization on the same successful course or to effect some change in course that will help it succeed where it had been in some sense failing or to take responsibility for not doing so. Only an individual can take moral responsibility, and being willing to do so indicates courage, just as it requires courage to stand in the box as a pitcher throws a baseball in one's general direction at lethal speed.

Thus there are both team and individual, cooperative and MEGA metaphors that fill out the conceptual scheme of capitalism. These individualistic metaphors, however, are somewhat newer than the others. This may reflect a recent change in the popularity of different sports and the styles in which they are played. Basketball has become the most popular sport in America in large part because of the tremendous individual talents of Magic Johnson, Larry Bird, and, most of all, Michael Jordan. Yet these players were popular in part because they were excellent team players, as well as individually skilled. Their immense popularity may be in large part because they were able to resolve in their own play the ambiguity of individual versus team to forge outstanding examples of cooperative competition within their own teams and the league itself.

CONCLUSION: CAPITALISM AS A COOPERATIVELY COMPETITIVE CULTURE

. . . Capitalist competition, if it is to be evaluated positively, can be seen as not only involving cooperation but also requiring some cooperative constraints on would-be winners to enhance future competition and the survival of capitalism as a viable and successful economic arrangement. As Marx suggests, the endless urging of capitalism to more and greater profits by the capitalist cannot be sustained. Furthermore, the related metaphors of the level playing field, playing by the rules, and teamwork reveal that the discourse of capitalism explicitly recognizes the importance of cooperation within competition. Hobbes showed us long ago that we can only escape the war of all against all by accepting the sovereignty of enforced legal constraint on our competitive, diffident, vainglorious natures. The sporting metaphors of capitalism continue to disclose that lesson in discourse. Finally, the metaphors of the slam dunk and stepping up to the plate reveal the degree to which individual achievement and responsibility are valued in our capitalist culture. The sporting metaphors that I have examined reveal ways that we may open up the conceptual space of our understanding of capitalism as unbridled, alienated competition for a more expansive and positive understanding of capitalism. These metaphors reveal that the very structure of our capitalist conceptual scheme already harbors the ancient idea that in striving together we reap the greatest benefits of capitalistic competition.

REFERENCES

1. Boxill, J. "Introduction: The Moral Significance of Sport." In *Sports Ethics*, J. Boxill (Ed.). Malden, MA: Blackwell, 2003, 1–12.
3. Greider, W. *The Soul of Capitalism: Opening Paths to a Moral Economy*. New York: Simon and Schuster, 2003.
5. Hyland, D.A. "Opponents, Contestants, and Competitors: The Dialectic of Sport." *Journal of the Philosophy of Sport*, XI, 1985, 63–70.
6. Jensen, M.C., and W.H. Meckling. "Theory of the Firm: Managerial Behavior, Agency Costs and Ownership Structure." *The Journal of Financial Economics*, 3, 1976, 305–360.
10. Mandelbaum, M. *The Meaning of Sports: Why Americans Watch Baseball, Football, and Basketball, and What They See When They Do*. New York: Public Affairs, 2004.
13. Palmatier, R.A., and H.L. Ray. *Sports Talk: A Dictionary of Sports Metaphors*. New York: Greenwood Press, 1989.
16. Suits, B. "The Elements of Sport." In *Philosophic Inquiry in Sport*, W. Morgan and K. Meier (Eds.). Champaign, IL: Human Kinetics, 1988, 39–48.

Questions for Discussion and Writing

1. Identify Cudd's thesis. Is her point about sports and capitalism positive or negative? Who is she speaking to? What is she trying to say about our assumptions?

2. Look at the metaphors Cudd offers as examples. Which had you heard before? Which ones are new to you? Why do you think some metaphors have become more prevalent in the language of business than others? What does Cudd argue?

3. Discuss Cudd's claim that sport and capitalism both rely on voluntary participation. What does she mean? Is she right?

4. How do *playing by the rules* and a *level playing field* impact sports and business? Are both sports and capitalism "fair?" Is fairness a prerequisite for good competition?

5. Read Cudd's analysis of the metaphors *slam dunk* and *step up to the plate.* Analyze a metaphor on your own. It doesn't have to relate to business, but should relate to sports and some other facet of life. Dissect the metaphor and see if it means the same in both sports and the other area of culture.

Making Connections: Writing

1. The readings in this chapter discuss a variety of negative uses of language, including profanity, insults, and sexist phrases. Which is most serious in our culture? Write an argument that claims one as most serious and support your claims with evidence and examples.

2. Keep a log of sports-related language you hear during the course of one week. Analyze your log and write about the positive and negative uses of language. Which seem more prevalent?

3. Eric Hoover claims that coaches sometimes encourage profanity from fans and David Haugh says that athletes voluntarily participate in trash-talking. Write a recommendation to the athletic director or an administrator on your campus arguing for a code of language (dos and don'ts) for your school's coaches and athletes.

4. David Haugh gives some humorous examples of trash-talking, such as Larry Bird's question, "So who's playing for second place?" Steve Rushin also relates some funny metaphors, such as the child who is "redshirting" by waiting until age 6 before going to kindergarten. Interview a psychologist or professor and write an essay examining the connection between humor and language.

5. David Haugh and Nancy Huppertz explore trash-talk and sexist language. Considering their arguments, is it possible to avoid offending anyone? Conduct a survey to find out what kind of language is offensive to people on your campus.

6. Choose two sports, either professional or college-level, and attend one game for each sport (i.e., football and volleyball). At each game, keep a log of any negative language you hear: profanity, insults, trash-talk, sexist or racist phrases. Compare the two experiences. Did one sport clearly result in more

negative language than another? Do particular sports lend themselves to negative language more so than others? Why?

7. Evaluate each author's use of examples in the readings in this chapter. Which author is most effective at using examples to support his or her argument or point? Why?

8. Choose a reading selection from this chapter, such as Nancy Huppertz's stance on gender-biased language, and write directly to the author. Support or refute his or her claims.

9. Examine a variety of Internet sources of negative language in sports. You might look not only at Web sites but also at blogs, wikis, and discussion boards. Analyze the use of language. Does a particular form of Internet writing seem to promote more negative language than a typical Web site? What about author and audience—what influence do they have on Internet language?

10. Examine metaphors related to sport and one particular discipline as Ann E. Cudd does with sports and capitalism. You might examine business, education, or health care, for example. Research the metaphors as Steve Rushin does and analyze the results.

Books Worth Reading

And the Fans Roared: The Sports Broadcasts That Kept Us on the Edge of Our Seats by Joe Garner. Narrated by Bob Costas, contains two audio CDs featuring some of the most exciting moments in sports history.

Fab Five: Basketball, Trash Talk, and the American Dream by Mitch Albom. An in-depth look at the publicly brash and arrogant all-freshman starting basketball team for the University of Michigan.

Hate Mail from Cheerleaders and Other Adventures from the Life of Reilly by Rick Reilly. Collection of columns from *Sports Illustrated's* Rick Reilly and his opinionated tongue.

I Never Played the Game by Howard Cosell. The controversial sportscaster writes about his own voice in sports.

Rammer Jammer Yellow Hammer: A Journey into the Heart of Fan Mania by Warren St. John. Author follows a community of Alabama fans from game to game to discover what "turns otherwise sane, rational people into raving lunatics."

Slang: The Topical Dictionary of Americanisms by Paul Dickson. Includes a chapter on slang related to sports.

Sound and Fury: Two Powerful Lives, One Fateful Friendship by Dave Kindred. Columnist for the *Sporting News* examines the banter and insults exchanged between boxer Muhammad Ali and broadcaster Howard Cosell, both friends of the author.

Sportcult edited by Randy Martin. Examines the impact of sports on cultural politics through metaphors and pervasive sports language.

Sporting with the Gods: The Rhetoric of Play and Game in American Literature by Michael Oriard. Traces cultural history of metaphors related to play, game, and sport in American literature and culture. Expensive to buy but available in libraries.

You Can Quote Me on That: Greatest Tennis Quips, Insights, and Zingers by Paul Fein. Tennis reporter compiles controversial quotations from tennis stars and argues tennis is not "the polite, countryclub sport where players shake hands over the net and offer congratulations."

Films Worth Watching

Though no sports film deals exclusively with words or language, several contain memorable, controversial, or significant speeches. Here is one of the more interesting scenes, quoted online at www.americanrhetoric.com:

Ali (2001). This film is based on one of the most outspoken athletes of all time, boxer Muhammad Ali. In one scene, Ali defends his decision not to participate in the military draft and fight in Vietnam, in language reminiscent of Martin Luther King's speeches: "I ain't draft-dodgin'. I ain't burnin' no flag. And I ain't runnin' to Canada. I'm stayin' right here.

You wanna send me to jail? Fine, you go right ahead. I've been in jail for 400 years. I can be there for four or five more.

But I ain't goin' no 10,000 miles to help murder and kill other poor people. If I wanna die, I'll die right here, right now fightin' you—if I wanna die.

You my enemy. Not no Chinese, no Viet Cong, no Japanese.

You my opposer—when I want freedom.

You my opposer—when I want justice.

You my opposer—when I want equality.

You want me to go somewhere and I fight for you. You won't even stand up for me right here in America for my rights and my religious beliefs. You won't even stand up for me right here at home."

Sites Worth Surfing

http://www.americanrhetoric.com
Site devoted to rhetoric, with an online speech bank and text, audio, and video versions of speeches, sermons, lectures, interviews, and more.

http://www.sportsfanmagazine.com
Online magazine with news, commentary, interviews, reviews, and a
directory of fan sites.

http://www.campusspeech.org
Site of the Center for Campus Free Speech, which protects and promotes free speech on campuses.

Billard, Mary. "NASCAR Nirvana: R.V.'s, Rock Bands and Jell-O Shots." *The New York Times*. Oct. 17, 2003. F1. Copyright 2003. Reprinted by permission of *The New York Times*.

"Boys to Men: Sports Media—Messages About Masculinity." Michael Messner, Darnell Hunt, and Michele Dunbar, researchers; Perry Chen, Joan Lapp, and Patti Miller, Children Now. Copyright 1999 Children Now. Reprinted by permission of Children Now.

Cudd, Ann E. "Sporting Metaphors: Competition and the Ethos of Capitalism." From the *Journal of the Philosophy of Sport*, Vol. 34, Issue 1, 2007: 52–67. Adapted with permission from A.E. Cudd. Copyright 2007 Human Kinetics. Reprinted by permission.

Curry, Jack. "Passion in Work and at Play." *The New York Times*. March 6, 2006: D1. Copyright 2006. Reprinted by permission of *The New York Times*.

Fimrite, Peter. "Danger on the Dome." *San Francisco Chronicle*. July 7, 2007: A1. Copyright 2007 *San Francisco Chronicle*. Reprinted by permission of Hearst Corporation through Copyright Clearance Center, Inc.

Gerdy, John R. *Sports: The All-American Addiction*. Copyright 2002 University Press of Mississippi. Reprinted by permission of University Press of Mississippi.

Guttmann, Allen. From *The Olympics: A History of the Modern Games, Second Edition*. University of Illinois Press. Copyright 1992, 2002 by Board of Trustees of the University of Illinois. Reprinted with permission of University of Illinois Press.

Haugh, David. "Trash-Talk? Hear No Evil: Barbs May Cross Line, But Athletes Hurt Only Themselves by Taking Bait." *Chicago Tribune*.

July 16, 2006. Copyright 2006 Chicago Tribune Company. All rights reserved. Reprinted with permission.

Hemingway, Ernest. From "Bullfighting a Tragedy." Abridged by permission of Scribner, an imprint of Simon & Schuster Adult Publishing Group, from *Ernest Hemingway: Dateline: Toronto*, edited by William White. Copyright 1985 by Mary Hemingway, John Hemingway, Patrick Hemingway, and Gregory Hemingway.

Hoover, Eric. "Crying Foul Over Fans' Boorish Behavior." *The Chronicle of Higher Education.* 50.31 (9 April 2004): A1–A37. Copyright *The Chronicle of Higher Education.* Reprinted by permission.

Huang, Thomas. "Sex Sells, and Many Athletes Are Cashing In." *The Dallas Morning News.* Aug. 22, 2004. Copyright 2004. Reprinted with permission of *The Dallas Morning News.*

Huppertz, Nancy. "The Importance of Language." Published online by the Women's Sports Foundation. Online at *http://www .womenssportsfoundation.org.* Copyright 2002 Nancy Huppertz. Reprinted by permission.

Kerr, John H. "Examining the Bertuzzi-Moore NHL Ice Hockey Incident: Crossing the Line Between Sanctioned and Unsanctioned Violence in Sport." *Aggression and Violent Behavior.* Vol. 11 Issue 4 (July/August 2006): 313–322. Copyright 2006 Elsevier Limited. Reprinted by permission of Elsevier Ltd. through Copyright Clearance Center, Inc.

Kim, Lucian. "Buzkashi—An Afghan Tradition Thrives." Originally published in *The Christian Science Monitor.* Copyright 2002. Reprinted by permission of the author.

Kindred, Dave. "Joe Louis' Biggest Knockout." *Sporting News.* Sports 2000 Moments. Feb. 10, 1999. Online at *http://www.sportingnews .com/archives/sports2000/moments/140271.html.* Copyright 1999 *Sporting News.* Reprinted by permission of *Sporting News.*

King, C. Richard, Ellen Staurowsky, Lawrence Baca, Laurel R. Davis, Cornel Pewewardy. "Of Polls and Race Prejudice: *Sports Illustrated's* Errant 'Indian Wars.'" *Journal of Sport & Social Issues.*

Vol. 26 Issue 4 (Nov. 2002): 381–402. Reprinted by permission of Sage Publications Inc. through Copyright Clearance Center, Inc.

Lipsyte, Robert. "March Madness—A Lot Like Life." *USA Today.* March 15, 2007. Copyright 2007 Robert Lipsyte. Reprinted by permission of the author.

Longman, Jere with Clifton Brown. "Debate on Women at Augusta Catches Woods Off Balance." *The New York Times.* Oct. 20, 2002. Copyright 2002. Reprinted by permission of *The New York Times* and Clifton Brown.

Martin, Christopher R., and Jimmie L. Reeves. "The Whole World Isn't Watching (But We Thought They Were): The Super Bowl and U.S. Solipsism." *Sport in Society.* Vol. 4, Issue 2, 2001. Copyright 2001 *Sport in Society.* Reprinted with permission of Taylor & Francis Ltd., *http://www.informaworld.com.*

Nelson, Mariah Burton. *Embracing Victory: Life Lessons in Competition and Compassion.* Copyright 1998 William Morrow & Co. Reprinted by permission of the author.

Nopper, Tamara K. "Asian America's Response to Shaquille O'Neal Riddled with Racial-Sexual Anxiety." Original essay. 2003. Reprinted by permission of the author.

Oates, Joyce Carol. *On Boxing.* Copyright 1987 *Ontario Review.* Reprinted by permission of John Hawkins & Associates, Inc.

Price, S. L. "The Indian Wars." *Sports Illustrated.* March 4, 2002. Copyright 2002 Time Inc. All rights reserved. Reprinted courtesy of *Sports Illustrated.*

Rhoden, William C. "In NFL, Violence Sells, But at What Cost?" *The New York Times.* Jan. 20, 2007. D1. Copyright 2007. Reprinted by permission of *The New York Times.*

Rosenblatt, Roger. "Reflections: Why We Play the Game." Originally published in *U.S. Society & Values,* electronic journal of the U.S. Department of State, Vol. 8, No. 2, December 2003. Online at *http://usinfo.state.gov/journals/itsv/1203/ijse/rosenblatt.htm.* In the public domain. Reprinted by permission of the author.

Rushin, Steve. "Sport Makes the Words Go Round." *Sports Illustrated.* Nov. 6, 2006. Copyright 2006 Time Inc. Reprinted courtesy of *Sports Illustrated.*

Ryan, Richard. "Where is the Budo in Mixed Martial Arts?" Published in *Black Belt* magazine, June 2007, and online by Dynamic Combat at *http://www.dynamiccombat.com/news/BBJun07.html.* Reprinted by permission of the author.

Sagan, Carl. "Game: The Prehistoric Origin of Sports." Originally published in *Parade,* September 1987. Copyright 1987 Carl Sagan. Reprinted with permission from Democritus Properties, LLC. All rights reserved. This material cannot be further circulated without written permission of Democritus Properties, LLC.

Sengupta, Somini. "A Cricket Match Bridges a Longtime Gap in Punjab." *The New York Times.* March 13, 2005: 3. Copyright 2005. Reprinted by permission of *The New York Times.*

Vignola, Patricia. "The Patriotic Pinch Hitter: The AAGBL and How the American Woman Earned a Permanent Spot on the Roster." *Nine: A Journal of Baseball History and Culture.* Vol. 12, No. 2 (2004): 102–113. Copyright 2004 The University of Nebraska Press. Reprinted with permission.

Wendel, Tim. "Latino Players Can Revive Baseball in America." *USA Today.* May 15, 2003. Copyright 2003 Tim Wendel. Reprinted by permission of the author.

Women's Sports Foundation. "Dropping Men's Sports—Expanding Opportunities for Girls and Women in Sport Without Eliminating Men's Sports: The Foundation Position." Online at *http://www .womenssportsfoundation.org.* Copyright 2000 Women's Sports Foundation. Reprinted by permission.